BEYOND THE LYRIC

NON-FICTION

*The Self on the Page: Theory and Practice of
Creative Writing in Personal Development*
(with Celia Hunt)

The Healing Word

Creative Writing in Health and Social Care (editor)

A Fine Line: New Poetry from Eastern and Central Europe
(with Jean Boase-Beier and Alexandra Buchler)

Writing: Self and Reflexivity (with Celia Hunt)

On Listening

A Century of Poetry Review (editor)

Poetry Writing: the Expert Guide

Music Lessons: Newcastle Bloodaxe Poetry Lectures

POETRY

Folding the Real
The Distance Between Us
Common Prayer
Rough Music

TRANSLATOR

Evening Brings Everything Back
(translations of Jaan Kaplinski)

Day (with Amir Or)

Beyond the Lyric

A Map of Contemporary British Poetry

Fiona Sampson

Chatto & Windus
LONDON

Published by Chatto & Windus 2012

2 4 6 8 10 9 7 5 3 1

First published in Great Britain in 2012 by
Chatto & Windus
Random House, 20 Vauxhall Bridge Road,
London SW1V 2SA
www.randomhouse.co.uk

Addresses for companies within The Random House Group Limited can be found at:
www.randomhouse.co.uk/offices.htm

The Random House Group Limited Reg. No. 954009

A CIP catalogue record for this book
is available from the British Library

ISBN 9780701186463

The Random House Group Limited supports The Forest Stewardship Council (FSC®),
the leading international forest certification organisation. Our books carrying the FSC label
are printed on FSC® certified paper. FSC is the only forest certification scheme endorsed
by the leading environmental organisations, including Greenpeace. Our paper procurement
policy can be found at www.randomhouse.co.uk/environment

Typeset in Baskerville MT 11/15.5 pt by
Palimpsest Book Production Limited, Falkirk, Stirlingshire

Printed and bound in Great Britain by Clays Ltd, St Ives plc

for Sean O'Brien

Be not afeard. The isle is full of noises,
Sounds, and sweet airs, that give delight and hurt not.

The Tempest, III. 2

CONTENTS

INTRODUCTION

This is a book of enthusiasms. Unlike the American modernist Marianne Moore, who famously wrote that 'I, too, dislike it', I love contemporary poetry. I enjoy reading it, hearing it, thinking about and writing the stuff – and have spent the last twenty years trying to get closer to it. I say 'trying' not because contemporary poetry is difficult to like or understand – it is not – but because it can be difficult to find a way into. At times it seems like a kind of club: only if you're already a member can you locate the entrance. Only if you already know lots of contemporary poetry will you be able to guess where it would suit you most to begin.

But it's not what's actually on the page, or in the ear, that keeps these things secret. Something comes between poems and their readers. Contemporary fiction and its fashionable true-life variants – travel-writing, life-writing – are relatively easy to get hold of. Just a glance through the broadsheet review pages, or in a bookshop window, will tell you what this month's must-reads are. These authors' names appear repeatedly on prize lists, at reading groups and on readers' blogs, as well as at festivals. But a poet needs a Nobel Prize before he or she can expect a similar level of recognition: what we might call the dinner-party test. Sometimes, even that's not enough. The announcement in 2011 of a Nobel Prize for Tomas Tranströmer, the great Swedish – and world – poet, was greeted in Britain by claims that he was an unknown.

Who does know what's going on in contemporary poetry? Well,

there are a lot of us reading and writing it. Every year more than two hundred volumes of poetry are published in the United Kingdom. *Poetry Review*, the country's largest specialist periodical, receives around ten thousand unsolicited submissions per annum. The Internet is even more crowded. Sheer volume is part of the problem: just dive in and the chances are you may not immediately come upon exciting, appealing work. Then there's a problem of taste: if you're in search of machismo you may not enjoy the metaphysical, and vice versa. And there's a further difficulty, one of the great unspokens of the poetry world. Poems, being man-made, vary in quality.

Still, a great deal of wonderful poetry, fit to convert the most casual explorer into a committed reader, is being written in Britain today. We're enjoying a period of tremendous richness and variety, and it's this new writing that *Beyond the Lyric* sets out to map. British poetry today is flowering and expanding, rather as our non-fiction did during the boundary-breaking Eighties: a period in which novels became non-fictional, travel writing explored the familiar, and essays turned lyrical and unscholarly. Or in the way philosophy and theory, particularly with a political or psychoanalytic orientation, took off and took over in France for the generation of '68. Or how the Harlem Renaissance expanded the range of Black American artists into a brilliant gamut. At each of these moments what resulted wasn't a single impulse or voice, but growing room for a terrific variety of work which led, in turn, to new ways of writing. Who would have thought that Bruce Chatwin's searchingly intelligent essay-novel *The Songlines* could lead to *both* Blake Morrison's formal family reminiscences *and* John Burnside's evocative, impressionistic memoirs? Or that what was hot off the Paris barricades would end up as either postmodern queer theory or a concert by the West-Eastern Divan Orchestra? Today's British poetry has undergone a similar game-changing shift, perhaps as a result of shaking off the ponderous shades of post-war gloom or because British culture itself is in vibrant transition.

And yet – this extraordinary cultural blossoming is a well-kept secret. There's much to say about the poetry being written here today. But all sorts of factors conspire to stop us from breaking ranks and doing so. British verse exhibits an endearing desire to stay closer to the life and practice of jobbing musicians than to that of readers in imagined library stacks, and we've fallen behind our counterparts, at least in Europe and North America, in terms of a robust, engaged critical culture. Fine books about poetry are integral to contemporary literature in the United States, where they're widely read as well as contributing to the serious task of canon-formation. In 1992, Dana Gioia's *Can Poetry Matter?* sparked a national debate because it challenged the public secret that poetry was no longer part of the North American literary mainstream. That debate was conducted not in the pages of tiny-circulation specialist magazines, but in broadsheets and the national broadcast media: the title essay itself had appeared in *The Atlantic.* Critics working with expertise and virtuosity on contemporary verse include some of the most distinguished in that country. Figures as various as Helen Vendler, Stephen Burt, Donald Hall and Christopher Ricks (who, admittedly, has also been the Oxford Professor of Poetry) feel uncompromised when they glance away from William Shakespeare, John Donne or John Milton towards their own contemporaries. In Europe major poet-critics are at work in every generation, from the beetle-browed Russian Yevgeny Rein to the baby-boomer intellectuals of the Hungarian publishing house and magazine *Jelenkor.* Yet in Britain only *New Bearings in English Poetry* (1932) by F. R. Leavis and Sean O'Brien's *The Deregulated Muse,* published with an accompanying anthology in 1998, have made any serious attempt to articulate what is admirable in the mainstream of contemporary poetry.

Could this be a legacy of Romanticism, two centuries on? In Britain the hope that poems are born not made, and may have a kind of natural grace, springs largely from Leavis's own desire to sweep away the fustiness and aridity of what we might call 'page criticism' and replace it with something feelingful and authentic. But this approach can seem defensive. For example, in the resistance to modernism we can hear discomfort at that movement's hands-dirty acknowledgement that poems are *made of something.*

When I started editing *Poetry Review*, after spending time with the literatures of Central and South-Eastern Europe, the poor quality of the critical writing appearing on my desk was a revelation. Acute, or even accurate, reading of the books under review was rare. Instead of stopping with the work itself, and assessing what it was trying to do, reviewers might evoke a volume's character through epithet and adjectival compound, producing copy closer to a publisher's blurb than to critical writing. Or they would resort to Rottweiler reviewing, which savages for the sake of 'excitement'. Any critical writing which doesn't proceed from close reading muffles, rather than clarifies; it damages the very thing it claims to promote. Yet canon-forming goes on willynilly. Those of us who work as poets are subject to repeated winnowing, 'Done because we are too many,' as Little Father Time's suicide note in Thomas Hardy's *Jude the Obscure* has it. Only a few are selected: by this particular trade publisher, for that BBC series, through the cyclical production of anthologies. At first glance, this makes sense. Poetry, it sometimes seems, is everybody's secret vice. Lots of people write it at some point in their life – for the band they form with classmates, as skits in birthday cards or as a form of confession in times of stress – just as all of us have probably kicked a ball about a park or a beach, though with no idea of becoming a professional footballer. This is touching and human and part of the point of the form. Writing poetry is something only totalitarian regimes try to ban. But poetry that serves its readers is a rarer bird altogether, and *as* readers we're able and entitled to find out what we want to read more of.

The trouble is that such selection doesn't always take place on grounds that are either explained or thought through. This mystifies both knowledge and power within the small world of poetry. As a result such knowledge comes to seem difficult and inscrutable. Yet emergent poets are better equipped today than ever before to articulate what is going on in a poem. The rise of a workshop culture, especially in universities, means that today's young writers are highly technically aware and accomplished. If they can apply readerly criteria to their own work they could, if they dared, apply them to the work of others.

Instead, a strange lack of confidence tempts many to adopt the reflexive position that successful achievement is all about power and influence, rather than springing from the writing itself. Sean O'Brien has described as 'grimly hilarious' a contemporary lack of awareness of:

> the fact that poetry might require an investment of time and patience, and that publication might come not as a result of wanting it but of deserving it. The preoccupation with 'being a poet' is part of the contemporary fetish of 'creativity', whereby an attitude and an identity as part of a scene are assumed to be the real thing, rather than the work itself.
>
> (in *Poetry Review* 100:2)

The development of open-mike evenings, increasingly competitive in format, runs alongside the way emergent poets use Facebook and the blogosphere to broadcast their poetry 'achievements'. But there's much more to an artistic manifesto than the bald *I want to be successful.*

The wider field of contemporary poetry also suffers from this failure to articulate what makes a poem good at what it does. Recent decades have seen several anthologies, each creating its own contemporary canon without *articulating* the critical case for the poets it includes. Blake Morrison and Andrew Motion edited *The Penguin Book of Contemporary British Poetry* in 1982. Michael Hulse, David Kennedy and David Morley's *The New Poetry* appeared from Bloodaxe in 1992. James Byrne and Clare Pollard's *Voice Recognition*, also from Bloodaxe, is a Class of 2010. For sound commercial reasons, the role of these volumes as de facto literary canon-formers is often obscured. Anthologies like Maura Dooley's 1997 round-up of women poets, *Making for Planet Alice*, and Linda France's *Sixty Women Poets*, both from Bloodaxe – or Bloodaxe's own house menus *Poetry with an Edge* (1988) and *New Blood* (1999), both edited by the publisher Neil Astley – are wisely marketed as a good read rather than as platforms for serious critical practice; yet they have of course been produced by literary critical judgement.

To some extent, such team sports are a legacy of the British little magazines of the last half-century. In the absence of true cultural decentralization, and thanks in part to the much later development of creative writing programmes in Britain than in North America, periodicals like the *London Magazine*, edited by Alan Ross from 1961 until his death in 2001, and, in particular, Ian Hamilton's *Review* (1962–72) and *New Review* (1974–9), have traditionally operated something of a monopoly on literary patronage. This means that critical-editorial practice has become deeply linked, in the minds of many protagonists, with the partisan development of particular schools of writing. At the end of his career Ian Hamilton talked amusingly to Dan Jacobson in the *London Review of Books* about his time as simultaneously poetry editor of the *Times Literary Supplement* and the *Observer* and the editor-in-chief of the *Review*:

> There were lots of protests about my –
> *Omnipresence. Ubiquity.*
> Yes. And quite right too. Except of course it seemed to me that this was completely all right; the more of me the better for the good of the cause, so to hell with these sniping charlatans and so forth. That was my position then, you understand.

Given that poetry has been written in every culture and era, and therefore in many widely differentiated ways, not to mention languages, this kind of belief that there's only one way of writing is clear folly. However, it's a folly encouraged by the fantasy that poetry always proceeds by 'movements'. This old-fashioned concept is a legacy of modernism. Wedded to the early twentieth-century idea of an avant garde, it suggests that we can only read literary practice as a chrono-logical series of unified movements, each occupying the entire poetic foreground and sweeping away whatever came before. True enough, poetry *is* written in its own contemporary context. But that context is more nuanced, even fragmented, than this fantasy suggests. That's particularly the case in twenty-first-century Britain, at a time when globalization has made us more open to cultural multiplicity, as it develops both within national borders and through digital communications. Poetry is no longer the dialect of a relatively small, white male middle-class, tribe (with a few interlopers), nor the product of a homogenous education system, culture and society. Contemporary literary writing is porous: susceptible to many influences, from junk TV to international travel.

One of the patterns this book uncovers is the way that, while some current tendencies in British poetry are the result of friends developing alongside each other and sharing influences, other equally distinctive approaches are shared by poets who are peers only in the narrow sense of being alive at the same time. These more individuated figures seem to have emerged from the wider field of poetry in general; that's to say, they've developed their own reading of all that's come before. I have to admit a particular sympathy with this approach. Perhaps it's my training as a performing musician – an interpreter, whose own professional failing it is if I can't 'get' a particular piece – that makes me return repeatedly to the importance of understanding that there's more than one kind of poetry in the world. I enjoy reading things I can't do myself; that are unexpected as much as familiar; that ask me to try out a different way of reading or listening. My enthusiasms are like a series of poetry crushes, that feed off and are never gainsaid by each other. One minute I want nothing but numinous North American verse that uses speech patterns which lie easily on the breath. Then I find I'm missing the muscular *kerr-ching* of assonantal, rhyming poems. I spend some time reading 'thinky' contemporary French poetry, then go looking for the clear-as-a-bell micro-narratives of certain middle-generation British poets.

Enjoying so many different kinds of poetry frees me from feeling I should be obedient, even to the tastes and types of the poets I most admire. It is also the opposite of old-style editing, in which to be combative and to govern by personal taste is taken as a sign of strength. The fine poet and editor Hugo Williams once said to me, 'You seem to like everything.' Which, as far as *ways* of writing go, is pretty much true. The point is just not to hang on to the dead wood that clutters each approach. Our poetry landscape isn't a jumble so much as a scene of more or less balancing variety: more Capability Brown than the competing front gardens of surburbia. Unless we poets accept difference, and learn to see beyond variety to excellence, we're doomed to an unending Punch and Judy of 'That's the way to do it' rival positions. Unless our readers enjoy lots of different things – as a good meal includes more than one food group, or a wardrobe more than one colour – we will limit our audiences to the diminishing returns of repetition.

But how to manage this? After all, it is true that poems written one way 'fail' to do what those written in another can. Free verse 'fails' to sustain regular form, and confessionalism 'fails' to exercise impersonality of the kind T.S. Eliot looked for in a poem. Which is where enthusiasm comes in. Rather than this kind of glass-half-empty reading, suppose we see the glass as half-full and concentrate on what a poem *does*, rather than what it *doesn't* do, reading and enjoying it on its own terms?

Reading poetry isn't a duty. It should be an enrichment, a bonus. Reading 'half-full' means seeing what's actually going on, in all its pleasurable variety, instead of complaining about what isn't; or what we imagine ought to be. It means being non-partisan, open and excited by the range of contemporary British verse. How, then, can such an optimist find a way through the tremendous variety of today's poetry – and the sheer number of aspiring poets? The answer, of course, is to read a poem on its own terms. Poetics mark out what a poem wants to do. Mapping living British poets according to the *kinds* of poetry they write, rather than by their thematic concerns, shifts the focus back to the poem itself.

This book tries out a quasi-Linnaean classification of poets. By observing poems and grouping them according to type, it identifies thirteen tendencies (or species) in contemporary British poetry. It doesn't value poems for the 'issues' they raise or read them for their geographical or political contexts; though it does accept that such content can form part of a poetic project. It also embraces the fact that poets have written about sex, love, death and loss in every culture since the time of Sappho – and that they have done so in countless different ways because these universal subjects remain unexhausted.

Naturally, not all of the poets who appear in this book will see themselves as specifically or solely belonging just where they've been located on its conceptual map. But, since I regard no school as better than any other, no disparagement is intended. My plan is to steer the reader through contemporary poetry, rather than to create a fantasy league of The Nation's Best Poets. A few anomalous figures who smudge rather than clarify the plan play a smaller part in this book than they rightly do in British poetry, though I have tried to signpost them. These significant, unusual figures include Anne Stevenson, whose formalism, too early developed and arguably traditional for her to belong among the new formalists, nevertheless distances her serious, and quietly elegant, work from that of her plain dealing peers. Another to be insufficiently tipped-in is Wendy Cope, that light-fingered virtuoso of full rhyme and sometimes comic charm. Her poetics matter: her writing plays an important, albeit polarizing role in British poetry today. But she belongs, with American exile James Fenton, in a tradition so secure and so oddly hermetic that it seems to require another kind of map: one much more chronological than contemporary. The poet-novelist Bernardine Evaristo is experimenting with new, hybrid forms, although it is fiction, rather than poetry, that is arguably being most refreshed by her work. Roma stories and vocabulary stud David Morley's touchstone verse; Robert Crawford uses scenes from and sites of Scottish history as symbolic currency. Colette Bryce, Jacob Polley and John Stammers belong with the anecdotalists, yet their achievement is largely in the sheer discipline and sophistication of their execution. They are refining, rather than redrawing, the poetic map. Most significantly of all, technically quieter poets like Jamie McKendrick, Stephen Romer or – despite the expansive beauty of his recent *Small Hours* – Lachlan Mackinnon, who make their important contribution in the calibre of each thoughtful turn of phrase, have had to be omitted altogether. These poets, in particular, deserve a different, non-Linnaean approach.

Also signposted but not discussed are the poetries of other countries.

Since it is written largely in English, the 'world' language we share with a superpower, British poetry has long lived in the shadow of North American, as well as Irish, verse. Our national prizes are open to the whole English-speaking world, providing it publishes here. This can make us feel we're more successful than we are, as when we co-opt the Caribbean and Irish Nobel Laureates Derek Walcott and Seamus Heaney to British verse. At the same time it can overshadow, and indeed stunt, the writing actually going on in this country. This has nothing to do with a poet's country or culture of origin but everything to do with actual participation in culture-making in the UK. So, poets from Northern Ireland are included in this book not for complex political reasons but because they work and publish under the same conditions as the rest of British poetry (no tax-breaks or life-time pensions from the Aosdana for them). Poets with a Caribbean background, and from every other part of the world, are included when they live and work here. They play a key part in what's going on in British poetry: often working against the historical grain to change the balance of what's published.

Missing, too, are some of today's young poets. This is not because they're uninteresting. Nor are they doing something new and inscrutable which is about to render this book out of date. Far from it. Emerging poets, however brilliant, grow into their own poetics only gradually. Even retrospectively it's hard to spot, in debut collections, what will become the defining project. Who would have thought, reading Seamus Heaney's 'Bog Poems' or the talky early verse of Michael Longley, that either would become a touchstone lyricist? Or that Sylvia Plath's early technical brilliance would turn to the rangy, form-busting late masterpieces? Occasionally, I have pencilled-in likely inheritors of current tendencies. But this project is not about compiling exclusive lists. It is designed to do the opposite, unpacking possibilities and opening up growing room for new poets.

First and last, therefore, this is a book about reading. It is a story of pleasures taken; it aims to identify, demystify and share some of those pleasures. Though I find the joys and challenges of writing poetry inseparable from those of reading it, this book is for *anyone* interested in dipping a toe into contemporary British verse. Poetry has changed over the centuries; but it changes and develops at a slower pace than modernity might have had us believe, a century ago. Many of the same puzzles that poetics argue over – is rhythm fundamentally metrical, or related to speech? Can a serious poem be anything other than lyric? – were being struggled with two and three hundred years ago. And since they have to do with the nature of language itself, they are unlikely to go away any time soon; even though we may have moved from pitting John Keats against Percy Bysshe Shelley to lining Don Paterson up against Alice Oswald. British poetry is, as it has been for a very long time, cantankerous, quarrelsome, fascinating – and extraordinary.

1

THE PLAIN DEALERS

Sometimes a way of writing emerges from a particular moment or movement and simply keeps on going, though the original nexus has long disappeared. That's more or less what happened to the plain dealers of British poetry, a generation now in their eighties. Dannie Abse, Alan Brownjohn, Ruth Fainlight, Elaine Feinstein, the late Herbert Lomas, Anthony Thwaite and (a couple of years younger than the rest) Fleur Adcock would probably all claim that their straightforward, bread-and-butter diction and emotional intelligence is not so much a conscious strategy as an absence of affectation. Feinstein has even called this way of writing 'modest' (modestly, she was not referring to herself).

But beware any poetics that protests its innocence too vigorously. No poem is ever entirely an Honest Joe, doing what it says it does without reflection. By definition, it is the result of artifice – even when that passes itself off as nothing more than technique, control or indeed intention. The plain dealers write commonsensical verse; but as the Italian Marxist Antonio Gramsci said, 'Common sense is the sense of the ruling classes.' Perhaps this generation no longer presides over British poetry. Yet common sense's claim to be straightforward, decent and true can imply that other approaches are pretentious or even false. Perhaps chary of fancy specialism, it characteristically feels entitled to speak on any and every topic. Plain dealing poetry certainly ranges widely, from pronouncements on human destiny – such as Alan

Brownjohn's millennial 'We are going to see the rabbit', Dannie Abse's hospital poems, especially those from *Funland*, or Ruth Fainlight's *Sibyls* – to detailed domestic observation by Anthony Thwaite or Fleur Adcock. Not least because they use familiar, lived-in language, these writers seem to come into their own when dealing with human relationships particularly. Elaine Feinstein, Dannie Abse and Herbert Lomas, for example, have all written moving collections about widowhood, while Alan Brownjohn's *Ludbrooke* emerged in 2010 as an antiheroic Everyman, closer to the rueful scapegraces of the Central European tradition, like Zbigniew Herbert's *Mr Cogito* and Jaroslav Hašek's prose *The Good Soldier Švejk*, than to North American models of the conflicted psyche such as John Berryman's Henry in *The Dream Songs*, or Robert Lowell's use of his second wife Elizabeth Hardwick's letters in *The Dolphin*.

These plain dealing roots in everyday lived experience could seem to threaten the ancedotalists of poetry's baby boom, who made up 1994's controversial New Generation promotion – of twenty poets who were at or around the second collection stage – or else emerged, like Carol Ann Duffy, Jackie Kay and Neil Rollinson, just before or after it. Both generations enjoy using anti-adjectival narrative: the plain dealers are above all storytellers. Their stories may not be particularly extended; they may recount a fable, an anecdote or even a thought process. But the sequential 'and then . . . and then' of narrative, rather than, say, textural exploration, remains a shaping principle. If, as the American critic Harold Bloom suggests in his family album 'theory of poetry' *The Anxiety of Influence*, all writing emerges through an Oedipal struggle with influential precursors, then these two generations need to discover complex, subtle differentials if they're to live and let live.

That's not always easy in the rough and tumble of the literary schoolyard. Only one plain dealer, Fleur Adcock, appears in *The Deregulated Muse*, 1998's seminal reconfiguration of British poetry by baby boomer Sean O'Brien. And the older generation have resistances of their own. Alan Brownjohn, reviewing New Gen-er Don Paterson in the *Sunday*

Times, claimed that his books 'are famously "difficult" and tend to leave readers uncertain about how to take the personality that inhabits them'. However, one useful distinction between these poetic projects is the difference in their political and cultural contexts. The laconic, hands-in-pockets New Generation are very much of their Cool Britannia time; an era when the political establishment sought to prove its grasp of the zeitgeist by inviting anoraked Britpop stars to Downing Street. Their predecessors had emerged as New Elizabethans, the citizen generation that participated in a collective renaissance in the post-war era of the Coronation and the Festival of Britain. Plain dealers often seem engaged *in,* rather than simply *by,* what they write. The poets of the Nineties on the other hand famously adopt framing, alienating devices, such as the language of instruction manuals, to distance their material from the narrator: think of Simon Armitage's 'Very Simply Topping up the Brake Fluid' or 'Phrase Book' by Jo Shapcott. But the plain dealer is often the spokesman in the crowd.

The Fifties idea of the poet as an exceptional Everyman was no plain dealing innovation, however. It goes back at least as far as William Wordsworth's preface to the 1802 edition of the *Lyrical Ballads,* where the poet is 'a man speaking to men'. Some European poetry has been able to accommodate this apparent paradox through the part played by a literate, literary language in the the development of national identity and, thus, the creation of nation states. Nineteenth-century national poets like Mihai Eminescu in Romania, France Prešeren in Slovenia or Adam Mickiewicz in Poland are celebrated not merely as cultural orna-ments but as nation builders.

The British plain dealers are associated with social reconstruction through *educational* democratization. In the wake of that radical moral shift which was the founding of the Welfare State, their post-war era was articulated by such studies of class and conditions as Richard Hoggart's *The Uses of Literacy* (1957) and Raymond Williams's *Culture and Society* (1958). This progressive, if unglamorous, sensibility persisted into the Seventies: in his *Mercian Hymns* (1971), Geoffrey Hill made King Offa 'overlord of the M5'. The plain dealers have remained the bards of public libraries and state education; systems which expanded exponentially in the wake of the 1944 Butler Education Act and the 1964 Public Libraries and Museums Act. Their poetry acknowledges this above all through tone. No lilies are to be gilded here. In Fleur Adcock's 'Against Coupling', 'There is much to be said for abandoning / this no longer novel exercise – / for not "participating in / a total experience" – when / one feels like the lady in Leeds who / has seen *The Sound of Music* eighty-six times'. This is cardigan-wearing, nylon-shirted verse, from a workaday generation: Alan Brownjohn and Herbert Lomas taught in Further Education; Dannie Abse, perhaps not coincidentally raised in a radical political family in the Welsh heartland of industrial silicosis, was a clinician specializing in chest disorders. Though the working lives of women in any case often follow a different trajectory, Elaine Feinstein taught at the University of Essex and for the Workers' Educational Association. Of this group it is only Anthony Thwaite who has held more traditionally 'literary' day jobs, first in the Drama Department of the BBC and later as the Literary Editor of *The Listener* and the *New Statesman*.

If the work of the plain dealers has a particular context, its texture and intention are distinctive too. The *poetic* origins of that particularity lie with two post-war schools, The Movement and The Group. Both these somewhat dour titles suggest a kind of sensory rationing, a refusal of anything effete or baroque, by a generation whose sensibility had been forged in austerity. Yet both are also oddly grandiose: it is as if there could only ever be *one* movement or group. For, despite a certain dowdy, lined-exercise-book aesthetic, the Movement and the Group were each, in their own terms, gestures of passionate resistance and creativity. As the Second World War's communitarian ethic pushed Britain one step further away from the mystifying ideal of an aristocracy, elevated diction must have seemed like a dead language. The Movement – led by Philip Larkin and including Kingsley Amis, Donald Davie, D.J. Enright, Elizabeth Jennings, Thom Gunn and John Wain – refused the rhetorical flourish of poets like George Barker as much as the classic lyricism of Stephen Spender. In favour was not just the famous demotic of Pop Larkin's 'This be the Verse', but a diction full of concrete particular and 'classless' language. In Anthony Thwaite's 'Mr Cooper' there is no polysyllabic, undemocratic, showing-off:

> Two nights in Manchester: nothing much to do,
> One of them I spent partly in a pub,
> Alone, quiet, listening to people who
> Didn't know me. *So I told the bloody sub-*
> *Manager what he could do with it . . . Mr Payne*
> *Covers this district – you'll have met before?*

And yet, ironically, even this poem can't avoid overhearing the famous modernist pub dialogue in T.S. Eliot's *The Waste Land*: 'You *are* a proper fool, I said. / Well, if Albert won't leave you alone, there it is, I said, / What you get married for if you don't want children? / HURRY UP PLEASE ITS TIME'.

Philip Larkin was born in 1922, the year *The Waste Land* was published. For poets born before the Second World War but still working today, the Group was more contemporary than the Movement. Alan Brownjohn, Fleur Adcock and occasionally Anthony Thwaite all attended Philip Hobsbaum's London meetings. Other key members of the Group were George Macbeth, Edward Lucie-Smith, Peter Redgrove, Peter Porter and Martin Bell. They were exciting times. The house of poetry had only just been spring-cleaned. In a much-cited 1961 letter to Hobsbaum, Lucie-Smith wrote that 'we have no axe to grind – this isn't a gang and there's no monolithic body of doctrine to which everyone must subscribe'. But this urban, brainy, take-no-hostages set did have older rivals of its own to resist. Naturally, these included the Movement, with whom they were nevertheless united in opposition to the post-Blakean New Apocalyptics, those Roaring Boys of the Forties, who included Dylan Thomas and his acolyte Vernon Watkins, George Barker, Henry Treece and Norman MacCaig.

When Hobsbaum and Lucie-Smith edited *The Group Anthology* in 1963 they characterized the work it included as 'frank autobiographical poems' and 'direct experience'. Today's plain dealers have carried a version of these values forward through successive eras. Alan Brownjohn's then position as Chair of the Poetry Society put him at the centre of the Poetry Wars of the Seventies, waged by Eric Mottram, Bob Cobbing and other avant-gardists of the 'British Poetry Revival' against the lyric mainstream, which saw competing claims about relevance and accessibility. 1965 had seen the International Poetry Incarnation at the Royal Albert Hall – a kind of triumphalist precursor to what survives in today's storytelling and performance poetry movements – and the Seventies would be coloured by the Albert Hall Poetry Live events and Michael Horovitz's anthology *Children of Albion: Poetry of the Underground in Britain* (1969). Both brought together diverse elements, including free-verse translations of poets like Yevgeny Yevtushenko, then-young British poets like Barry Tebb and Chris Torrance writing out of a non-linear tradition, political street verse from Tom Pickard and Michael X, and – trumpets at a distant gate – the American Beats.

Much of this relatively expansive, risky versification viewed itself as, perhaps counter-intuitively, a poetry of the people. The Liverpool poets Roger McGough, Brian Patten, Adrian Mitchell and Adrian Henri are often seen as the free-form heirs of these mass-access initiatives. But it is telling that, while they were influenced by rock music – most obviously, given their home city, by the Beatles – Poetry Live had been associated with jazz. Jazz, with its counter-cultural roots, made an unlikely precursor for poetry as 'the new rock 'n' roll': that lame hope of a much later Nineties promotional slogan. Its character of resistance – think of the rebarbative texture of much experimental jazz-funk – suggests a coterie addressing its initiates. And indeed this was just what was happening: the publishing mainstream was being challenged by a small, if publicity-hungry, counter-culture. The relatively easy-reading plain dealers, then arguably at their most established, were the poetic mainstream that both Bob Cobbing and Michael Horovitz sought to resist.

From 1962, readers' hunger for a more varied diet would guarantee the success of another development – Al Alvarez's Penguin Series of

Modern European Poets. However, apart from Feinstein's formative early contact with the Beat Poets Allen Ginsberg and Charles Olson, the plain dealers have remained largely uninfluenced by encounters with other poetic traditions. Home is where they start from. Here is Fleur Adcock in 1967:

> A snail is climbing up the window-sill
> into your room, after a night of rain.
> You call me in to see, and I explain
> that it would be unkind to leave it there:
>
> ('For a Five-Year-Old')

By 2009 the iambic pentameter has gone, but an apparently lucid concern with the local remains:

> My codependent,
> my precious parasite,
> my echo, my parrot,
> my tolerant slave:
>
> I do the talking;
> you do the typing.
> Just try a bit harder
> to hear what I say!
>
> ('Dragon Talk')

But how much light does this writing really shine on what it's like to *be* either a young mother or the older correspondent frustrated by voice-recognition software? Adcock typifies a very particular, and arguably gendered, privacy. Not everything is stated or displayed. For historical reasons – restricted access to literacy, Higher Education, employment and publication – women's experience was still some-thing of a poetic tabula rasa even in the second half of the last century: the point repeatedly made by Irish poet Eavan Boland's much-cited essays in *Object Lessons* (1995). In some ways Adcock addresses this blank. She is among the most consistent British poets of family life, and her use of, in particular, a child's-eye view – and especially the imaginative terrain of childhood – refutes the stripped-back utility aesthetic her work also flirts with. Later, Boland would tint domestic rituals with the sepia of historical resonance. But Adcock preserves a child's energetic make-believe. Anthologizing herself in *The Faber Book of Twentieth-Century Women's Poetry* (1987), she juxtaposes 'Blue Glass', a poem about 'the underworld of children' and their dream-play, with the similarly dreamlike science fiction of 'The Ex-Queen Among the Astronomers', as if to plot the sources of her imagination.

For women poets, gender is part of where we live; the familiar home of the self. It is a legitimate and indeed unavoidable subject matter. However, women's *poetic* identity has been under-explored. Adrienne Rich's *Diving into the Wreck*, which explicitly problematized *how*, as well as whom, to speak *as*, was published in the US relatively early, in 1973: when women poets – Marianne Moore, Elizabeth Bishop, Anne Sexton – were already counted among the major North American writers. But in British poetry even today the gender debate languishes at the level of numerology. Magical thinking is mixed with special pleading. As recently as 2008, Eva Salzman and Amy Wack could publish the 'anthology' *Women's Work*, really a miscellany which seems to have no literary raison d'être – questions such as quality or the chronological development of discourses are not addressed – other than to publish lots of poems which happen to be by women. And so, despite her portfolio of serious literary work (she also edited the *Oxford Book of Contemporary New Zealand Poetry*) and her OBE and the Queen's Gold Medal for Poetry, Fleur Adcock can sometimes give the curious impression of just dipping her poetic toe in the water. It seems nothing is to be pursued too strenuously. As if there is no need to ask who the speaker of the poems is, or what she might have to say, since the woman poet is already by definition a specialist in a subject which can only be herself. At times this even suggests that there is so much she has not yet explored that for a woman writer who let go of the side of the poetry pool and started swimming would be overwhelmed. For example, the wit of the well-known later poem 'The Video', about sibling rivalry, is almost too deft. It seems defensive. If it weren't so fluently rhymed, would we read this as 'literary'?

> After she had a little sister,
> and Mum had gone back to being thin
> and was twice as busy, Ceri played
> the video again and again.
> She watched Laura come out, and then,
> in reverse, she made her go back in.

If the results occasionally seem a little nerveless, a degree of self-protectiveness may be the price we pay for the courage to be pioneering. Adcock is not alone in being courageous. One striking link between the plain dealers is the extent to which they came from unprecedented or unexpected backgrounds. As a woman from New Zealand, Adcock sustained a double exile within British poetry of the Sixties, Seventies and Eighties. Other brave new starting points were closer to home. Both Alan Brownjohn and Herbert Lomas emerged from lower middle-class Methodism by way of grammar school and National Service; Jewish poets of this generation include Ruth Fainlight, who is also American, Elaine Feinstein, and Dannie Abse, who is also Welsh. Remembering this, it is possible to see in the diction of a poem like the sonnet 'Greenwich Park' by Herbert Lomas (1942–2011) a kind of camouflage, a willed dowdiness:

> Spring's come, a little late, in the park:
> a tree-rat smokes flat S's over the lawn.
> A mallard has somehow forgotten something
> it can't quite remember. Daffodils yawn . . .

In this downplayed vocabulary, even neologism ('tree-rat') becomes an understatement, one that doesn't have ideas above its station. And note the setting: expansive Greenwich Park commands a slope overlooking the Thames and the Royal Naval College, and is the home of the Royal Observatory. Yet the poem – for all its witty charm, and it *is* charming – contracts its attention to just a flowerbed and a couple of pigeons:

> A cock-pigeon is sexually harassing
> a hen: pecking and poking and padding
> behind her impertinently, bowing and mowing.
> But when he's suddenly absent-minded –
> can't keep even sex in his head –
> she trembles, stops her gadding, doubts
> and grazes his way. He remembers and pouts.

All the same, it seems, you can't keep inventiveness down. It's not only those close-packed participles that so deftly set Lomas's pigeons in motion; it's the way movement shifts to a stationary present tense when their absorption is temporarily broken. The enjambment that creates a hesitation after 'doubts' helps, too.

'Greenwich Park' appeared in *Trouble* (1992), published when the poet was sixty-eight: a late collection by most standards, but one which marks only the halfway point in Lomas's Collected poems, *A Casual Knack of Living* (2009). There's a kind of productivity that seems almost conscientious at play, as in the work of many of the plain dealers. Ruth Fainlight's *New and Collected Poems* (2010) runs to more than five hundred pages. To date, Elaine Feinstein has published fourteen poetry collections – as well as novels, translations and biographies – Anthony Thwaite sixteen, and Alan Brownjohn, who is also a novelist, more than twenty. It is salutary to remember how highly motivated such a generation, who lost portions of their youth to war, must be.

However, if we're to read attentively, we need to avoid anachronism. This means not assuming that, for example, utility diction is the whole of a poetic project. In Lomas's early 'Something, Nothing and Every-thing' the vocabulary is willfully unexceptional – the poem's built on a simple turn of phrase – but this is also the literary trope that enables the central conceptual shift:

> There was nothing between us
> then something took off her dress
> something took off my shirt
> . . .
> there was nothing between us
> we touched each other
> everything was touching between us
> . . .
> there was everything between us
> there was nothing between us

Never mind if this seems slightly naive; 'everything was touching between us' a hostage to snigger. The clumsiness marks the spot at which the writer resists what's too easy, that ready-to-hand-ness which means the writing hasn't gone as far as it could. For Lomas is a surpris-ingly restless poet. He lacks an automatic music: and it is as if he has to convince anew, with each poem, through a freshly coined tonality. 1974's *Private and Confidential*, for example, includes 'The History of Love', all delicate rhythmic balance though its subject, childhood crushes, is as British as John Betjeman; the long post-Kipling poem 'Lord Suspends Law of Karma for Lucky Luciano' – an onomatopoeic translation of a Finnish poem about fish; and the lapidary, or at least pebbly, 'Olives'. And it is the same in *Nightlights* (2007), a collection of complicated questions, both indirect:

> Dear Darkness, it's so hard
> to believe in you
> because I can't see you.
>
>   ('Three Prayers for Children')

and direct:

> His wing purring like a little cat,
> he picks a crumb in sunlight
>
> and sings *No, no, a bird's*
> *not an egg's way of making an egg.*
>
> And I ask *What is it, then, is it*
> *death makes you want to generate?*
>> ('All that's Transitory is only a Trope')

Yet a measured voice, completed by certainty, can after all emerge from all this, under pressure from grief:

> Tomorrow's your new birthday,
> the day you were born into death.
>
> Other things will happen, a visit
> to the doctor, perhaps, a glass of wine,
>
> and sometime, at nightfall, I'll pour
> a glass of Bombay Gin on your grave.
>> ('The Month of Holy Souls')

Lomas's language is programmatically egalitarian. There's nothing in his poems that demonstrates whether they're written – or 'spoken' – by a man rather than a woman (though it would certainly have to be someone in love with women). The dream of a classless society lingers in the work of this author who once published a book asking *Who Needs Money?* (1972). Though virtuous as a social belief-system, the trouble with this as a *poetic* strategy is, of course, that words are *not* either equal or similar. Peter Redgrove, who was born just eight years after Lomas, was an altogether different class of exhibitionist even near the end of his life. The poems of *From the Virgil Caverns* (2002), published just a year before he died, are cascading triplets of stepped lines. In 'At the Old Powerhouse', this striding lineation drives energy through a poem about (electrical) power and movement – a swan strides the water as it brakes and lands – and is mimetic, certainly; but also evocative. To read the poem is to have a sensation of energy. There's more going on than the straight metrical mimesis famous by Alfred Lord Tennyson's galloping 'The Charge of the Light Brigade'.

Because Redgrove's charged atmosphere isn't simply mapped out by that kind of sound-diagram, it feels to the reader or listener as if she has discovered it for herself. It seems *authentic*. That's because its evocation is multi-centered. This sound-scape is created not just by phrasal rhythm but at the level of individual words, which cluster in slant alliterations: of stretched *etch/eck/etre*, and tight *stri/switch/stock*, sounds. The verse bounces with this sound-sense of alternating release and capture. And the bounce, like a musical inflection in an interlocutor's voice, makes its sound engaged and animated. The language is symbolically and semantically engaged, too. The poet is unafraid either of a slightly mannered antiquity – he uses words like 'javelin' and 'whipstock' – or depth-charges of meaning; as when he uses an adjective, 'stridor', which evokes both his swan's landing strides and its stridency.

This multiplicity to Redgrove's writing, in which a poem is at the same time a sound-world, a linguistic adventure and a study in symbolic meaning, sets it at an acute angle to that of his plain-dealing peers. That is no accident: his are the poetics of quite another belief system. His strongly held beliefs, partly elaborated in such prose works of mythical psychology as *The Wise Wound* (co-written with Shuttle) and *The Black Goddess and the Sixth Sense*, were invested not so much in helping to build post-war British society, as in a conscientious and radical critique of that way of life.

In 2003, Anthony Thwaite's 'The Art of Poetry' satirized the conventional advice:

> . . . Adopt
> Current demotic, yet be wary of

> Brand-names, and proper-names
> Limited by time. The Latinate
> Is out, except for satire.
> Ease yourself into the vernacular.

Plain dealing may be straightforward, but that doesn't mean it is spontaneous. Poems like Thwaite's 'Leavings' (from 1967's *The Stones of Emptiness*) can seem uninflected. Lacking distancing devices, especially irony, the language is wholly present to itself and therefore to the reader:

> Emptying the teapot out
> Into the drain, I catch sight
> Suddenly of flies at work
> On some rubbish by the back
> Of the shed . . .

This fly-on-the-wall reportage is married to a commitment to localism, whether in 'At Dunwich' (1967), *Letter from Tokyo* (1987) or 'Lines Lost in Antwerp' (2007). There's also a propensity to examine the State of the Nation, notably in poems about the British Council and Higher Education: 'I have spent a lifetime picking away at remains' ('Spring', 2007). But this commitment to what's really going on isn't so much argued for as taken for granted, by poetry whose nostalgia (collection titles include *Victorian Voices* and *The Dust of the World*) could also sound like resistance to the new.

Nostalgic resistance has a characteristic music. A continual narrative present tense plays its part: scenes from the past are often folded into a question or present-day reflection. So does repeated use of an opening clause with no active verb. We start in the middle of things, with the material of the poem already a given:

> The exhaustion of museums, of libraries:
> It is nothing to do with dust, or being old, or dead.
>
> ('Accumulations')

A Larkinesque note of regret can be heard in the subject matter: an uncelebratory quotidian, in the first books, already being lapped in *The Owl in the Tree* (1963) by images of 'A house gone derelict where, splayed / Like metal branches, pipes jut out / Where once the Ascot hung'. By the Seventies, 'The hazed meadows on England grow over chancels / Where cattle hooves kick up heraldic tiles' in the attractive, but oddly arc-less, poem 'Reformation'. This is a world of receding satisfactions. Even the teaching of literature seems a folly, especially when attempted abroad. Not surprisingly, given his role as that poet's literary executor, Thwaite (*b.* 1930) can read like a younger Larkin. But he is one for whom gloom is an affair of poetic good manners rather than existential necessity. There's too much *give* to create necessity in a voice which elsewhere mimics translationese, or ventriloquizes Victorian prose. In *New Confessions* (1974), its engagement with Augustine of Hippo inescapably echoes those English modernist classics *Briggflatts* and *Mercian Hymns*. Thwaite's vocal flexibility is both his strength – and a clue that his poetic sensibility might be to some degree learnt.

Like any other poet in our book-lined, literate age Elaine Feinstein (*b.* 1930) also writes amid a welter of influences; but her two great clarifying encounters are with the Beat and Black Mountain poets, who blew the formal cobwebs out of her writing, and with Marina Tsvetaeva, the great Russian whom she was the first to translate into English in 1971. Tsvetaeva was a lyric modernist, and Feinstein might have been expected to resist her bunched, formal diction. But this relationship was *ad feminam* from the outset:

> When I read Simon Karlinsky's account of her character, in his early book, I recognized in her many of my own faults: domestic eccentricity, impracticality, and a febrile nature. She existed only in Russian, so I began to make versions of her poems, with the help of Angela Livingstone from the Russian Department of the University of Essex, at first only for myself.
>
> It was a transforming experience. The violence of her emotions and the ferocity of her expression of them released me from

English defensive caution. She taught me to see irony as a way
of keeping deep feeling at a distance.

('Close to the Bone', in *Poetry Review* 96:2)

Perhaps the finger-slow reading all translation involves allowed
Feinstein to hear these poems as forceful expressions of experience. Or
perhaps it was the sheer rarity of other women's experiences in English-
language poetry that made this recognition vivid. As she says in the
Introduction to the 1992 edition of her Tsvetaeva versions, 'Men of
comparable genius often find women to look after them.' It is interesting
that, despite her early understanding of the relevance of American
poetry, with its many new speakers, Feinstein didn't develop in dialogue
with her transatlantic peers, such as Adrienne Rich or Alice Walker.
Instead, she (re-)makes a Tsvetaeva, perhaps somewhat in her own
eventual image, who is clear-spoken, wry and emotional:

> How do you live with one of a
> thousand women   after Lilith?

> Sated with newness, are you?
>   Now you are grown cold to magic,
> how is your life with an
>   earthly woman, without sixth

> sense? Tell me: are you happy?
>   Not? In a shallow pit? . . .

('An Attempt at Jealousy')

Compare this with Feinstein's account of 'A Visit' from her late husband,
in *Talking to the Dead* (2005):

> And early this morning you whispered
>   as if you were lying softly at my side:

Are you still angry with me? And spoke my
name with so much tenderness, I cried.
    I never reproached you much
that I remember, not even when I should;
    to me, you were the boy in Ravel's garden
who always longed to be good,
    as the forest creatures knew, and so do I.

T.S. Eliot was right to suggest, in his essay 'Tradition and the Individual Talent', that reading other poetry with a sense of recognition is a form of self-recognition. Feinstein's Tsvetaeva speaks with her translator's own living accent.

Equally important to this writer's poetic identity is a capacious, though highly personal, internationalism. Feinstein never forgets that her grandparents were from Odessa, and as she enters her eighties has set herself the task of exploring and avowing her sense of the East. *Cities* (2010), an autobiography in verse snapshots, has rapidly succeeded *The Russian Jerusalem* (2008), in which prose and poetry alternated to tell the – episodic, nightmarish – story of what happened under Stalin and Lenin to the great Russian poets, and to those other inhabitants of Feinstein's world, her own family:

    It is London, pale sunshine,
    here and now. Already
    we are their immortality.
    Their spirits enter us,

    and those who come after,
    in other cities, other languages.
    May the Lord in his long silence
    remember all of us.

                                        ('Heaven')

There's an un-English emotional freight to these word-choices: *immortality, spirits, cities, languages, Lord*. What makes this possible? Certainly, Feinstein writes about history, the Holocaust, bereavement, and these are big topics. But topics themselves don't produce good verse. One source of her writing's strength might be its refusal to perform. There are no special effects, only a story told in terms stripped bare of textual indulgence; of adjective, unnecessary detail and wordplay:

> When Czeslaw Miłosz read in London
> you told him his voice was like
> your grandmother's. His smile resembled yours.
> You were never scared of genius
> and he was gentle with you, explaining:
>
> *The Polish accent sticks to the palate*
> *across three languages.*
>
> ('Lublin, 1973')

This touching encounter within an émigré community manages to avoid name-dropping. Miłosz functions precisely as a sign of remoteness – a potentially scary 'genius' – rather than being *appropriated* as a famous friend. The poet is in the poem simply because he really happened – he is part of a texture of well-furnished experience.

Ruth Fainlight (*b*. 1931) turns this inside out – or, perhaps, outside in. She writes, for all the apparently autobiographical character of her material, from behind a series of masks. One of her best-known collections, 1980's *Sibyls and Others*, includes as its title suggests an extended sequence about those mythic creatures. Written largely in the third person, these are not persona pieces, but employ those figures to bring a range of world cultures, from Shinto to Norman Gothic, to bear on the idea of feminine authority. *What would a truth-telling female voice be like?* they seem to ask. Perhaps we don't yet know; but the exploratory care of Fainlight's portraits makes later projects, like Carol Ann Duffy's volume *The World's Wife* or Jo Shapcott's *Mad Cow* poems, seem like relative jeux d'esprit.

Still, Fainlight has a double problem to solve: how can she *describe* feminine authority, and how should she *deploy* it? Her writing attempts to resolve the question of who speaks by working from the page backwards to the author:

> What I'm describing is privilege: the actual physical
> State of one who expects and depends on such luxuries
> As acknowledgement . . .

This is from 'My Position in the History of the Twentieth Century', surely one of the most challenging titles in the history of slim volumes. That it doesn't read as hubris – and it's certainly not irony – but as a straightforward label for what the poem is thinking about, is a clue to Fainlight's most successful mask. She is the plain dealer *par excellence*, whose imperturbable speech patterns allow her to explore and depre-cate without compromising the apparent reliability of the narrator. 'Or Her Soft Breast' is an oddly formal poem from 1983 that inches towards the Elizabethan when it uses a metaphor of forbidden desire for death. It also admits 'the slow fire /of self-despite'. Nearly two decades later – in 'Brush and Comb' – 'I must prefer the role /of victim. (Though sometimes not.)' And it's through Fainlight's forcefully level-pegging lines that we can most clearly see how plain dealing is, in its own way, unstoppable. Solomon's desire for Sheba, a fleeting domestic memory or the not-unexpected feminist symbolism of the moon are all made to move at the same speed. This 'masked' autobiography gives nothing away.

Fainlight's self-discipline extends to her descriptive strategies. Although she has been exposed, as an Hispanicist, to headier poetic mixtures than those of her British poetic contemporaries, her sleeves-rolled, hard-working verse resists the tempting shortcuts that adjectives offer. It is also led by meaning, rather than the ear. The well-regulated lines do not wax and wane, but bear an equal weight of meaning and emotion at every point. In a poem of orphanhood:

> I spread my hands on the desk.
> Prominent tendons and veins
> on the back, like hers;
> red worn skin of the palm
> that chaps and breaks
> so easily, inherited
> from my father. Even without
> the rings, the flesh of my hands
> is their memorial.
>
> ('My Rings')

Sylvia Plath, Fainlight's contemporary and friend – a fellow-American who had also found herself married to a well-known British writer – raised the stakes for the authoritative female voice in poetry by shifting registers towards intensity, even hyperbole. If Plath split the atom, however, Fainlight's project has always been to mend it. In poems like 'My Rings' symbol and message have become so tightly fused that the whole image speaks as one.

Alan Brownjohn is a flâneur, a role he adopts with zest. Like Fainlight he delights in masks, among the most recent and ludic of which is 'Ludbrooke', the protagonist of sixty sonnets in *Ludbrooke and Others* (2010):

> A friend says, 'Ludbrooke, you're a conniving sod.'
>   . . . Yes, he's felt exactly that
> For many decades. He knows his instinct for finding
> A devious route to any given objective
> Other men would approach by motorway,
> Breaking down en route . . .
>
> ('His Compliment')

Ludbrooke is a playful figure, but one inflected by a closely character-ized emotional complexity, which Brownjohn's more wholly owned verse doesn't aim for in quite the same way. The persona allows

Brownjohn to explore both vanity ('His Classic Modesty' compares his
lovemaking to the Acropolis, which '*Intelligent girls* adore') and humili-
ation (an Oxfam shirt), in their fleetingness and proximity. Personality
seems to serve as the prism which splits experience into ambivalent
complexity. By contrast, the omniscient narrator of the same volume's
final poem – not a Ludbrooke piece – conjures 'an odd affirmative
spark' from a pigeon visiting a Tube train carriage, and gets his money's
worth out of the metaphor: 'Could we not ourselves form a flock /
Migrating to common sense?'

Yet Brownjohn's earlier poetry deploys a careful mono-linguality, its
focus tightened in order to sustain complex thought. 'Of Dancing',
published in 1975, starts with characteristic jauntiness:

> My dancing is, in my opinion, good,
> In the right, cramped circumstances, and provided
> Other people are too preoccupied with
> Their own to notice mine . . .

Yet it arrives, via a beautiful portrait of the natural world, at the
surprisingly metaphysical:

> . . . Vanity is so sad pretending to represent
> Nature with humans dancing. Those who can move
>   need not dance.

This isn't a reprise of Larkin's 'Home is so sad', though it echoes that
poem's famous opening construction, but the sketch of a larger horizon.
Both its piquancy, and its authority, lie precisely in that distance between
the workaday diction and the scale of its conclusion. It is a very British
piece of existentialism.

What makes it so British is the modesty that is, after all, a metonym
for good manners, especially among Brownjohn's generation. His
unprotesting examinations of social class include 'Incident in 1912'
– a strange morality tale – and the much earlier 'Common Sense',

a found poem published in *Sandgrains on a Tray* (1969) and taken
from '*From Pitman's Common Sense Arithmetic, 1917*'. These textbook
puzzles bluntly record the costs of low pay and of war-time casualties, and Brownjohn lineates each to produce a five-line stanza. The
technique would still be regarded in some quarters today as avant
garde. And yet another poem from the same collection, the wry
social commentary of 'Somehow', uses the mild, steady tones of
blank verse to ventriloquize a provincial letter-writer. These stanzas
may have eight lines but they refuse to echo Lord Byron's heroic
ottava rima:

> The North Lancashire Ballet Group is coming
> Next month, and Miriam Granger-White is giving
> A Francis Thompson reading in the Public
> Library. So we are all well catered for, culture-wise,
> And don't really miss London . . .

The wry, even sly, humour (how Brownjohn must have observed and
detested 'culture-wise') is not much different from that accompanying
the anti-heroic Ludbrooke onto the page some forty years later. Such
steadiness, of vision and in the line, bespeaks real discipline. Sustained
over numerous volumes and many decades, it acquires an almost moral
quality.

A more expansive, riskier writer, Dannie Abse (*b.* 1923) is in some
ways the outlier in this company. His verse has only gradually distilled
itself from the more ornate, specifically Anglo-Jewish tradition, of
which Isaac Rosenberg's highly referential modernism might be the
ultimate example. Feinstein and Fainlight allude to the Jewish cultural
experience, but the Abse of *Walking Under Water* (1951) explicitly seeks
out a heightened, psalmic prosody. In 'Epithalamium', for example,
the opening couplet – 'Singing, today I married my white girl / beautiful in a barley field' – may sound like Dylan Thomas, but that white/
barley imagery is biblical rather than Anglo-Welsh, something that's
made yet more explicit in 'Song for Dov Shamir':

> Working is another way of praying.
> You plant in Israel the soul of a tree.
> You plant in the desert the spirit of gardens.

Easy enough perhaps in a poem about a kibbutz; but South Welsh smokestacks are characterized with similar pastoral allegory and a hint of corresponding rapture: 'The straw-coloured flames flare still, / spokes over the long horizon' ('Leaving Cardiff'). Formal devices like these can't be divorced from the poetry's content. 'Red Balloon', from 1961, appropriates ballad metre for a parable of anti-Semitism.

'Remembering Miguel Henandez' is inflected by Hispanic speech rhythms and imagery:

> The noise of many knuckles on metal,
> We do not hear it.
> There is lightning when we are asleep
> And thunder that does not speak;

But in the poems of late middle age the colours shift and Abse embraces more Anglo-Welshery, as the title of *Welsh Retrospective* (1997) makes clear. Topic, and imagination, both seem more concentrated on the close-at-hand. By 1972's 'Portrait of the Artist as a Middle-aged Man':

> . . . oh half my life
> has gone to pot. And, now, too tired for sleep,
> I count up the Xmas cards childishly,
> assessing, *Jesus*, how many friends I've got!

Here, in a crafty bit of cross-cultural finger-crossing, the name 'Christ' lurks under a 'crossing'-out in the abbreviation 'Xmas', and the only '*Jesus*' is a demotic exclamation. This wit stirs up a cross-current of meaning and colour that allows an emotional, and intelligent, personality to disturb the surface of the verse. Abse's poems never read as technical exemplars; there is always something whole-heartedly inhabited about the writing. By 2010, in his 'Lachrymae' for the death of his wife in a car accident, this could not be clearer: 'I went to her funeral. / I cried. / I went home that was not home.'

Grief, like other kinds of truth, is economical with words. Reading old 'Letters' after his wife's death, Abse finds that 'Now I read sweet words / I daren't repeat. (You would not want me to.)' This kind of writing, which takes no hostages but still *makes* something out of the simple – or not so simple – matter of experience, is the plain dealers' trump card. Consistency, allowing us to *know where we are* as readers, and a kind of 'trust me' plain speech which offers itself as a code for decency, are the strategies through which it gains, and earns, authority.

If that authority can seem a little in love with the quotidian, and with the truths of Everyman and -woman, it is worth remembering how powerfully this generation of writers, emerging in the immediate post-war era, resisted the twin pulls back to a mystifying, aristocratic literary past, or forwards to dangerously utopian visions of transformation. Their poetics of proportion measures up to big abstractions – and indeed to difficult moral and emotional experiences. Producing clarity from the chaos of experience, it lays the best possible foundation for the diversity and eclecticism that has followed.

2

THE DANDIES

In Sixties Britain, style came off the ration. Even if London only swung for the coteries, the pleasure principle was re-emerging after decades of Depression, war and rationing, and it would become widespread in the Seventies. British poetry, too, diversified and took on colour. One legacy of those permission-giving decades is the dandy swagger with which some poets greeted the plain speech – and moral high ground – of the utility era. Swagger is the classic street aesthetic, concerned with lightness of encounter and recognition at a stroke. It does more than is strictly necessary – and does so ostentatiously. Yet, even though it seems to be entirely on display, there's something self-referential, even hermetic, about dandyism. Whatever it deems pleasurable or cool is transferred into a closed system of codes, to be read by initiates. To *notice* the breadth of either a lapel – or an irony – is to *understand* its excellence.

Dandyism offers a way to feel special; but its mechanism is attractively simple. After all, nothing is fundamentally disturbed by a little style. Poetic swagger sets off none of the depth charges of a modernist reappraisal of culture. It doesn't go in for surrealist rearrangements of logic, or postmodern scepticism about the capacities of either language or thought. Instead, dandyism accepts plain dealing's fundamental contract: an unproblematic, realist view of language and experience. But, in the spirit of carnival, it contains our unease about how that might limit what a poem can do by offering us a little linguistic fancy dress.

In fact, all poems swagger. Even plain dealing pulls at least one trick, creating the illusion that poems lack a kind of interiority; something we might call self-consciousness. This isn't quite the same as believing they're artless: it's obvious that a poem isn't a spontaneous occurrence or a natural fact but a man-made object. Not even plain dealing shied away from the fact of fabrication. In his poem 'In 1936' for example, Anthony Thwaite plays the judicious craftsman:

> It was in Leeds in 1936,
> In Roman Terrace, by our red-brick house.
> I stood there with a boy, who said to me:
>
> 'That house just opposite – take care
> You don't walk near it on a Saturday.
> They're Jews . . .

Pentameter makes clear that this poem is controlled rather than spontaneous, and its title defines a unified focus. Yet the narrator plays the Honest Joe, juxtaposing sentence after sentence as if they were so many bricks in a wall, and had no *internal* relationship to each other – even though it is precisely the relationship of childish gossip to the era of European fascism that's telling. It is as if the poem wants to pretend it is simply the sum of its parts. As if poetic logic were purely grammatical or even arithmetical, and the poem as a whole had no interior life, no cumulative atmosphere or tone.

Yet as readers we rely on the ways a poem is composed in relation to itself to get our bearings. Some connectedness of purpose – what we might loosely call a meaning project – unites every element within a poem. If J.H. Prynne's connections sometimes seem purely tonal, or if Selima Hill's narrative steps can be surreal, that project has simply changed character, not nature. Formal connection works throughout a poem, in every direction at once. A sonnet can only *be* a sonnet when every line behaves in a particular relation to every other. (Free verse operates in similar ways, even though the pattern it follows is of its own devising: it might have to do with aural balance or the exposition of an image, for example.) This working-togetherness haunts William Carlos Williams's idea, first announced in his Introduction to 1944's *The Wedge*, that 'a poem is a small (or large) machine made of words'.

In Don Paterson's much-quoted variation, the poem becomes 'a small machine for remembering itself'. We might go further and call it a 'small machine for admiring itself'. All poems swagger. But the dandy poem, which carries a swagger-stick under its arm, exploits rather than struggles against its own inherent artifice: acting out in ways it might take an experienced reader to decode, but which we can all enjoy. This doesn't imply that either its form or its content are superficial. On the contrary, working *with* the poetic grain and employing virtuoso attention to detail, dandified writers are able to explore both poetic form and their chosen topics more deeply than would otherwise be the case.

It is a flamboyantly individualized approach. The dandies aren't a single, unified group. Their strategy emerges periodically, perhaps in reaction to poetry it finds dreary or artless. Today's influential dandies include Hugo Williams, Craig Raine, Glyn Maxwell and Jo Shapcott, but these poets certainly don't see themselves as belonging to a single school or movement. Craig Raine and Jo Shapcott, for example, speak for different generations. Raine represents the Martianism with which the Seventies closed, and Shapcott the New Generation that sprang up in the Nineties. Although neither actually named the movement with which they are associated, each was active in the early identification of a peer group. An Oxford University faculty member and an editor – not only as Poetry Editor at Faber from 1981 to 1991, but of *Quarto* and latterly *Areté*, the magazine and edition he founded – Craig Raine has been well-placed to cultivate a group of like-minded mentees and colleagues. This community adopted many of the mannerisms of, in particular, his second collection, *A Martian Sends a Postcard Home* (1979), and so gave a movement an identity and a name. By contrast, Jo Shapcott was a member of the London poetry workshop run in Notting Hill by Robert Graecen, and later Matthew Sweeney, from which a number of poets emerged sharing a respect for cool and elegance. Also among them were Don Paterson, Vicki Feaver, Sarah Maguire, Ruth Padel, Maurice Riordan, Lavinia Greenlaw and Michael Donaghy.

Since they didn't develop within the academy or, as would have been the case fifty years earlier, through literary or journalistic apprenticeship to one form of print or another, several of this group have earned their living by leading creative writing workshops. As a result, they've had a disproportionate influence on the way poetry has been taught, and so written, in Britain in the last twenty years; their legacy includes such fine, slightly younger, poets as Paul Farley. Their very Nineties model of cool was for some time so ubiquitous that it was difficult to identify its specific qualities. However, many of these poets have since developed far from their common aesthetic roots and come to appear unlikely stable-mates. In remaining closer to the point of common poetic origin than, arguably, any of her peers, Jo Shapcott has come to be the repository of that aesthetic.

Dandyism is every bit as inconsistent in its outcomes as in its origins. Glyn Maxwell's flamboyance extends to choice of forms: he has tried to rehabilitate the verse play and, despite denials, a book like *The Sugar Mile* (2005) closely resembles a verse novel. On the other hand, Hugo Williams (*b.* 1941) is the master of the distilled short: lyrics that manage to shake off the cloying aspects of sincerity, even when his recent work, in particular, takes the form of a series of autobiographical 'spots of time'.

Williams was encouraged by poet-editor Ian Hamilton at two magazines, the *Review* and the *New Review*, whose dominant note (in verse: the *New Review* published across genres) was the short, 'feelingful' poem. Hamilton opposed this to the expositional seriousness and heavy-handed rhetoric of much that had gone before. He positioned his magazines at the other pole of post-war poetry to that occupied by the New Apocalyptics clustered around Dylan Thomas. Hamiltonians (who included such lesser-known figures as Colin Falck and Michael Fried) were distinctive enough to earn the composite sobriquet *Hugo Harsfried*. Yet, beside Hugo Williams, those still central to British poetry include Alan Jenkins and David Harsent – whose work could hardly differ more from his and each other's. These poets do have in common, though, a lack of patience with what they might call the humbug surplus. They avoid emotion that hasn't been earned by the poem itself. Confessional poetry, with its high-register entry point, tends to leave them cold; all three exercise a fine linguistic discipline. Ian Hamilton's own poems were famously few – his *Sixty Poems* (1998) pretty much a lifetime's oeuvre – and were marked by an economy so exquisitely judged as to be almost fey. They stand in contrast to the ferocity of the criticism he practised and encouraged, and whose seriousness of mission seems to have been internalized by his heirs, all three of whom have worked as editors. Williams, who started his working life at *London Magazine* under the late Alan Ross – another highly influential and sui generis editor – is currently poetry editor at the *Spectator*.

Hamilton's dark advantage, in his advocacy of the personally felt lyric, was that the material he had to draw upon from his own personal life was difficult and unhappy. Hugo Williams's emotional territory of ruefully remembered love affairs, a theatrical childhood, offers no such short cuts to high seriousness. Instead, he resorts to tone – his is dry and wry – to bounce away from the dying fall of self-absorption. *Billy's Rain* (1999) is well-known for the sequence of end-of-the-affair poems which make up the second half of the book. They are much less well behaved than earlier missives from the affair itself, which explore some forms of understatement and devise others. 'Interval', for example, cleverly transfers the poem's entire narrative responsibility onto a few pieces of furniture:

> A couple of cushions on the floor,
> the angle of a sofa,
> are all we need to know
> about a missing hour.

Elsewhere, the eponymous 'Rhetorical Questions' of a much-quoted poem about female orgasm deploy tonal paradox. The answer the tone of these questions seems to entail – 'How do you think I feel / when . . .', 'And how do you think I like it / when . . .' – is emphatically (yet so *un*-emphatically) not the one implied by their content: 'you make me talk to you / and won't let me stop / till the words turn into a moan' and 'the blank expression comes / and you set off alone / down the hall of collapsing columns'.

The poems of sexual jealousy that follow are more shamelessly direct:

> It looks at first like a horse
> failing repeatedly to clear a fence,
> rearing up, stalling for a moment,
> sinking down between her thighs.

('Congratulations')

But even here, in characterizing his imagination as a voyeur, Williams is dressing up in a jaunty persona, as he had done nearly a decade earlier in *Self-Portrait with a Slide*. That book's anti-hero, Sunny Jim, has a routinely disappointing life. A rare LP 'is going to be "Absolutely great, thanks" – / until I get it home' ('Wow and Flutter'); while in a dream of hipness 'flares trail a year or two behind' their wearer, and fashion, along the King's Road. *Self-Portrait* also includes two great set pieces of generalized human self-disgust. 'When I Grow Up' is a portrait of confused and cathetered old age. 'Toilet', funny about the self-deceiving lust of a passenger on a train, ends with a fantasy that when the woman from the seat opposite goes to use the train toilet, it is a 'sign' that 'she likes me' and 'is lifting / her skirt, taking down her pants / and peeing all over my face'. As the boundaries between the narrator's fantasy, his actual surroundings and the blonde's imagined imagination are removed, the distinction between appearance and truth disappears, too. To see is to make real: Williams comes from a family of actors and it is impossible to shake the sense that these stories are something like appearances or roles.

The same volume's 'In the Seventies' is a quieter, echt-Hamiltonian homage to Williams's apprenticeship at that 'fine but / slow-moving publication', which must find its place among these corner shops' quick-selling 'canopies of soft porn':

> It shouldn't be such a bad day. Tony and I
> are delivering copies of *The New Review*
> to newsagents in North London.

This fragment of memoir stands out among the surrounding poems, with their accent on somewhat surreal and sealed-in themes or ideas. Since *Billy's Rain*, poems in its mould have lapped and overtaken the often slightly longer fictional verse. A kind of distillation has been conducted through *Dear Room* (2006) and *West End Final* (2009). The tone becomes more certain and more ready. The non-literality of his earlier work could seem like a form of evasion, but since the millennium Hugo Williams's poetry has come closer, in both diction and content, to the largely autobiographical prose he has been writing 'with his left hand' since the Eighties. Often leaving the 'point' of the story apparently open, the organizational strategy of these poems resembles his popular *Freelance* column for the *Times Literary Supplement*.

This is not to say that Williams's writing has become prosy. Air moves through the deft lineation of 'A Conjuring Trick' (2009), a poem about his mother's cremation. In its closing stanza the funeral director's formality is captured by laborious, cumulative line breaks. Then the final three lines take us outdoors to the 'natural' feeling of a narrator's own experience; the line break's rhythmic pause after 'turn' creating the volta:

> He takes me aside
> and whispers that her ashes
> will be waiting for me in Reception.
> As we crunch back to the cars, we turn
> and see smoke spiralling into the air,
> while something difficult is imagined.

In that 'something difficult' Hugo Williams uses the gallant understatement we might expect of an Old Etonian.

By contrast, Craig Raine – self-identifying 'scholarship boy' – is all
baroque extravagance. The brief prose self-portrait that forms the
centrepiece of *Rich* (1984) reveals that 'Inspiration ran in the family':
an invalided veteran, the poet's father became 'a Spiritualist and a
faith healer, talking about his negro spirit-guide, Massa'. But the same
piece gives us a somersaulting eleven year old who had to learn that
'the self-confidence he'd given me, genetically and by example, to other
people was mere boasting'. There's nothing languid in this portrait of
the artist as a young upstart. A similar, distinctive sense of lived density
is apparent even in the slim poems of Raine's slimmest volume, 1996's
Clay: Whereabouts Unknown (easily construed as a mere counterpoint to
his verse novel *History: The Home Movie*, which had been published a
couple of years earlier). And his famously scatological work of
mourning, *A La Recherche du Temps Perdu* (2000) has no trace of
Hamiltonian pursed lips in its celebration of:

> hairs like an icon's
>
> calibrated nimbus,
> your black smoking bush,
>
> the dark brown lips
> labyrinthine as a molten iris.

A La Recherche is held by some readers to be writing in crisis,
approaching too nearly some unpalatable truths that make it voyeuristic.
Voyeurism's gratuity, they feel, militates against poetry. This is an argument that takes two steps back from a robust sense of poetic health.
Neither death nor sex could plausibly be excluded from the canon of
poetic subject matter: that would be to ban most poetry, from *The Epic
of Gilgamesh*, the Song of Songs, and in this country *Beowulf*, onwards.
Raine is far from being the first poet to write about genitalia, which

can be found in both the anonymous mediaeval bawdry of 'I have a gentle cock' and William Blake's and Rainer Maria Rilke's considered roses. What Raine's critics are really saying is that, as they read this thirty-eight-page elegy for a lover who died of AIDS, they have a heightened awareness of *themselves* contemplating the poem's subject matter. It is *they* who feel like voyeurs. Yet all poems invite the reader to follow their gaze. Here, an enlarged sense of this experience simply aligns itself with the project for which this poet is best known, and for which Martianism is named: such poetry aims to show things 'as if for the first time', in T.S. Eliot's words; as if, in fact, through extra-terrestrial eyes.

The estranged, innocent, mystifying eyes of poetry do render familiar things strange. Sex and death, probably its most-examined themes, can become oddly quotidian. Raine's early exercises in Martianism were designed to make our daily life unexpected once again. (Middle-period Raine sometimes seems to rely on the sheer speed of the poet's intellect to keep things fresh.) Still, some things are regarded more repeatedly than others. Raine has a Freudian's preoccupation with the pursed character of orifices: 'a gathered eyelet / neatly worked in shrinking violet' ('Arsehole', from *Rich*); 'I looked out the sex: // female, a little black-eye, / too tender to touch, / which only looked at me / and I was crushed // and had to look away' (this sex belongs to 'Redmond's Hare', a creature the narrator is preparing for supper).

Why does this looking matter? One answer might simply be that it's the way this writer's mind works. But that would be to suggest artless inadvertence, and a poet who has been both editor and scholar surely has little inadvertence left. Another response is that observing the world is one way of being alert and intelligent within it: rather as students are taught close reading to help them read critically, as alert citizens. Raine's looking is close reading done out loud. There's no place, his Martianism seems to suggest, for the consolatory familiar. Besides, this poet born in 1944 is at home in a baby-boomer aesthetic, where everything is available, always and all at once. Nothing is any longer protected by rationing – or taboo. So, in Raine's world, historiography means Walter Raleigh digging a symbolic potato patch, an equally symbolic fag in his mouth.

Unsurprisingly, the shadows of a parents' war and of the Cold War haunt this imagery: 'The mind is a museum / to be looted at night' ('The Grey Boy'). But Raine also addresses those ghosts head on. At first reading, *History: The Home Movie* (1994) is striking both for its generous canvas – it is a socio-political history of Russia and Britain in the twentieth century – and for its refusal to guide the reader. In subsequent books an integrated emotion opens out the poems: a stated or implied 'I feel' informs both *A La Recherche* and 'I Remember My Mother Dying', the key uncollected poem of *How Snow Falls* (2010). The reader's struggle with *History*'s cast of thousands, however, is only slightly ameliorated by the family tree printed at the front of the book. A poem should be entire unto itself, but general levels of historical ignorance make it difficult to follow, or care about, everything that's going on in this verse novel.

This is partly down to Raine's refusal to let what counts as common knowledge contract. Just as we must know Christian doctrine to follow the *Four Quartets*, or Homer to understand how Derek Walcott's *Omeros* (1990) draws out the dignified, archetypal experiences of small fishing communities, *History: The Home Movie* demands that we keep an eye on historical truths, and acknowledge that they *are* the context in which we live now.

But *History*'s occasional hermeticism is heightened by a technical difficulty. Poetry, the cliché goes, shows not tells; yet the storyteller's obligation is precisely to tell. How, then, can a poem make things happen? Raine's solution is to tell his story as an intricate series of static instants. Occurrence follows occurrence, without much explicatory use of conjunction. In this continual present tense we're not always sure how we have arrived at each scene: like the book's characters, we live within an unsignposted present.

Here is Lydia Pasternak, in 1921, failing to secure the family's exit visas from Russia:

Shocked, she cannot speak.
Will she be able to walk
on her beautiful legs,

out through this ordinary door
and back into Russia for good?
Never to be abroad again?

Hammer and sickle. Forever.
Gilt on red. Cloisonné. Blurred
emblem of the ampersand.

She might be the North Star,
Sarah Bernhardt herself,
making an entrance:

everyone waiting watches the door,
as if the door were God,
as if the door were a loaded gun.

This series of instants isn't simply a technical strategy. It is quite specifically Martian. Like the 'metaphors' of Raine's earlier poems, the images and comparisons ('as if . . . as if') aren't similes, but symbols. It's not only a resemblance, but a resonance, that has been condensed in the comparison. In *Rich*, a Steinway piano, a 'grinning grand / with its dangerous fin', isn't only conspicuous among an heiress's possessions but is 'possessed' by her attributes: since the desirable 'Rich' are indeed 'dangerous'.

Martian epithet doesn't simply let us see the world anew; it establishes a new set of connections between the parts of that world. It's this hidden motor of accelerated connection that some Raine imitators, like Oliver Reynolds, lack. Christopher Reid – discovered by Raine while still an undergraduate, and appointed his successor as Faber poetry editor – knows the accelerator matters. He can play the faux naif, but the exuberant references of his 1979 debut, *Arcadia*, are a young man's peacock display: 'nicotined eyes, and someone's squiggly hookah, / fendered in levers, wheezing the blues', 'He kept a retinue / of gloomy servants, guard-dogs / and (his confidant and spy) / a raucous white cockatoo'.

If these deftly done images seem familiar, that's surely because they're plundered, not exactly from what Philip Larkin disparaged as the myth kitty, but from the shared picture book of English eccentricity. *Arcadia*, that dream of privilege, here remains a Sitwell/Lord Berners world of cheerfully gentrified dysfunction. Martian freshness of vision has turned into a less fully executed, more stylish estrangement. Puzzled, yet still playful, early Reid wanders a terrain of mixed-up familiars: a floor-mop, cows, weddings, hair in curlers and 'a pair of glasses, / folded on a book / in lotus position'. Like those pre-war children's classics with their comforting reprise of midnight feasts and picnics, this poetry offers frequent pauses for refreshment: there are stilton and camembert, Jerusalem artichokes and peppers, a fishmonger and a butcher. And such pleasures seem to overflow in Reid's several collections for children, elegantly illustrated and produced by small presses including his own. Yet it would be an exceptionally precocious child who could enjoy the wit of poems like 'Liarbird', from *Alphabicycle Order* (2001):

> Some grand and gorgeous birds
>   emit the feeblest squeaks,
> while others, too drab for words,
>   from their unpromising beaks
>
> pour out entire operas.

Narrator and ideal reader alike, it seems, are adult children.

While Raine's Martianism reconnects apparently discrete parts of his world by resonance and resemblance, Reid's takes apart existing connections, alienating the objects of his poems from themselves like a child dismantling a watch or a fly to see how it works. This is most subtly and successfully done in his third collection, *Katerina Brac* (1985), with the adoption of an alter ego that is further estranged by being both cross-dressing and Central European. The book borrows the surrealism, riddles and games that Mittel-European writers like Miroslav Holub, then fashionable in Britain, used to outsmart the censorship of Communist governments. Reid, of course, faced no such censorship; but a model of educated play, in which fantasy and archetype perform unexpected roles, clearly compels him. He puts his own finger on what he's doing with the early poem title 'A Whole School of Bourgeois Primitives'. A different kind of playfulness is evident in his verse novella *The Song of Lunch* (2009), a rueful tale of lost love versified in longish, informal lines we might call 'blank prose'. But Reid rightly judged that games could not sustain the emotion of *A Scattering* (2009), his collection of elegies for his late wife. In this book of apparently simple verse the poet seems undressed by grief.

Glyn Maxwell (*b*. 1962) frequently solves the problem of sustained poetic narrative by using personae. One early rehearsal is the title sequence of his 1992 collection, *Out of the Rain*, a forty-two-sonnet coming-of-age parable. More ambitious still is *The Sugar Mile*. An ensemble of voices gives an account of the London Blitz, and also refers to 9/11: an event of relatively immediate significance for Maxwell, who was living in the United States at the time of the atrocity. Juxtaposing a period from his own prehistory (Maxwell was born in 1962, two decades after the Blitz) with the events which put an end to 'The End of History' pre-empts the usual poor-taste rhetoric of disaster comparisons. It also avoids misplaced asides to camera, the kind Theodor Adorno's 'no poetry after Auschwitz' injuncts: cataclysm should not be reduced to an individual's reaction to it. Maxwell comes close to hubris when a barman talks about changing his job for one at the World Trade Center: 'Windows on the World. / Tuesday I start. Tomorrow's my last day.' But this brute pun is earned by the compression characteristic of the closing tercet of the sestina from which it comes. That form itself successfully mimics the circularity of bar work and talk.

Sugar Mile's 'numbers' could no more be read alone than could, say, the constituent sonnets of Vikram Seth's *The Golden Gate* (1986). Instead, they work as speeches:

> I thought I'd lost you, Joey, who are these
> > All over everywhere
> > Don't stand and stare
> At her she's had a shock, look at her eyes.
>
> Thought you'd joined the navy like your dad
> > I did just then I thought
> > He's off to war I ought
> To stop him he's too young I said . . .
> > > > ('Granny May at the Scene')

It is no surprise perhaps that Maxwell, who by this stage in his writing career had already published seven plays, should elect to tell a story in this way. He integrates the rhythms of East London into formal versification: Cockney slang *rhymes*, after all. These rhythms fill the poems with characterization: a survivor of the bombardment uses the terza rima (or a stalled form of it) of one who's seen Hell; an imposter breaks up a neighbourly chorus with prose; a schoolgirl's spelling works like an accent.

Maxwell has been a stylist since his 1990 debut, *Tale of the Mayor's Son*, its title poem a take on pentameter (and the occasional alexandrine) so characteristically jaunty it feels more like a form of appropriation. Usurping the omniscient narrator, the young poet's self-projection tries on the big boots of narrative authority:

> I could define Elizabeth. I will:
> > Every girl you ever wanted, but
> can't have 'cause I want. She was twenty-one.

This figure of the young poet matters. *Breakage* (1998) includes 'Letters to Edward Thomas', a fourteen-part homage to one of Maxwell's major influences. In Edward Thomas's own poems, such as 'March' or 'Lights Out', a flexibility and apparent clarity of voice identifies the speaker with the spoken. Thomas called this 'the sound of sense'. It implies that there is no barrier between thought and the external concrete world. *Sum ergo cogito*, they seem to say.

Maxwell's finest work from all stages of his career, such as the uncollected 'Come to Where I'm From' (2011), displays a related flexibility of thought and tone:

> Hard to remember now that it's all begun
> that it all began and, now that it's all over,
> hard to recall it's gone. Those who are gone
> arrive in a crest of steam and the late-lamented
>   help them with their boxes.

Something altogether stranger is going on in *Hide Now* (2008), whose poems appear profoundly internal, and dream-like with circularity. It is as if a shifting, urgent music has generated phrases which fill up each line and spill out to entail the next. In part this might be because of the familiarity of the metres Maxwell uses. In 'A Play of the Word' this is anapest tetrameter:

> Something was done and she ran from a town
> and I'm glad it was done or she wouldn't have come,
> but she wouldn't have gone and she's long gone now,
> so I'm wondering why and remembering how.

Elsewhere, blank verse remains a presence even in lines of uneven length. But there is also a sense of meaning getting slightly out of step with itself and carried away; something that is only enhanced by an increasing use of repetition as a kind of 'strong rhyme'. In 'Flags and Candles' for example:

Flags line up an hour before they're chosen,
wave back along the row at others like them.
Candles sit in boxes or lie still,

sealed, and each imagines what will happen.

This is a convincing enough representation of object-life. But what's actually going on in the poem? The eponymous flags and candles are resonant. Yet while the poem borrows that resonance, it doesn't seem to exploit or develop it. The piece remains inert, like one of Maxwell's waiting candles, and even its use of rhyme seems unpropulsive – perhaps because of the lines' strong-weak feminine endings. The poem's intention appears close-at-hand, yet never quite *in* the reader's hand.

Like Craig Raine's *History*, though using very different techniques, Glyn Maxwell is here exploring the freedoms and limitations of a continual present tense. Content and context may be an ever-rolling stream rather than accumulating significance. Without time for example there can be no consequences; so the continual present tense releases the poet from some kinds of moral meaning-making. It is the subtle exposition of this message through traditional forms and metres, as much as the flattening out of poetic pleasures into a rhythmic-melodic surface, that makes Maxwell the important stylist he is.

Jo Shapcott (*b.* 1953) has never presented her poetic self as either a life coach or a moral guide. *Of Mutability* (2010) is neither misery memoir nor confessional verse-fest. The most literal insight it offers into the experience of being treated for, and surviving, cancer is when it records the subtle realignments an individual must make when her body feels what we might call 'wobbly': as though it belonged to a watery city ('La Serenissima'), or were 'a drop of water' held together only by surface tension ('Deft'). Such images debunk the terrifying sensation of dissolution in serious illness, even as they evoke it. This steely modesty is central to Shapcott's technique. In this first sortie

since *Her Book*: *Poems 1988–1998*, the Selected poems she had published
a dozen years earlier, more than two-thirds of the poems are written
in the first person. But, far from self-aggrandizement, this signals a
form of limitation. The self is merely individual. Despite its Big Theme,
the volume refuses to universalize.

This refusal is key. It is a postmodern turn, away from messy numi-
nosity or the idea of the poet as 'unacknowledged legislator', and
iterates that what you see is what you get. Unlike plain dealing's realism,
however, here 'what you get' has no automatic contract with the world
of daily experience, but exists *in* the world of the poem. That world
is logical and expressed with grammatical clarity, but the poem implies
neither that such a thing came before it nor that it exists after the
poem has ended. Resonance isn't the language's first criterion. This
makes pure sound – from internal rhyme to speed of diction – particularly significant. It also allows the poet to take lyric risks. She may
sound like Elizabeth Smart, that prose rhapsodist of the Forties:

> Look up to catch eclipses, gold leaf, comets,
> angels, chandeliers, out of the corner of your eye
>
> ('Of Mutability')

or the American contemporary poet of eco-spirituality Mary Oliver:

> I went outside and found the landscape
> which had eaten my heart.
>
> ('Viral Landscape')

But the verse never expands into expression or confession.

Shapcott has long adopted and adapted such crafty freedom. In the
'Mad Cow' poems of the Nineties, a persona that was both wild and
ridiculous allowed her register to rise:

> The police came once when I was doing my death dance
> to the amazing circular music which had entered a gap

near my cortex and acted as powerfully as a screwdriver
on my soul.

> ('The Mad Cow Tries to Write the Good Poem')

and fall:

>. . . I have been sad recently
>and now the weather has changed for good.

> ('The Mad Cow Believes She is the Spirit of the Weather')

This ventriloquizing is a hallmark. An Elizabeth and Robert Browning
sequence in her 1988 debut, *Electroplating the Baby*, has been followed
by appearances from Tom chasing Jerry around tourist London, Marlon
Brando, and even Superman. In 1992, *Phrase Book*'s title poem crunched
together military jargon and a period phrase book to implicate its
narrator in contemporary, inevitably post-colonial, warfare.

Yet in *Of Mutability*, whose theme is, overwhelmingly, ontological and
bodily insecurity, the use of the first person seems to set off difficulties
of its own. We expect it to indicate that the poet has put aside personae;
that the 'I' is somehow authentic in ways that raise the stakes. But
while some poets explicitly rehearse mental processes (C.K. Williams,
Jorie Graham) or emotional experiences (Pascale Petit, Sharon Olds),
Shapcott's poetic 'I' seems constructed to give as little ground as possible.
It repeatedly turns the poem's focus away from itself: 'It's two thousand
and four / and I don't know a soul who doesn't feel small / among
these numbers'; 'I breathe in and become everything I see'; 'surgery,
and all that mess / I don't want to comb through here'. It records its
own limits: 'I wanted to stay awake longer than / anyone else in our
student house'; 'and my transparent self / went about its business all
that day, the usual.'

At the same time, buoyant, regular diction constructs an unusually
coherent, apparently unitary speaker, whose language betrays no unconscious hinterland. It's as if this first person is another persona. In *Phrase
Book*'s 'I'm Contemplated by a Portrait of a Divine', the device of a

painting frames a clever portrait of a psyche havering on the cusp between ordinary embodied life and spirituality. This allows us to pretend the poem's metaphors are merely literal, ekphrastic representations of that picture: 'This pose . . . / It's so important for keeping the drawer shut / in case my heart should slip out, fly up.' And even this seems a device to limit, rather than to invoke, the writing's resonance.

It's the discipline of the aural patterning that stops this leading to flatness. When 'Brando on Commuting' includes the superhero's fantasy about meeting a girl on the Tube, he plans to 'cut through / her shyness like a crusader'. These sounds are economically organized. Vowels sink, between the alliterative snip of the *c*'s, into a matching *ou/y/e*, before rising to the high *a* that is the crux of 'crusader'. But the imagery is economical, too. It replaces fleshed-out description with the *principle* of the crusader's blade. *Mutability* is also economical in scale. Fifty-one pages include several variations on the sonnet form, as well as a series of landscape and townscape miniatures – and even a riddle – which are shorter still. Such modesty is a form of refinement. If poetry is traditionally seen as a heightened discourse, Shapcott makes hers distinctive by sweeping away the metrical and alliterative music, and such gestures as allusion or multiple meanings, that we have come to associate with this heightening. The effect is a spring-cleaned modernity. *Of Mutability*, despite the companionably familiar literary allusion of its title, is about as unfusty as it is possible to be. The only heightened vocabulary is scientific – 'layers of xylem and crushed phloem', 'octandrous', 'gut epithelium', 'latent inhibition' – and if poems occasionally shift out of the present tense, nothing is in the passive case. From the disobedient, 'itching' cells on the book's first page to the imagined 'jet stream' of 'piss' on its last (a jet 'so intense my body rises / a full forty feet and floats // on a bubble stem of grace': not 'is raised', in other words), everything is *done* rather than done *to*.

It might signify a quiet formal repudiation of victimhood, but the use of the active case also indicates the poetics of the influential Nineties generation. So does a largely un-adjectival prosody in which imagery, often jokey or surreal, takes on the descriptive function:

And what are they doing there, those flowers
with the faces of bereaved dogs and scared kittens?
Bindweed, made of paperwork and damp beer mats,
is flourishing in the shadows . . .

('The Death of Iris')

Shapcott uses rhyme and slant-rhyme with unostentatious ease, as
in her two 'Abishag' poems after Rilke, and several of *Mutability*'s
un-metrical sonnets employ occasional rhyme or an interlocking
matching of letters, not quite alliterative or indeed aurally explicit:

There is a tower of the winds as tall
as this one in another city, a steeple
filled with fire . . .

('St Bride's')

Don Paterson, pre-eminent advocate of this kind of music-making, has
long been one of Shapcott's closest colleagues. It was at the height of
their collaboration in the Nineties that, as well as co-writing a column
on computer games and co-editing their *Last Words: New Poetry for the
New Century* (1999), she published the two collections, *Phrase Book* and
My Life Asleep (1998), in which her voice, as refreshing but dry as an
afternoon gin, first explored its own range.

Allusive, discreet, joke-telling, here as in the most recent work her
surfaces – both aural and semantic – are shiny with lack of obfusca-
tion or hubris. The macabre narrative of 'Electroplating the Baby'
and *Of Mutability*'s straightforward seriousness seem equally confidently
to fill that gleaming language. To strain for affect would contradict
the poet's demonstrated belief in what poetry is, and her solution is
to delegate any gestures towards capital-M Meaning. The 'Mad Cow'
poems are not, after all, *quite* feminist. Their playfulness stops them
short. And as Shapcott points out in her Acknowledgements to *Mutability*,
'The artist Helen Chadwick is the presiding spirit' of a collection in
which ekphrasis becomes, as it is so rarely, poetically structural: many

poems describe Chadwick's work, from 'Viral Landscape' to 'Piss Flower'.

Shapcott's consistency makes her a steely exemplar of the virtues of stylish writing, but she is far from being the most recently emerged dandy in British poetry. The swagger is no less of a young poet's gait now than it has ever been. Of course, that makes it hard to tell which of today's younger writers will turn out truly to have adopted this poetics, and which are simply writing sharp. The process of differentiation is further complicated by Don Paterson's rapier-sharp editing at the Picador poetry list since 1997. The press issues a steady series of stylishly dandified collections, varied in tone, from Colette Bryce's and John Stammers's street machismo to the cool pastoral of Jake Polley and Katharine Towers, by way of Annie Freud's self-abjecting humour. Chill fingers of cool can also be felt at work in the writing of new poets like Joe Dunthorne, Tim Turnbull and Sam Riviere, from other stables. Will they turn out to be as elegant and emotionally intelligent as their precursors? Time will tell.

3

THE OXFORD ELEGISTS

Poet dandies flaunt their style. But *no* technique can avoid expressing its notion of what an ideal or at least a satisfactory poem might be. Sometimes, for example in strict forms, this ideal resembles a ground plan. At others, it seems closer to metaphysics: a belief, rather than an opinion held on argued grounds, that one particular strategy or style captures the 'true' nature of poetry. Poets of all kinds hold such beliefs about the sine qua non of poetry. Plain dealers believe a poem's accessibility is a near-moral form of accountability. Dandies hold that, though comprehensibility is important, it isn't enough: a poem expresses itself through its style. For both, what defines a poem is something that, though it may be articulated in technical terms, has to do with tone and purpose.

The poets this chapter groups together – John Fuller, the late Mick Imlah, Alan Jenkins and Andrew Motion – share a poetics that is principally a question of tone, though this produces technical similarities. Three are strict form virtuosi, capable both of extended riffs and of incorporating rhyme into the very structure of their thought. Unlike dandies, the Oxford elegists do share a network of friendship, collegiality and mutual influence: only one of this quartet did not study at the University. Their writing hasn't remained tethered to Oxford, but it does borrow resonances from that institution. Chief among these is a broad sense of poetic practice as above all literary. As a result, these poets share a degree of relative estrangement from certain contemporary developments, not so much in the writing but in the reception and promotion, of British poetry. It would be difficult to find a group less suited to the inverted byline, fashionable in the Nineties, that omits any suggestion of writerly apprenticeship or expertise but glamorizes manual or other unrelated work, however briefly done. Embedded for most of their working lives in explicitly literary day jobs – editing and university lecturing – all four omitted to go on the road, 'gigging' and workshopping, with their more band-wagoneering peers. This means that none has contributed regularly to the formative creative writing workshop culture of the last two decades (although Andrew Motion is now a Professor of Creative Writing). As a result, the generations who have emerged from that culture are often less aware of this group's work than they should be.

The Oxford elegists also share a concern with the high cultural past and are at their best (as the moniker suggests) when they strike an elegiac note, midway between nostalgia and sensibility, in poems which record both shared and individual experiences of change. Though a far from gloomy read – rich cultural allusion tends to combine with respect for beauty – their emotional register is tuned pretty consistently to certain keys: truth, decency, restraint. And, as a shared public form, elegy is always both permissible and appropriate. Its lightly ritualized character functions something like a dress code: the format, already agreed, can both contain and present even difficult material. Moreover, linking the present occasion with every other grief elegized in cultural history, it supplies resonance by association.

In any case, elegy is curiously contagious. Like tragic catharsis, it allows an audience to borrow mourning. Just as we need do nothing more than follow the drama in order to take part in tragedy's cathartic explosion of emotion, elegy's mood-altering capacity to draw the reader into emotional agreement pre-empts any more critical response. For example, in his 'Fantasia on a Theme of James Wright' (2006), an elegy for the mining communities lost to Thatcherism as well as to pit disasters, Sean O'Brien exclaims, 'O my brothers.' Though he's addressing his

readers, he seems briefly to address those lost miners too: the exclamation bespeaks solidarity between us and them. No other form is so
purposefully collusive. Even love lyrics don't require the reader to join
in with the lover's desire. We may identify or sympathize – but we
don't get turned on.

Elegy is associated with a familiar phrasal music, a feeling that the
individual poem joins in with something that's always already going
on. In short, it has a sense of tradition. The Oxford elegists don't
set their faces away from the past. Instead, like the modernists, they
exploit the ways in which, because of the contexts in which they've
already been used, words and phrases can evoke resonances or
secondary information. Alan Jenkins appropriates riverbanks, and
Mick Imlah cricket pitches, as metonyms for unspoilt youthfulness
– these images are already full of symbolic correspondences – while
John Fuller's 'God Bless America' (1972) delegates meaning-making,
or at least exposition, to quoted material.

Which isn't to say that these poets trot out pastiche or fail to engage
with actual lived life. John Fuller, born in 1937 and arguably their
presiding spirit, writes verse of warmly contained emotion. Even *Ghosts*
(2004), his collection most 'haunted' by explicit, returning thoughts of
death, contains its theme within the comforts of form and of a stabi-
lized register. 'Excitement', for example, balances its opening, 'We
should give thanks to be living with infants', by ending, 'For there
comes a time when we no longer / Wish we could go on sleeping for
ever, / Because we are asleep for ever.' Two-thirds of the book's poems
eventually arrive at the idea of death, though each frames it differently.
Among these is the title poem, which imagines those who fell from the
Twin Towers as 'Handlocked divers, impossible stars'. A Shelleyan
wind, and sparks from the cottage hearth where the poet sits contemplating these events, resolve this poem – even though such literary
allusion runs the risk of appearing too bookish and decent a response
to the events of 9/11.

Possibly Fuller's most revealing collection is his next, *The Space of
Joy* (2006). Eight long poems, each meditating on the 'space' that

creative work takes up in its practitioners' lives and in the world, move from Petrarch to Samuel Taylor Coleridge, then Matthew Arnold, Johannes Brahms and Wallace Stevens. Within this chronological frame-work, each poem portrays the simultaneous cultural and geographical forces that create the relationship between an individual's life, love and work. 'The Solitary Life', a discursive prologue whose title is echoed in the book's closing stanza – 'To be alone / Is a condition of the observing brain' – has the poet in a hammock 'with a cushion and some books', 'slung' between trees, the shadows of whose leaves form a virtual laurel wreath:

> My head is full of shadowy characters
> In whom I ponder similarities
> Of restlessness and longing and a quest
> For peace . . .

For a contemporary British poet to place himself in a canonical context – even by thinking through it as Fuller's poet-guide does here – is unexpected and seems, for a moment, startlingly unfashionable. The light touch of Fuller's musicality can best be heard elsewhere in *Pebble and I* (2010): poems include 'Newspapers', which subverts the spirit of blank verse, and 'Pomme', which sustains it. But *The Space of Joy*, shot through with the poet's love of music, exuberantly runs the risk that its use of musical techniques might appear knowing. A note explains how 'the metre of ["Arnold in Thun"] is Arnold's invention for "Rugby Chapel" and other poems'. A meditation on Petrarch, father of that form, is a sequence of thirty-five – what else? – sonnets. And when, in the book's seventh poem, Wallace Stevens plays Brahms, he is made to speak through a number of forms, including that of his own 'Le Monocle de Mon Oncle'. Speaking *as* his subjects – who ventriloquizes whom? – allows Fuller to characterize them more fully. Each character comes to realize that the essentially unfulfilled nature of love is a rehearsal for death: 'We wait in vain to be emparadised.' All loss prefigures loss and necessitates resistance. For composers and poets this means writing: 'And after all, paper is all we know.' It is a transcendent pragmatism, in which 'joy' comes from acceptance and work.

This sort of secular redemption is neo-Romantic, and Fuller's canon is indeed broadly Romantic – if questioningly so. *The Space of Joy*'s comedic 'Coleridge in Stowey', in which the eponymous poet is busy 'Wrestling the challenge of Infinity / To Personality' while eschewing domestic responsibilities, reveals a self-pitying solipsist. This foreshadows the Martian caricatures of 'Piano Masterclass' (2010), in which that instrument 'sits forward on its knuckles / Glossy as a gorilla.' But *The Space of Joy*'s four final stanzas reveal this eponymous space is found not in art, but in human relationships:

> . . . what
> My parents built for me in reaching out
> Towards each other, something like an arch,
> A space of joy . . .

This is almost Fuller's *ars poetica*: that love is authentically remade by art, since 'something that's remote is better seen, / Like stars or mountains. And the heart goes out / Fiercely if frailly from its uncertain darkness, / Like coloured fires along the terraces.'

Playing the father in this happy family portrait is the poet Roy Fuller (1912–91), who served as Oxford Professor of Poetry from 1968 to 1973; a period when his son had recently become a Fellow and Tutor at Magdalen College and was publishing collections of his own almost annually. It would be all too easy to assume John Fuller's poetry existed within a perpetual Oxbridge of thought and influence. But his first academic post, held after National Service, was at the State University of New York; and though his capacious, sensitive writing builds on his father's work, it also differs from it, lacking altogether those lightly modernist tones.

Nonetheless Magdalen, of which Fuller is now Emeritus Fellow, has long seen itself as the cradle of Oxford poetry. It is home to the John

Florio Society (sometime members include the poet and editor Jon Stallworthy and James Fenton, former Oxford Professor of Poetry) and periodically the magazine *Oxford Poetry*, frequently edited by its graduate students. Seamus Heaney joined the College while he held the Professorship of Poetry. In short, it is the kind of establishment that lets insiders assume entitlement's languid air. Some of that languor seems to have been discerned in Mick Imlah by his friend Alan Hollinghurst, who wrote the Introduction to Imlah's posthumous *Selected Poems*:

> It was typical of Imlah not to be troubled by the career pressures which naturally affect most young writers. He had a sensible belief in his own gifts, but he was as indifferent to status as he was to money . . . He was wonderfully quick-witted, funny, several steps ahead in exact and ironic understanding of any matter being talked about; but he was equally and happily prone to a dawdling, quizzical slowness.

Imlah, who at his death in 2008 was only fifty-two, is a link figure among the elegists. A protégé of John Fuller's, he had stayed on at Magdalen College to write an ultimately never-submitted PhD on Victorian versions of Arthurian legend. Fuller's Sycamore Press issued his first pamphlet, *The Zoologist's Bath and Other Adventures*, in 1982; and in 1988 Imlah published his first full collection, *Birthmarks*, at Chatto, where he became Poetry Editor the following year. Like his immediate predecessor Andrew Motion, he had moved to this post from the editorship of *Poetry Review*; he stayed until 1992, when he became Poetry Editor of the *Times Literary Supplement*. He would remain in that chair until his death nearly two decades later. This chain of roles is significant because, though not himself a highly productive poet, Imlah had an important influence on contemporary British verse as an editor. (The poet and editor Ian Hamilton, who was arguably even more influential, displayed a similar costiveness.)

The map of the Oxford elegists' world that all this implies stands some clarifying. It is unusually editorially led. All four poets – Fuller, Imlah, Jenkins and Motion – were published by Chatto; that is, until two 'went upstairs' to Faber. Motion moved a few years before becoming Poet Laureate, Imlah with a long-awaited second collection when he was terminally ill. While both Motion and Imlah served terms as Poetry Editors at Chatto as well as at *Poetry Review*, Imlah and Jenkins have between them held the poetry editorship of the *TLS* since 1981; Jenkins is also that paper's Deputy Editor. Fuller published early pamphlet collections by both Imlah – who became a junior colleague of his at Magdalen – and Motion. A fifth figure, that of Blake Morrison, hovers like a deus ex machina close to these overlapping realms. Jenkins's predecessor as *TLS* Poetry Editor, where he would be responsible for the younger man's appointment, Morrison collaborated with Motion on the generation-defining *The Penguin Book of Contemporary British Poetry* (1982). As young writers, Morrison and Motion both wrote loose-limbed, short narrative poems with a consciously English tone; in retrospect, we can see in them Morrison's later success as a prose memoirist. However, as he effectively ceased to publish new poetry after 1990, his verse lies beyond the scope of this book.

The point is not, of course, that these are felicitously ramifying coincidences. This is how a school establishes itself. The spectacle is always both encouraging – enthusiasms are shared and junior colleagues helped along – and bracing. In particular, it demonstrates how practical the effects of a poetic belief system can be. Friendship, after all, arises from like-mindedness. In these repeated professional interactions we see not laziness but a kind of quiet intellectual passion at work. Of course, all young poets feel that other ways of writing simply don't count. It's how the dialect of the tribe develops. Without furious hubris who would dare make a start at poetry, in which so much that's wonderful already exists? In Ted Hughes's earliest letters, not only to Sylvia Plath but to writer friends who have since failed to emerge – as in Robert Lowell's letters to Elizabeth Bishop – the repeated message is that all other poets, beyond the charmed circle, are fools. Even the younger Larkin, for all his deprecation, seems not to have demurred at Monica Jones's response to a 1955 broadcast: 'Oh, I am sure that you are the one of this generation.' But the poet in his or her professional prime – and especially the poet-editor, who has a professional responsibility to turn outwards towards the other – has outgrown that early, Oedipal struggle for survival. By this stage of a writing life, to dismiss alternatives just because they *are* alternative is clearly irrational and, as an editor, Mick Imlah was far from proselytizing. His role among the Oxford elegists was something more akin to keeping the faith.

And Imlah kept the place for his own kind of poetry. His second collection, *The Lost Leader* (2008), is characterized by dense lines that remain in thrall to pentameter; and by an odd sense of equidistance. The poems are largely stories, from either Scottish or literary history. They're packed with fact, yet lack the push and pull of affect. As a whole, the book reads like a play on becoming Great through sheer 'greatness' of topic. It was, perhaps, the only way to go. When his debut appeared in 1988, *Birthmarks*'s 'ambitious young toerag' was still in his early thirties and already plundering history, especially imperial history, for topic and theme. 'Tusking' has 'the tinkle / Of ice and Schubert' on a verandah, while 'Visiting St Anthony' is a traveller's tale, both tall and rueful, that could have been recounted by any of the travel writers *Granta* magazine was making famous at the time; sons of Empire (or progeny, anyway, of adventure stories such as the *Biggles* books) like Bruce Chatwin and Colin Thubron.

It isn't the settings so much as his protagonists that most clearly demonstrate Imlah's Oxford colouring. The 'Mountains' sequence gives us a series not of geophysical phenomena, but of explorers. Yet his importance among the Oxford elegists is far more than simply connective. Technically robust, he could be a rumbustuous rhymer. In 'Cockney', a skit on the haywire vowels of the British class system, a set of tercets develops some of the most outrageous rhymes in the literature: from *fancy/Finzi/fiancée* and *Mahler*/milieu/*Millwall* to *Seychelles/seashells/satchel* and *Salome/assail me/salami.*

Imlah's early poem 'Secrets', with its cleaned-out vocabulary and end rhymes, its faintly arch diction and use of nostalgic tropes – a game of cricket, a drink in the pub, an imagined field of corn – could have been written by Alan Jenkins:

> Where no one flushed the grass
> A six-hit from the cricket,
> We dealt in shallow sighs
> Till hush! – she let her dress
> Unbutton to the locket
> And parted secrecies.

Compare that opening stanza with another, this time from Jenkins himself:

> I have led her
> Through long grass
> To the spring
> Hidden by willows;
> A childhood
> Haunt of mine,
> Herons lifting
> Off its shallows.
>
> ('Climber')

Despite the resemblances, Alan Jenkins (*b.* 1955) performs a very different role within this group. He differs profoundly from Mick Imlah not only in the way he emerged as a poet, but in his deployment of poetic affect. Imlah's poems – both the early pieces with their leaven of wit and the later 'loan stories' from other people's lives – could be read as sophisticated displacement activity, and all their craft as a kind of screen between the speaker of the poem and lived experience. Jenkins, on the other hand, has been profoundly influenced by Ian Hamilton, whose *Collected Poems* he edited in 2009, and by Hamilton's doctrine of the feelingful. Feeling *is*, for Jenkins, the point of the poem; form, its writerly accompaniment, brings emotional experience into focus by creating resonance.

A short poem from *The Drift* (2000) gives us the teenager in his bedroom:

> Riverside allotments, avenues of beech and oak,
> grass-smells drifting over gardens, bonfire-smoke
>
> in the autumn: the Surrey we had been allotted.
> I argued with him, stumped upstairs and plotted
>
> revolution or escape, watched by the eye of Che
> who recited Baudelaire's *Les femmes damnées*
>
> from my bedroom wall, and I took up the theme
> in wet dream after dream after dream . . .

This should be a piece of ephemera, as slight as it is short, but the rhymes that bolt it together show us it's here to stay. They shift, and shift the poem, from the conventionally evocative *beech and oak/bonfire smoke*, to the brief but intense burst of *Che/damnées* – a pairing which gives a satisfying sense of collusion, since the reader must know how to pronounce both, and of something virtuoso since it rhymes across languages – and arrive at that final *épatent* coupling of literary theme and wet dream. And these end-rhymes don't work in isolation. The first couplet's criss-cross alliteration, between 'Riverside allotments' and 'Grass-smells drifting over' (as if that 'o' itself drifted over from 'allotments'), becomes diffuse in the second's *autumn/him/stumped*. In the last couplet, 'from' and 'theme' frame the following line – which is nothing but the internal-rhyming repetition of 'in wet dream after dream after dream . . .' These formal fixatives make us stay with the poem. They also fix the experience of the poem's present; the very fixity that is at the heart of teenage miserablism.

Nine years later and 'A Canterbury Tale' is altogether longer. Its twenty-five stanzas, each an octet with its own unique rhyme pattern, revisit a summer teaching job taken decades earlier:

> Thirty years since I last did this, since I sat
> In a hot window-seat on the slow train down,
> Ashford-Hastings-Canterbury, stopping at
> Each leaf-occluded halt, each dormitory town;

Ostensibly, however, nothing else has changed. The same fine ear is brought to bear, in the second line, on the prolonging 'ow's; the metre works flexibly to produce a regular six-foot line. But something *is* different. Now description is casually incorporated, merely another form of evocation – 'leaf-occluded halts' – for a poet who has acquired the confidence to let information, such as place names and train timetables, do the tonal work. The sestrameter is a further element of prolongation in this more sustained verse. It's almost as if Jenkins is challenging the line, or the reader's ear, to let him prove just how much he can keep going. He makes it sound easy by incorporating his long lines into longer sentences, which fluently and almost blatantly (that 'stopping at/') enjamb. Like the give-and-take of varied feet that stops this formal, if not positively numerological, verse falling into the jog-trot of regular metre, Jenkins's sentences – or are they his thoughts? – exert a kind of tidal pull on his lines. Fittingly, given the subject matter, that pull is evocative of longing. More generally, it evokes the movement of emotion, its arhythmic pull and push.

This movement of sentence structure against, but within, the formal elements of lineation and full rhyme brings the poems to complex life. It is also the source of their music. Reading later Jenkins – from 2005's *A Shorter Life* onwards – one often senses a subterranean tune; a kind of basso profundo counterpoint to the poem's primary thought or story. Increasingly, that bass note has become the loss of something that is both personal (youth, love) and general (losing touch with English tradition). In *The Lost World*, a small-press edition of seven poems published in 2010, these losses are conflated not in a gesture of solipsism but so that we come to understand abstract, historical decay through a world of personal feeling.

This is, if you will, feelingful public verse. The loss it marks has to do with something, perhaps paraphrasable as innocence, which is prior to, but symbolized by, both its protagonists' remembered youth and the unchanging nature of traditions. Jenkins unifies these symbols by placing a youthful protagonist *among* things that are time-honoured. The boy in 'Little Men' dreams of being an explorer; in 'The Boys' Book of Sport' a youngster is at play; while the title poem is furnished with familiar, familial touchstones, from a father's 'unfashionable 'tash' to the way 'A smell of creosote comes off the garden shed / In puffs of dust when my best shots hit it –'. He is repeatedly, even insistently, explicit about loss:

> . . . And now? What can I feel,
> As Canterbury comes to a stop outside,
> But envy for that boy, and gratitude,
> And grief for whichever one of us has died?
>
> ('A Canterbury Tale')

> The summer rain . . .
> That falls and falls and washes it all away.
>
> ('The Lost World')

> Time, the clever thief
> Taking all we have but grief.
>
> ('Little Men')

Yet of course those memories have not disappeared. The work is stuffed with them: this counter-truth echoes the way versification and sentence-structure lie at a slant to each other.

In fact, Jenkins's poems have always proceeded 'awry': like those Renaissance paintings, such as Hans Holbein's *The Ambassadors*, in which the viewer needs to stand to one side, not taking the thing at its word, in order to glimpse the deep message. In elegies such as 'Orpheus' (from *A Shorter Life*), emotion denies or contradicts itself. Written for the poet's mother, this triptych of twelve-line rhyming sections records the failure of the narrator's love (after all, by lacking self-restraint, Orpheus consigns his beloved to hell), but is powered, as elegy can be, by love and longing. After the son has taken his mother 'to that suburban high street where / you sat for your last wash and perm',

> . . . you were young again,
> touching your new hair, and I was without guilt
> and loved you as on that first day of term,
> as if I had won you back by this huge success.

If that 'huge success', echo of 'success so huge and wholly farcical' in 'The Whitsun Weddings', didn't signpost Philip Larkin, the 'as if' of the last line should do so, since it works, like the conclusion of Larkin's 'An Arundel Tomb', to double the poem back into ambiguity. Jenkins's 'Orpheus' doesn't say its narrator has *not* won back his mother, simply that appearances aren't everything in matters of the heart. At the same time – 'you were young again' – it also says that they are. In 'An Arundel Tomb' Larkin's 'hardly meant' is a smudge of ambiguity: does it mean the couple in the tomb didn't mean to be faithful or that they did, but only just?

> . . . The stone fidelity
> They hardly meant has come to be
> Their final blazon, and to prove
> Our almost-instinct almost true:
> What will survive of us is love.

Jenkins's smudge works in a similar way: the poem in fact more radically open than its 'final blazon' of 'huge success' suggests.

Of the poets in this chapter, the one most closely associated with

Philip Larkin is Andrew Motion. His first lecturing post, which he took up in 1976 when he was just twenty-four, was at Hull University. Larkin was then still the University Librarian; and this conjunction would eventually lead to the ambiguous, ambivalent biography *Philip Larkin: A Writer's Life* (1993). Yet Motion, like Imlah, first studied under John Fuller at Oxford. All the more surprising, then, that it is Alan Jenkins – who read Comparative Literature, rather than English, at the University of Sussex – who has emerged as Fuller's true heir, publishing work that, though emotional, can handle extended rhyme with virtuoso ease: his 2007 translation of Arthur Rimbaud's *Le bateau ivre*, conjuring both a strict rhyme scheme and all the original material, keeps full rhyme aloft; the long, nostalgic poem *Blue Days (The Sailor's Return)* (2010) juggles ten sections and two forms.

Both Fuller and Jenkins have also published bagatelles – though Fuller's *Song and Dance* (2008) seems almost disingenuous beside Jenkins's risqué *The Little Black Book* (2001) – but it is hard to imagine Andrew Motion producing any such thing. The ten very public years of his Poet Laureateship, assumed at the age of forty-seven, seem to have over-defined his poetry life. Though Motion is also a literary biographer and has held professorships at a series of universities, poetry is at the heart of his writing life. He has produced editions of Thomas Hardy and of Edward Thomas: twin pilots of a lyric tradition that is customarily held to continue through Larkin, who admired both. This lineage may seem hard to trace in the latter's blunt, nubby, Movement diction and general lack of tunefulness, but Motion has drawn (for example, in his end-of-laureateship lecture) on Robert Lowell's helpful distinction, drawn in 1960, between 'the raw and the cooked' in verse: some poetry is built with formal care, some seems less carefully prepared if more spontaneous. Larkin's use of measure, his economy and even his adoption of stanzaic forms, all produce a highly traditional music. That economy can make Larkin an evasive and demanding role model; especially for a young poet, likely in love with possibilities of language, thought, feeling and form, and whose instincts may tend to the elaborate. Larkin's whole poetic – and world

– view sometimes appears more attuned to the limits than to the capacities of verse.

His lesson for Motion, though, may have been a commitment to sincerity. Motion's earlier verse – up to *The Price of Everything* (1994) – is often scrupulously narrative. Emotions past or fictional may be named, but the poem itself does not *express* those emotions. Instead, it seems to offer itself as a clear lens through which to observe them, as if undistorted. This first-person speaker is a reliable, though not an omniscient, narrator. *Natural Causes* (1987) is one clear example of this approach. The book's three major poems conduct extended emotional explorations. They evoke the way experience and sensibility press on each other. 'This is your subject speaking', the collection's epilogue, gets Larkin to speak his own lines of regret and fury:

> *You see, there's nothing to write*
> *which is better than life itself, no matter*
> *how life might let you down, or pass you by,*

and:

> *The trouble is, I've written*
> *scenes like this so many times*
> *there's nothing to surprise me.*
>
> *But that doesn't help one bit.*
> *It just appals me. Now you go.*
> *I won't come out. I'll watch you.*

Motion lineates this (presumably, allegedly) reported speech pretty much as Raymond Carver would lineate Chekhov's words in *A New Path to the Waterfall*, the deathbed collection he published shortly after in 1989. Both Carver and Motion were performing an act of homage, but also releasing the poetic lineation already within the prose. To do so requires an adept's ear, and the sort of formal acuity underlined by Motion's later increasing use of pentameter. It also releases something of the values of prose into verse – 'prose' standing, here, for a kind of unblink-ingness in the face of what must be said plainly if the pre-emptive falling away of a too-musical phrase is to be avoided.

By now in his thirties, in this volume Motion is already a convincing elegist. 'Scripture', a long poem about the death of a prep school friend, is '*Commonly called The First Book of Myself*'. Unlike many poets, Motion has always had 'a subject'. The death of his mother, the result of a riding accident when the poet was seventeen, informs much of his work: it is revisited in poetry, prose memoir and even a novel. The school friend, given the biblically apt name Jonathan, was 'the first I knew to die', and the poem's subtitle acknowledges that bereavement produced Motion's particular poetic first person; one pared back to something freed of bluster or rhetoric.

The title poem of *Natural Causes*, which juxtaposes 'a stupor of joy' at the birth of a son with 'the man / with no memory . . . prowling his tucked-away hospital room', is more emotionally mature and flex-ible still. Of course, these two scenes are linked by the riskiness of life, a conclusion Motion draws out through related images, rather than finger-wagging emotion, but the poem's true causal connection is its observation of how this insight arrives:

> nervously, slithering into my mind
> like a dog on a heavy painful rope,
> yet lazily too, like a dog on a dusty day

Part Churchill's black dog, partly an image of disgust, this 'thought-dog' represents threat transferred, like an epithet, from observation to understanding, and from adult patient to new-born infant.

The death of the poet's mother most haunts 1997's *Salt Water*, the second part of which is a prose account in which he retraces the dying John Keats's trip to Rome: 'I sit in the front of the bus drinking beer and thinking about my mother.' A particular kind of clarity, seeming to suggest actual experience, gives Motion's poetry its edge.

Salt Water's opening sequence 'Fresh Water', which follows the River Thames to its source as well as into the narrator's memory, is an elegy for a friend drowned in the *Marchioness* riverboat disaster. In its closing lines, the drowned girl swims 'back upstream, her red velvet party dress / flickering round her heels . . . until finally she is sliding uphill / over bright green grass and into the small wet mouth of the earth, / where she vanishes.' It's a beautiful, moving and also tidy metaphor for the burial of a friend; and this is what carries the poem's affective freight. For, double adjectives notwithstanding, the language itself – all those monosyllables – is limpid, even fluvial. (When Dylan Thomas wrote, in his 'Refusal to Mourn the Death, by Fire, of a Child in London', that 'After the first death, there is no other' he was perfectly wrong. It is the first death that lends each subsequent one reality.)

'Fresh Water' is written in the present tense; as many of Motion's most apparently personal poems are. The slimmer pickings of 2009's *The Cinder Path* include elegies for the poet's father, and – in a set of five blank verse sonnets – a celebration of the life of 'Harry Patch, "The Last Fighting Tommy"'. Sometimes, the lens blurs with the shift into a communal poetic persona; as if there's been some loss of the poet's individual perspective through which to concentrate sufficiently on its material. Motion was a generous and expansive Poet Laureate, who refused to form a protective coterie around himself, and spent the decade from 1999 to 2009 broadly at the disposal of poetry in Britain wherever it might be found. However, a writer whose authority and technique are founded in the authenticity of direct witness might well be daunted by a perceived need to adopt the more impersonal standpoint public speech demands. In *Cinder Path* the role of public poet seems to insert itself between the disinterested diction and the crystalline, highly personal, import of Motion's best verse; as if the reflexive consciousness entailed by a public role levered his technique away from its work of private reparation. For, unlike the other elegists with whom this chapter deals, Motion at his very best is not in exile from his subject. His verse may be tender, even unflinching, but it never trades in longing. It is always present *with* its subject. It doesn't deal in touchstone trope or symbol, but uses actual memories that are all too powerful and resourceful enough to fuel the verse. If that sometimes seems to produce a kind of quietism, even simplicity, then the technique has achieved its goal.

Elegy is a subtle, collusive form, whose effects range from the highly individual to the broadly collective. However conservative the symbolic vocabulary of the Oxford elegists – there's not a skyscraper or an iPhone to be seen in their poetic city-state – their relationship with the genre itself is anything but static. It's not immediately clear who their heirs will be. Yet something, at least, of their poetics is shared with the touchstone lyricists – and it is to these that we turn next.

4

THE TOUCHSTONE LYRICISTS

Gillian Clarke, Sarah Maguire and Michael Longley write a kind of verse that has been naturalized by antecedents as various as the Romantic landscape poem, Edwardian literature of nostalgia, and the nineteenth-century reclamation of national 'folk' icons, from Morris Dancers to druids. But these touchstone lyricists in fact negotiate complex relationships with meanings that they must trust are stable, but which vary with time and experience. Their poetry keeps a faith that is currently under pressure, both from those who do not share it and from contemporary poets, like Alice Oswald or Frances Presley, who carry its themes and preoccupations forward in their own more technically exploratory writing. For the touchstone lyric looks over the shoulder of much self-consciously contemporary imagery in search of a universal register of Beauty as Truth.

All artistic tradition includes a conservative element: a belief not that the old ways are necessarily best but that the past has produced great work from which much can be learnt. Ideas of craft and apprenticeship suggest that there *is* something to learn. Yet sometimes a misplaced sensitivity conflates traditional craft with social tradition; it can also confuse culture's two gazes, the look forward and the look back. These distinctions are helpfully maintained by the bi-focal lens with which modernism plunders the past in order to refresh its contemporary artistic and formal vocabulary. Poetic modernism was imported to Britain by its great masters: both Ezra Pound and T.S. Eliot were

active in the canon-forming London literary magazines of the early
decades of the twentieth century. Eliot founded *The Criterion* in 1922
and edited it for its entire run until 1939; Pound was an editor of the
shorter-lived *The Egoist*. But, significantly for British poetry's relationship with tradition, the transplant failed to take. Modernism, like those
who practised it, remained a blow-in. (Or, in the case of David Jones,
Welsh.) Traces of this alienation remain in even the best-known works
of 'English' modernism. T.S. Eliot's 'East Coker' is more universal than
local. Its villagers are endowed with the dignity, but also the unreality,
of archetypes as they join the round dance of time; its narrator is a
visitor. As we'll see, those who did apply modernism to the matter of
Britain, including Basil Bunting and Geoffrey Hill, have produced
poetry of extraordinary power and resonance. But they have never
captured the castle. Modernism never became the central tendency of
our national poetry, as it did in other countries. Instead another aspect
of conservatism has made itself felt. 'Common sense', which confines
thought and imagination to what is already familiar, has often demanded
that British verse stick to a lyric, realist brief, and decried experiment
as pretentious or obfuscatory.

So, the backward glance can be radical. But the look forward sees
a British society made up of hugely more various backgrounds and
experiences than in the past. Rupert Brooke's church clock standing
at ten to three no longer evokes all our yesterdays. Poets writing in
Britain today have a greater range of imagery than ever before to
draw on; and that the view ahead differs from that behind is not
merely normal, but exciting. Readers sometimes assume that a poem
in traditional form must have a conservative social agenda; and that
new writers, for example those with hyphenated, 'British plus' backgrounds, will prefer to avoid such techniques. But this is to misunder-
stand the role of conservatism within *craft*. Looking back in order to
learn about formal tradition is enriching; it's only looking back where
we should look forward, at today's life-world, that is a form of false
consciousness.

All this means that touchstones, which face both ways at once, need to be handled with care. Making a scene or an object into an unchanging, continuing repository for significant personal, emotional or metaphysical meaning is an explicitly conservative way to create a symbol. It brings the past into the present. Poets in socially and culturally unified communities – the Palestinian Mahmoud Darwish, or Vasko Popa in the former Yugoslavia – have access to symbols that can be read in the same way by most members of that community, from surgeons to labourers. Darwish's touchstone symbols include any mention of those contested territories; Popa's a still-immediate folk iconography (raven, harvest, forest). Their verse gains from these shared symbols the power and perhaps the right to speak, at least to their own society, in universal terms.

Every poet longs to do just this. But each also uses a private, personal mythology and symbolism to make sense of the world: even Darwish, for example, sometimes plays strange games with gender. The temptation is to substitute the one for the other, as if what fizzes with resonance for the individual is going to be just as exciting for everyone else. It's here that exclusivity, and its cousin hermeticism, can creep in. The Oxford elegists reveal some of the resources and the limits of context-specific touchstones. Mick Imlah's image of a cricket pitch at the close of play in 'Secrets' is a symbol of lost innocence *precisely* because of its cultural association with an honour code. But that code is class- and culture-specific: the line 'Play up! Play up! and play the game!' comes from Sir Henry Newbolt's 'Vitai Lampada', which is set in the private Clifton College. ('There's a breathless hush in the Close tonight / Ten to make and the match to win / A bumping pitch and a blinding light / An hour to play, and the last man in.') If you don't know this poetic staple of a particular time and class, you won't hear it in Imlah, nor read his summer scene as anything more than a familiar metaphor for youth. This relatively private iconography doesn't matter, providing Imlah is writing not national poetry but lyric verse: that avowedly personal genre is always concerned to some degree with characterizing the narrator. But even the lyric must unpack each symbol enough to involve a general reader, keeping track of what he or she can reasonably be expected to know.

Gillian Clarke makes the natural world and traditional rural ways of life her own material. No simple documentary, her writing gains lyric lift by attesting to her own implication in that world. A similar approach has allowed Sarah Maguire to move through cultural borders as if they were porous; personal experience collapsing distance and trumping her own standpoint as a white Londoner. Clarke has always been a touchstone lyricist; but Maguire, who started to write with conventional New Generation crispness, has revealed her own lyric expansiveness more gradually. It's only in reading back from 2007's *The Pomegranates of Kandahar* that we notice it at work, like a premonition, in her writing from a decade earlier. Meanwhile Michael Longley, the creatively if not chronologically senior poet of this triumvirate, writes both within and at a distance from the persuasive, and pervasive, Irish pastoral of the later twentieth century. He has moved through that tradition and into a verse which, while it can be transcendent in its celebration of the natural world, is also able to contain a wide range of social and political themes.

So it is with Gillian Clarke (b. 1937) that we start. She represents the confluence of two influential poetics. The incantatory, and not un-hippy, poetry that emerged in the Seventies was bound to appeal to this daughter of Anglo-Welsh verse: whose predominantly pastoral, nostalgic perspective represents a seam of touchstone lyricism running through contemporary British verse. The 'second son' in a national culture that was for centuries preserved largely by *yr iaith*, the (Welsh) language, Welsh poetry in English both is and is not the inheritor of a national identity. Its 'bardic' role has become increasingly secondary with the success of the Language movement. After the civil disobedience of the Seventies, Welsh became an official language, now accorded social primacy especially in the northern heartlands. Since the advent of Welsh-language media, and with Welsh-medium education the norm in large areas of the country, Wales no longer needs to be spoken up for by English-language verse.

Nor do all Welsh poets writing in English take part in this tradition. Despite his exuberant 'Fern Hill' evocation of rural Wales,

Dylan Thomas was always on the high road to life as *A Young Dog*, and to London, where his ambitious diction and imagination made him one of the new Apocalyptics. R.S. Thomas was more influenced by modernism than his supporters probably care to admit: the satire-portraits of the early collections, where 'Iago Prytherch' and 'Cynddylan on his Tractor' become principles of time and place, are not, after all, so far from the despondent, generic housemaids of T.S. Eliot's 'Preludes'. Gwyneth Lewis, a genuinely bilingual poet who has shifted 'English forms' such as the sonnet into Welsh, has portrayed Welsh-speakers as a kind of secret society in her English verse ('Welsh Espionage'), but she favours the cosmopolitan pentameter over the Anglo-Welsh repertoire of:

> daft Ianto
>
> . . .
>
> Left to recite the Complete Works of Sir Lewis Morris
> To puzzled sheep, before throwing himself over
> The edge of the abandoned quarry.

(This from Harri Webb's gloriously wry 'Synopsis of the Great Welsh Novel'.) As its residually colonial prefix suggests, Anglo-Welsh writing is a tradition that seems preoccupied by, and unable to resolve, its own Welshness. It has a tendency to protest too much, overloading its lines with allusion to local place names and traditions, and failing to question what has become clichéd. Gillian Clarke, however, is *Cymru Cymraeg*, Welsh Welsh, as the genealogy at the end of *Letting in the Rumour* records, and she is comfortably bilingual. As well as translating the canonical short story writer Kate Roberts, she has collaborated on translations with her younger friend and neighbour, the Welsh-language poet Menna Elfyn; contributing in particular to Elfyn's bilingual collections *Cell Angel* (1996) and *Cysan Dyn Dall* (2000).

Despite volunteering in the language movement in her youth, Elfyn herself cuts a controversial and pioneering figure in Welsh-language circles. Not merely a woman who has the temerity to write poetry, she has repeatedly addressed women's experiences of domestic life: her strategy parallels Eavan Boland's. Nearly two decades before Gwyneth Lewis, she introduced another 'foreign' formal tradition – free verse – into Welsh-language poetry. Yet while Elfyn, and successors such as her niece Elin ap Hywel, have been loosening up the Welsh-language tradition, anglophone Welsh verse seems to feel the lack of the vigorously structured Welsh-language *cynghanedd*, a half-line alliterative form. The regional speech-rhythms and word-order that inflect 'Wenglish', once seen as lending national colour to Anglo-Welsh verse, in fact smudge it:

> I have, my only remnant of the past's wreck,
> A book of your *barddoniaeth*,
> With Nain's writing, beside the *in memoriams*,
> Telling of the dead, for me, in English.
>> ('To Ioan Madog, Poet, Ancestor', John Idris Jones)

Since the Fifties there have been many poets writing this kind of cosy sentimentalism, full of a second-hand *hiraeth* (longing) that an increasingly urban and media-savvy Welsh-language culture has outgrown. Its closest equivalent is, perhaps, the middlebrow hinterland of today's lesser-known Irish poets. In the immediate post-war era Anglo-Welsh poets included Vernon Watkins, Roland Matthias, Emyr Humphreys, Leslie Norris, John Ormond, T. Harri Jones, Raymond Garlick and John Tripp: a masculine roll-call. The exceptions escaped: Alun Lewis to his tragic destiny as a war poet, Dylan Thomas to Soho, Keidrych Rhys and Lynette Roberts into a modernist European mainstream, and Dannie Abse to London and lyric plain dealing. But there *was* also Harri Webb, who carried the wrought quality of Welsh-language verse across to his English poetry. His elegy 'Thanks in Winter' brings together T.S. Eliot and the fourteenth-century Dafydd ap Gwilym, two poets who 'purified the dialect' of their tribes:

> The day that Eliot died I stood
> By Dafydd's grave in Ystrad Fflur,
>
> . . .
>
> A pilgrim under the yew at Ystrad Fflur
> I kept my vow, prayed for my country,
> Cursed England, came away.

Dafydd ap Gwilym's grave at Strata Florida ('Ystrad Fflur') is a touch-stone for Welsh-speakers. Invoking it in the Welsh way, using the Welsh poet's first name, but keeping an estranging formality to 'Eliot' in this English-language praise poem, Webb forces the new language to adopt some of the rules of the old. This is no cosy 'ear-worm', but the formal adoption of a technical trope. Its quality of technical transposition can be measured against the unstoppable name-calling of Webb's Anglo-Welsh near-contemporary, Ruth Bidgood:

> Now as I went down Rhiw'r Ych alone
> and turned west over the ford of Nant-y-Neuadd,
> I knew there was only darkness waiting
> for me, beyond the crags of Cwm-y-Benglog.
>
> ('Burial Path')

The next wave of Anglo-Welsh poets was little different. Children of the long 1940s, who emerged in the Seventies, they include Meic Stephens, Chris Torrance, Jeremy Hooker, Tony Curtis, Duncan Bush, Steve Griffiths, Nigel Jenkins and Christopher Meredith, a handful of women – Gladys Mary Coles, Ann Cluysenaar, Christine Evans, Sheenagh Pugh, Hilary Llewellyn-Williams, and latecomers Jean Earle and Sally Roberts Jones – and the faux naif Robert Minhinnick with his chaotic post-Dylan Thomas homages.

It is to this generation that Gillian Clarke belongs. Like them, she avows a rural Welshness, 'Down at Fron Felen / in the loaded barn' ('Haymaking'). Yet in writing about her own 'sweet especial rural scene' she manages to look over the shoulder of one tradition to another:

> Only walking the path
> in my blue dressing-gown,
> seeing bright breath where the river is,
> the house calm and white in the rising sun,
> a glittering loop of swifts about the barn,
> could I believe the world unbroken.

('Dream')

This is pure pastoral. It's not the natural world, but rural life (the house, the barn), which by enduring proves the world 'unbroken'. And, for all its specificity, this tableau vivant supports a universal meaning. Partly that's because its images don't clot. The quality of light associated with each keeps them congruent, but gives them the space to stand alone. It is also because the poem doesn't rely on resonances shared only within a club of Welshness, but deploys universal touchstones: dawn, a river, bird flight, a house and a barn. There's nothing here that might not be glimpsed and equally under-stood in Sussex, or Serbia.

But Clarke's lucidity has to do with more than images of light. Part of the fresh feel she brings to familiar topics comes from her diction. This passage is largely monosyllabic, apart from its verbs, until we come to the big concept, 'unbroken'. She has the necessary ability to see afresh. In other early poems, hands doing the washing-up have 'bracelets of hot water', a racing pigeon a 'collar of opals', and the moon is a 'full-blown' dandelion clock: observations which are almost Martian. All that muffles them is a tendency to beautify. Yet this rural world does have an authentically shifted centre of experience. Clarke is unafraid to apply beautification – or beatification – to death, whether human or animal. It's in natural settings, her poetry insists, that we're most exposed to the real nature of life. 'In January', from *Letting in the Rumour* (1989), jet fighters practise over the apparently empty hills of South Cards:

> The cities can forget on days like this
> all the world's wars. It's we

out on the open hill who see
the day crack under the shadow of the cross.

The first line's unnatural word order preserves the formal pattern of
this slight sixteen-liner, in which loosely patterned slant-rhymes create
an echoing sense of relatedness between the parts of the scene and of
the poem, as well as recreating the way jet engines echo: *Aberporth* /
dragonfly / *south* / *day* are followed by *cries* / *pair* / *air* / *crows* and my
favourite, *field* / *falls* / *filled* / *wings*.

Clarke's earlier poems, blurry with language-music, are relatively
indistinguishable from much Anglo-Welsh verse. 'Blaen Cwrt', from
The Sundial (1978), is driven not by original perception but by the lilt
of enjambment, a repetitive music that almost writes itself: 'We warm
our hands / With apple wood. Some of the smoke / Rises against the
ploughed, brown field.' There was, then, a middle-period renaissance;
and key to it is that the other great influence on Clarke's work, her
exact English contemporary and friend Frances Horovitz. Horovitz
died in 1983, aged forty-five, and her poetry epitomizes the 'feather,
stone, bone' school then current. It is easy to see how this developed,
as the Seventies converted middle-class bohemia into more widely
accessible hippydom, and the rise of folk and folk-rock gave younger
poets a steer towards country life. A certain idealism about, and ideal-
ization of, freshness took hold in British poetry. Ted Hughes was
pioneering poetry in schools, and the Arvon Foundation, with which
he was closely associated, was expanding its vision of going into the
country to write. Indeed, Hughes was something of an encouragement
to all this himself. A part-time farmer, living outside both the metropolitan coteries and academia, he unabashedly granted the natural
world a quasi-mythic status in his work.

Frances Horovitz emerged from a group of poets who expressed
this rural zeitgeist in resolutely free verse. Broadly settled in the rural
west of England, these new ruralists included Michael Horovitz (her
first husband), Roger Garfitt (her second), Lawrence Sail, and the
founders of Arvon, John Fairfax and John Moat. If the transformations

carried out by Hughes's poetry sometimes appear shamanistic, this group's writing displayed a pseudo-shamanic belief in the simple virtue of *naming*; and a post-Romantic belief that the natural world is apt for secular revelation. *Primus inter pares*, Frances Horovitz produced work which bears a particular affinity to the studio ceramics then becoming fashionable. Pared down, it resists the temporal shifts that grammar generates, and is clearly influenced by an Eastern sensibility: 'Zen' was arguably the orientalism of the Seventies. Indeed, 'often, she made her notes in the form of haiku or near-haiku', as her widower Roger Garfitt notes in his edition of her *Collected Poems*. 'Vindolanda – January' opens:

> winter light
> a track through trees
> leaning with frozen snow;

while a stanza from the unfinished and posthumously published 'Orkney' has:

> a roofless cottage
> from the dark door space flying
> lapwing or whitemaa

This delicate, static quality has re-emerged in the poetry of Pauline Stainer, whose first book appeared in 1989. However, perhaps the most surprising thing about Horovitz's verse is the for-its-time revolutionary ability to be uncompromising. Analysts of speech-patterns tell us that women use more non-informative (prompting, supportive) speech acts, and tend to hedge their assertions with more qualifiers, than men do. Simply and repeatedly asserting an objective standpoint, allowing herself to be the observer and namer of touchstone creatures and objects from the natural world, Horovitz travelled a real distance from both 'authentic' speech-rhythm and the temptations of language-music. *It is a fact*, her poems aver, *that these things matter*. She doesn't shelter behind familiar symbols, but nominates, new, shared touchstones: 'soap-wort and figwort, / the lilac and the brown' or, at the British Museum, 'the room of clocks'. Frances Horovitz continues to matter because she was a distinctive practitioner of a kind of writing that idealized the material world and found revelation in concrete detail; and whose belief in the primacy of sensory over mental and emotional experience has profoundly influenced contemporary fashions.

Twenty years after Horovitz's death we find Sarah Maguire (*b.* 1957) writing, like Gillian Clarke, at a confluence of traditions. Her first two books, *Spilt Milk* (1991) and *The Invisible Mender* (1997), are broadly typical of the best work of her ('New') generation. Using stripped-back diction they tell short, often autobiographical, stories about such reso-nant topics as sex, travel and her own adoption. But after a visit to the Palestinian territories for the British Council in 1996, and her subse-quent foundation of the Poetry Translation Centre in 2004, she has become increasingly involved with contemporary poetry in Arabic, and from the Middle East and Africa more generally. The Arabic tradition, which values beauty for its own sake and is less concerned with narra-tive and argument than with the quality of the language, has broadened her line and softened her diction.

In the 'Nursery Practices' section of *The Invisible Mender* this former professional gardener writes, with intimate and telling attention, of how on 'The Mist Bench' in the greenhouse:

> Bare leaves are downy
> turn blurred
> and glaucous
>
> as the fine fur plumps
> and sleeves itself
> with water

The detail is tight, but the voice aims for lucidity. Maguire avoids big-gesture simplicity and over-reliance on monosyllables. Instead it is the

short line that performs the refining role. A decade later, in her poem
'Europe', young men in Tangiers dream of crossing the cultural divide:

> Each night, they climb these crumbling ramparts
>
> and face north
> like true believers, while the lighthouse of Tarifa blinks
>
> and beckons,
> unrolling its brilliant pavement across the pitiless Straits.

These alternating line lengths are elective. But the writing is less
concerned than formerly with seeing fresh. After all, ramparts always
'crumble', and all believers are 'true'; the Straits of Gibraltar have long
been known as 'pitiless'. This is a poet who has settled into her own
skin and no longer has anything to prove.

  This new confidence intensifies both a trust in music and an interest
in those points where meaning lifts off to produce emotion – both
qualities for which 'lyrical' is often used as short-hand – which was
always more pronounced in Maguire's work than in that of many of
her cool contemporaries. By the standards of the Nineties she had
always been a confessional poet. Her first two collections take their
titles from an emotional life: respectively, an act of love-making and
imagining her birth mother. This relatively softened, vulnerable tone
equips her to look outwards. *The Pomegranates of Kandahar* are hand
grenades, but they are also fruit:

> If you answer the phone, the sea at Killiney
> will sound throughout Palestine.
> If you put your head out the window (avoiding the snipers, please)
>
> a cloud will rain rain from the Liffey
> and drench all Ramallah, drowning the curfew.
>
> ('From Dublin to Ramallah')

This is almost cavalier in its refusal to sound 'crafted': 'rain rain'? Could Maguire really find no synonym for this kind of weather? Of course she could. The micro-pause that the repetition introduces allows us to glimpse the ghost of a half-line break, which moves throughout this poem – a trace of the parallelism of some Arabic verse. The pattern is broken only by that disobedient 'throughout' unfolding its long vowels in a deft piece of mimesis.

But this is still the Horovitz-Clarke gesture, a kind of 'to the things themselves' that underplays the role of language in *creating* our pictures of those things. Maguire is gazing over language's shoulder to her touchstones. In 'Landscape, with Dead Sea':

> The lights come on in Jericho:
>
> I imagine what I cannot see –
> > barbed wire threaded with jasmine,
> > > sharp enough to smell.

In 'Petersburg':

> At midnight, the Winter Palace is on fire –
> one thousand molten windows
>
> scarlet with the agonies of sunset
> igniting in the west.

The political imagery may be schematic, but when one line – 'At midnight, the Winter Palace is on fire' – does almost as much as Alexander Sokurov's entire ninety-six-minute film epic *Russian Ark*, such shorthand is a hotline to significance.

Touchstone lyricism may be unfashionable, but it has a tendency to recur. Lightly transformed or partly appropriated, touchstones play a role in other kinds of writing, particularly mythopoesis and the expanded lyric. They provide an entry point for emerging poets like

Frances Leviston and Fiona Benson, meeting expectations about musicality, references to the natural physical world and formal ease. Most significantly, touchstone lyricism is hospitable to a particular kind of poetry from a whole range of cultures; in particular, celebrations of traditional life, from Scotland to the Caribbean. It informs the work of some of the key figures in recent free-verse developments, including Grace Nichols and Fred D'Aguiar. It also colours poetry by the 'Scottish Muslim Calvanist' poet and artist Imtiaz Dharker, who writes evocatively about her Pakistani and Glaswegian heritage; and the Kurdish poet and translator Choman Hardi, who writes primarily in her mother tongue. Paul Henry is Clarke's principal Welsh successor. Even for these middle-class writers, details of daily domestic routine represent an authenticity to particular ways of life. For poets from traditionally impoverished communities this kind of record can be a form of reparation. Something that seems at a glance like simple 'pastoral' may in fact represent a first attempt to harmonize and dignify a tough lifestyle that has been hard to make sense of.

Touchstone lyricism might not have taken the direction it did without the particular influence of Irish poetry. Though it falls outside the scope of this book, our neighbours' literature plays a key role in British culture, and Seamus Heaney is the indisputable touchstone lyricist. From the early Bog Poems of the Sixties – and their affinities with Eugène Guillevic's 1961 exploration of the Neolithic *Carnac* as much as with the work of Heaney's close contemporary Frances Horovitz – to the brilliant, transformative *Seeing Things* (1991) and beyond, in the later revisitings of Heaney country, his poetry fills a memory tray with touchstones. *Stepping Stones* (2008), Dennis O'Driscoll's exhaustive volume of interviews with the poet, underlines how important their specificity – a *particular* old implement, a *particular* farmhouse called Mossbawm – is to Heaney's imagination.

Nobel distinction means his poetry is read everywhere, including in schools, and this alone produces imitators; but Seamus Heaney's influence on future British tradition was consolidated by his time at Oxford, where he was Professor of Poetry from 1989 to 1994. His friend Bernard

O'Donoghue was then teaching Mediaeval English at Wadham College. Publishing a debut full collection in his late forties, in 1991, when Heaney's practical sway in Britain was at its height, O'Donoghue's modest verse emerged fully formed, its influences all risen to the surface:

> A chapel in a graveyard in a fort,
> And Denis Hickey, sitting by the gate
> With his knuckle-headed blackthorn

This is from a 1999 poem whose title, 'Kilmacow', is pure touchstone; but which slips, unfortunately, out of reach for the reader who doesn't know, or can't imagine, the place. Part of the conservative power of touchstones comes from this inflexibility. They're charged with the given, and what's already been made of it. They don't generate thought-experiment or a restless search for 'what lies beyond'. O'Donoghue's poems of a cosy quotidian offer little more than 'getting out / Of doing things' or 'Redwings' being mistaken for 'strange thrushes'. 'Happiness writes white', as Henry de Montherlant said.

Another, slightly younger, Irish pastoral poet living and working in mainland Britain, Maurice Riordan tries somewhat harder, leaning back on lyricism in his 2007 collection *The Holy Land*. The result is genuine poetic achievement. The book's central sequence of 'Idylls', set on the family farm of his childhood, are that rare thing, true prose-poems. They make for satisfying prose and also have the finely judged diction and conceptual range of poetry. In 'Idyll 6':

> It was mid-morning. The Harvester still hadn't showed. The men patted the dogs and lazed about. The Bos'on was sitting up on the driver's seat. Suddenly the machine started into life. The engine revved and belts and flywheels began to turn. The worm rotated. Then the combine set off bouncing across the stubble ground. But 'Son steered it round to face the uncut field. He lowered the blade into the standing barley.

Despite the familiarity of this imaginative territory Riordan, who has
co-edited anthologies of poems about science and ecology, demonstrates a genuine commitment both to the reality of the natural world
and to the labour and complexity of farming tasks. His combine
harvester and dogs aren't appropriated as symbols, but released into
the authenticity of whatever they mean in their own world. This
relinquishment of his narrator's hold on things ultimately sets him at
a slant to the touchstone tradition.

The Northern Irish poet Michael Longley writes verse that is rinsed
clean of overt intellection. In fact, one of the things the reader first
notices is the way that his writing doesn't seem to take heed of itself.
Poetry that's overtly self-referential often seems to be in parentheses;
something interrupts the poem's underlying, rapt music. By contrast,
Longley creates a bell-clear single line:

> I'll hand you six duck eggs Orla Murphy gave me
> In a beechwood bowl Ted O'Driscoll turned . . .
>
> ('Phoenix')

Born, like Heaney and Clarke, at the very end of the Thirties, Longley
sprang to heightened life with his sixth collection, 1991's *Gorse Fires*. In
this book his verse relaxes into his exceptional signature clarity.
Everything is earned, nothing unresolved, and images and stories lie
at the surface of the words, rather than in their shadow.

The poems up to this point, though thoughtful and well-judged,
often seem more simply to be leading exemplars of the well-behaved
pastoral verse that still dominates the Irish lists on both sides of
the border. Contrast the first stanza of a Seventies parable on war
poetry (the poem's epigraph is from Edward Thomas's diary at the
Front):

> Who bothers to record
> This body digested
> By its own saliva

> Inside the earth's mouth
> And long intestine,

('Mole')

with the whole of 'The Exhibit', from 2000's *The Weather in Japan*. The later poem appears in a sequence of short lyrics that move from the Troubles to the second, and then the first, world war:

> I see them absentmindedly pat their naked bodies
> Where waistcoat and apron pockets would have been.
> The grandparents turn back and take an eternity
> Rummaging in the tangled pile for their spectacles.

What has shifted in the quarter-century between these two poems is the earlier need to suggest that subtle, emotional reactions are unusual or hard-won. The mature Longley's mastery lies in so staging his material as to imply or demonstrate that no right-thinking person could disagree with what he presents as *communal* truths. In this brief poem after Auschwitz, Longley doesn't have the temerity to suggest, as a lesser poet might, that he has exceptional rights over, or insight into, our inevitable responses. Instead his attention is all on the victims themselves, and on rendering them as neighbourly familiars: those patted waistcoat pockets.

This dignified and also modest role as a communal spokesman is what in fact makes Longley a political poet: one who repeatedly protests the Troubles, even in poems written after the 1998 Good Friday Agreement. These poems are anti-war but, far from the rhetorical performances of poets like Adrian Mitchell, for whom war is an abstract cause, his verse takes no prisoners. It is unshifty and steely. In 'Harmonica':

> A tommy drops his harmonica in No Man's Land.
> My dad like old Anaximines [*sic*] breathes in and out
> Through the holes and reeds and finds this melody.

Not a word of this is less than necessary. The harmonica is individuated by its backstory, the micro-narrative of the first line (we can guess
what happened to the 'Tommy'). Anaximenes of Miletus, the Pre-Socratic
who held that air is the source of everything, is a marker of continuity:
war, like poverty, is a constant. The 'holes and reeds' bring the trenches
and the craters of No Man's Land into the very mouth of the poem's
Orpheus, 'my dad'. 'Harmonica' legitimates this tragedy, of fighting
men recruited by the British from a divided community, through the
links it makes with the 'poor bloody infantry' of 'Flanders fields'. It is
subtly done. But the writing doesn't admire its own subtlety. Its crystalline diction is un-knotted by adjectives: in general, the only epithets
Longley uses are the names of colours.

Unity of voice and content make Longley a truly lyric poet. Song
doesn't trump his message: it takes ownership of it. To stage communal
truths he uses images or stories that will be universally understood.
Agreement, rather than simple recognition, is what turns these scenes
and accounts into symbols: they are *already* freighted with emotion and
meaning. The Tommy missing in action, the awful hoarding at the
concentration camps, are touchstones that we as a society have been
forced to agree.

But Longley also has personal touchstones: creatures and plants, the
taxonomy and territory of 'Carrigskeewaun / (A remote townland in
County Mayo, I explain, / Meaning, so far as I know, The Rock of
the Wall Fern)', as he spells out in 'Heron', an elegy for the New York
School poet Kenneth Koch. Yet this country home and all it represents
is handled with a light touch. Or rather, we are allowed to see that
touching *going on*: 'I am writing too much about Carrigskeewaun, / I
think, until you two come along, my grandsons, / And we generalize
at once about cows and sheep.' Longley comes at the matter of shared
place the other way from Popa and Darwish. Instead of claiming that
we can all belong to this small, local ecosystem, he shows us how the
feeling of belonging itself is made out of this relationship with the place;
and suggests that we can all share this feeling – about somewhere. His
touchstone just happens to be a place called Carrigskeewaun.

These poems attest the importance of touchstones themselves: of belonging, of understanding, and conversely of the significance of loss. But Longley's gentle tip, setting the touchstones rolling, is an immensely anti-conservative gesture. Whatever 'the leveret breakfast[ing] under the fuchsia' means for him, in showing us the *workings* of such symbols he modernizes them, and so frees future poets to write with equally tender directness about their own vicinity, whatever it may be: suburban neighbourhood or city tower block. Some of this is already happening. It can be seen at work in the quiet neighbourhoods and interiors that feature in recent collections by Jamie McKendrick, including *Crocodiles and Obelisks* (2007) and of Stephen Romer's *Yellow Studio* (2008). And Longley's heirs, the inheritors of touchstone lyricism's power to rearrange and recharge experiences and cultures, even include Paul Farley and Michael Symmons Roberts as they collaborate on a prose vision of urban *Edgelands* (2011).

5

FREE AND EASY?

Some poets believe that poetry's meaning is inseparable from its
sound. They feel that it is impossible to translate verse because the
original sound-scape is by definition lost. Or, less uncompromisingly,
they think that translated poetry can be successfully recreated only
when the new sounds of the 'host' language are used to real effect;
and hence that the translator of poetry, far from being peripheral,
plays a role of the utmost importance. This belief that the sound
of poetry *creates* meaning isn't confined to strict formalists. John
Burnside, writing somewhat in the tradition of Percy Bysshe Shelley,
holds that rapture creates 'true' form; while J.H. Prynne uses lyric
music, rather than a conventional relationship with meaning, to
propel his verse.

For others, though, the central characteristic of poetry isn't its sound
but its sensibility: the *kind* of thing it says, and the *sort* of occasion or
theme it says it about. Poets who take this view are intuitively hospitable
to international writing, even from languages they can't pronounce and
never hear. W. N. Herbert and Pascale Petit, two of our most prolific
poet-translators, exemplify this approach which does, however, mean
a further struggle with the question of appropriate *content*. Can it ever
be too 'highbrow' or too 'low'? One form anxiety about tonal content
takes is a preoccupation, which marks the last two poetry generations,
with sounding contemporary – for example, urban:

Beneath a fractured intercourse of shadow
and streetlamp, two people are foregrounded, black
                                       on white.
                        (John Stammers, 'Mother's Day')

Walking down Newgate Street on a Saturday morning
I saw a rasher of fatty bacon lying curled
on the pavement like an ear and thought:

who'd rather have bacon when they could have earholes,
an audience of thousands falling accidental as snow,
and what if snow is not an accident?
                        (W.N. Herbert, 'A Breakfast Wreath')

Since the Nineties, contemporary terms and objects, and the slightly distanced sensibility of untouched youth, have been widely used. A familiar strategy is the reflexive ponder, not quite post-modern but certainly distancing:

My father at the sink
like his father before him
softening two flints
of soap, then squeezing
the yellow into the pink.
                        (Jacob Polley, 'Economics')

This kind of tone-setting generates poetic strategies of its own. The naming of parts from cultures other than the largely Western, urban default becomes a gesture of significance, and therefore 'poetic'. Collections like Kate Clanchy's *Samarkand* (1999) and Sasha Dugdale's *The Estate* (2007) reassert the Anglo-Saxon norm by exoticizing the alternative: this used to be called orientalism. But poets with a genuinely international or minority-cultural background of their own do, simply by naming what's characteristic or feels significant in that background, enlarge English-language culture. These enlargements are interesting poetically as well as culturally, since they heighten the shared vocabulary of both word and image.

But naming something as apparently ordinary as a family meal, or a piece of domestic furniture, within the frame of a poem always means paying renewed attention to that detail. This is the point William Carlos Williams was making with his familiar red wheelbarrow, upon which 'everything depends'. To put it another way, a poem and what it names are mutual framing devices, which lend each other dignity:

> This poem began after
> the wild turkeys walked across
> our garden in Connecticut.
> >   (Sujata Bhatt, 'A Poem Consisting Entirely of Introductions')

> With low sky catching alight from streetlamps
> there Billy is, workshying, dribbling a football to the shopfloor.
> Inside, the cleaners sluice the floor of its blue dye.

> In the yard, rain rinses – 'that's where the foreman Dan
> chucked up' – clots of human flesh. Eel-flesh, peas, fired potato.
> >   (David Morley, 'November the Fourteenth, Nineteen Forty-one')

Free verse is particularly well-suited to poetry of this kind, which brings one culture into another, because it is both content-led – the form *adapts itself* to what the poem wants to say – and able to slip past the specific cultural resonances of strict form. Of course, free verse is itself culturally specific; but it brings a narrower (if admittedly Western) present to bear on its content in place of the rich history foregrounded by forms such as the villanelle and sonnet.

Indeed, often free verse does not even acknowledge itself as a form. This is especially useful when it is involved with poetic transference:

letting new things work as symbols. In Pakistan-born Moniza Alvi's 'Fighter Planes':

> I . . .
> thought I could fly
> and peck at little
> bits of the world,
> beat my wings
> where I was born
>
> try looping lines
> between the hemispheres.

This innocent-looking piece of writing from Alvi's second collection, *A Bowl of Warm Air* (1996), is in fact doing several complicated things at once. The form is both apparently artless, so as to appear 'spoken' and intimate – not all the lines have only four syllables or two stresses, nor do those stresses fall in a regular pattern – yet also manages to be studiedly mimetic. Its short lines show us how 'little' the speaker's 'bits of the world' are, and how a 'looping line' must fly down the page. The piece also states directly that its business is cultural transition. Those 'hemispheres' are in the world as much as in the brain, and the poem starts with an image of peace-making in an international context: 'I saw the bright / green parrots / make their nests / in fighter planes'. *Look*, the narrator says, *how I reconcile the two nations I'm a part of.* And yet that swords-into-ploughshares image, of bomb-bays turned into nests, is so quickly articulated that it is almost subliminal. Alvi (b. 1954) doesn't flesh out a detailed concrete 'reality' for her reader. The image is as part of the poem's (internal) train of thought, not ours.

So this poem is about the making of poetry – as the saying is, it problematizes the process – in ways which are both overt and counter-intuitive. We expect reflexive rationalisation to produce knotty, theory-driven verse, not this informal, talkative approach. Alvi's poems are filled with this kind of lightly worked metaphor, as easy to decode as a dream and, like dream, there *to be* decoded. In 'Rolling', also from what is arguably Alvi's richest collection to date:

> In my dreams I roll
> like the holy man
> who rolls two thousand miles
> down the middle of the highway
> who rolls for eight months
> to a Himalayan shrine.

Although the long, thin, unrolling poem will pass 'through my father's house / before he fled to Pakistan', 'through my family name' and 'right into the girl / I might have been / growing up here', where it ends is strangely under-determined: 'Somewhere I think I might have been / but it's not a Himalayan shrine / and no goddess expects me.'

This is neither polemic nor political theory. It names puzzles, but doesn't attempt to solve them. In other words, Alvi shows the reader that to be engaged in cultural transition is to deal with Keatsian 'uncertainties, Mysteries, doubts'. For all its plain-speaking – from her debut *The Country at my Shoulder* (1993) to *Europa* (2008) even her volume titles 'locate' her – the writing opens up topics, rather than pins them down. Nowhere is this more true than of her use of symbol and metaphor. In 'You are Turning Me into a Novel', from her first collection, 'You are travelling towards me //at the speed of an idea', but 'I hope you don't think / it is my life', because 'Somewhere in each chapter / I do something terrible'. This is both a fuzzy metaphor – is the narrator a book or a character in a book? – and a declaration of intent. The speaker refuses to be reduced to something singular and controllable. Like many poets before her, from the John Masefield of 'Cargoes' to the Ted Hughes who could write such dreams for children as *Moon-Whales and Other Moon Poems,* Alvi wants to keep an 'elsewhere', a strategic evasion, as an element in her poetic identity. That her 'elsewhere' might also be a historical, biographical fact is merely, as far as poetic strategy goes, a lucky trump.

Even in the relatively through-composed collections *Carrying My Wife* (2000) and *Europa*, Alvi's metaphors do not stabilize as they extend. *Carrying My Wife* splits off the self/not-self of a hyphenated identity into the figure of a wife, observed in a series of twenty-five poems through the narrative of a 'husband'. If this weren't role-play enough for a female poet, the couple in these poems role-reverse, even shape-shift: 'My wife took to walking on all fours', 'Man Impregnated', 'we fell in love // many times / in the course of our marriage'. We're left with a dream-like, glancing sense of love, desire and nugatory femininity; and this is further explored in *Europa*, which uses Ovid's shape-shifting myth to explore both rape and Europe's forcible appropriations of the Indian subcontinent. It is gradually becoming clear that these twin assaults are Alvi's founding myths, and that her poems explore and pair these uncertainties about and violations of human boundaries, often looking at both at once.

If symbols don't click shut in Alvi's verse, neither does form. Her rhythms aren't regularized as metre. On the contrary, they seem to make some effort to be imperceptible:

> Two centuries ago
> I thought I heard a rustling
> in my stomach – trees grew there
> swishing gentle-fingered branches.
>
> ('Storyteller')

This opening, typical for the poet, follows the discreet conventions of free-verse lineation, which in Britain often traces phrasal structure. The occasional use of what we might call secondary enjambment, when a clause but not a phrase is broken across the line – 'I thought I heard a rustling / in my stomach' – helps stop the structure from becoming intrusive through repetition. But there's no *additionality*. It doesn't create more tension or interest. Alvi's titles are equally deprecating. On the contents pages these look tempting – 'Nothing Too Passionate at First', 'Giants with Tender Hands', 'The Airborne House', 'Man of Tree and

Fern', 'The Air Was Full of Starfish' – but, like greengrocers' labels, they name what is already in each piece.

A very different challenge is thrown down by W.N. Herbert. *Cabaret McGonagall* (1996) and *The Laurelude* (1998), are knowing, ludic names for collections grainy with references, but busy with cheerful chatter. Much of this chatter is in persona; ascribable, its author seems to suggest with a shrug, to the cast of irrepressible characters that fill Herbert's collections. Some are English speakers, some Scots: and their allusive wit is, it seems, the slightly hangdog form that Dundonian humour takes. Herbert was born in Dundee, in 1961, and now works at Newcastle University; but he completed a doctoral study of Hugh MacDiarmid at Oxford, where a resulting volume, characteristically titled *To Circumjack MacDiarmid*, was published by Oxford University Press in 1992. The socialist, nationalist MacDiarmid might presumably have preferred almost any other university in which to be revalued, but this feat of cultural appeasement on Herbert's part is both surprising, and interesting for the light it sheds on his own writing.

Unlike fellow Scots-identifying poets, such as Mick Imlah or Robert Crawford, Herbert doesn't disappear among the accumulated cultural referents of that country's history. Instead, he retains an inviting presence through his style, which seems to take its responsibilities to introduce reader and material to each other, and to charm both, seriously. 'No Joy' opens:

> Black didn't know the difference between
> Gaelic and Scots, not even when you told him,
> but it was his bookshop we were reading in,
> so we didn't.

Which is a smartly collusive way to remind the anglophone reader of just that difference. But as the poem goes on, it turns, seeming to switch sides as it wryly questions whether Scottish culture is, as an Irish character suggests, joyless:

> I checked my Harris tweed jacket for joy,
> I checked my Donegal overcoat, since
> it was a cold night for a northern boy
> in the metropolis.

Back again the mockery turns on itself – or is that on its speaker? – as 'a northern boy' is, of course, supposed to cope better with meteorological than with emotional cold. Stitching to and fro go the English and the Scottish perspectives. The risk is that this produces poetry which, for all its line-by-line vigour and condensation, slips out of the memory because it lacks the clarity of the thumping conclusion. Cultural negotiation might, it seems, be subtle and piece-meal.

On the other hand, it means that Herbert is dealing with questions of identity poetics every bit as distinct as those developed by the other writers in this chapter. His chief strategy is to elide difference. In *The Laurelude*'s 'In Memoriam Bill Burroughs', that writer is memorialized with the 'Coronation of Bill's Corpse as the Shit-Click King': a subtitle that neatly sidesteps the Orange problem inherent in calling him 'King Bill'. But though the poem itself may be a Beat-inflected hyper-list, it is set not in the American culture that William Burroughs celebrated, but in cyberspace: that panopticon, ever ready with malapropisms, which offers 'denim pasties, / dairy telegraphs, advent colanders, and laminated drizzle'. These crunched pairings are a speeded-up version of the Scots-English alternations in 'No Joy'. Unlike the touchstones employed by Moniza Alvi or (as we'll see) Fred D'Aguiar and Grace Nichols, Herbert's imagery never seems unchanging. Instead, each citation and trope, including the grammatical, is tampered with and turned: 'So why not raise a glass of white so blond / it catches like his beard' and 'Hard cheese, hard as Pecorino' are puns which turn on category error. Even similes shift from description into a kind of appropriation. 'Cromag' starts 'in David Craig's old office', but quickly slips outdoors:

> . . . a dead fly on its back with its legs drawn together
> like a man's fingers when he's trying to evaluate
> something it's hard to reduce
> to a quantity.
>   It is
> a shrewd gesticulation, like
> the copse of trees protruding from Millbuies' brim,
> that Victorian loch . . .

Herbert's attempt to solve the problem of how to produce universal speech from locality is manic and often very funny: but the project is serious. The restless verse it produces seems a signal that the British cultural status quo is not yet representative in the balance it strikes.

Neither W.N. Herbert's nor Moniza Alvi's apparently spontaneous versification is wholly their own invention, of course. It is a legacy from those poets of the Seventies and Eighties who shook off the cautious, formal diction of the Group and its plain dealing successors. The public perception of poetry changed in those decades; free verse became the expected norm. By the Seventies Ted Hughes (who would be Poet Laureate from 1984 until his death in 1998), was already being taught in many British schools, alongside Seamus Heaney. Especially after the 1981 edition of her *Collected Poems* had been published, Sylvia Plath was widely adopted by women readers. The Eighties marked a further period of poetic transition. By the end of that decade, figures as diverse as Michael Donaghy, Matthew Sweeney and Selima Hill had emerged. Though each revealed a discrete set of influences, they shared an enthusiasm for free verse. Widely read figureheads then still alive included R.S. Thomas, George Mackay Brown and Norman MacCaig, all three of whom used free verse (though Mackay Brown also borrowed traditional song forms). This gave even their late work what was then a contemporary feel, and allowed them to refresh material as age-old as spirituality (the later Thomas), epiphanies of the natural world (MacCaig), and traditional working life (Mackay Brown). Its contemporaneous, apparently transparent form also made their writing feel organic, as if its origins in those places and cultures were 'natural' and spontaneous.

And there was more. Neil Astley founded Bloodaxe Books in Newcastle in 1978. Bloodaxe's original list included the Northern modernists Basil Bunting and Martin Bell, as well as other key figures overlooked by the London trade publishers, including Barry MacSweeney. The press was a form of resistance to metropolitan fashion. But it went further than that. The look of Bloodaxe books was then fresh, even mildy astonishing, with full-bleed, full-colour covers, more than one poem to a page, and Bodoni typeface: an anti-effete font with resonances of street poster print. Bloodaxe's almost counter-cultural energy demystified poetry and made it feel like a newly vernacular form. Astley supported poets, like the mountain-climbing Andrew Greig and the prison-visiting, working-class Ken Smith, who demonstrated that readers and writers did not need long years of university education to see the point of poetry. From the outset the press displayed a tendency to create alternative literary canons, and specialized in anthologies of women writers: Jeni Couzyn's *The Bloodaxe Book of Contemporary Women Poets* (1985), Carol Rumens's *New Women Poets* (1990), Linda France's *Sixty Women Poets* (1993), Maura Dooley's *Making for Planet Alice* (1997), Robyn Bolam's *Eliza's Babes* (2005) and Deryn Rees-Jones's *Modern Women Poets* (2005). E.A. Markham's *Hinterland: Caribbean Poetry from the West Indies and Britain* appeared in 1986 and was soon joined by anthologies of Finnish, Hungarian, Polish and Indian poetry, among others. The idealist anthologies began to appear a little later: *Staying Alive* (2002) and its successors *Being Alive* (2004) and *Being Human* (2011) and the eco-anthology *Earth Shattering* (2007) are high-selling volumes which repeat that poetry can have a message. Of course, humanly and socially valuable poetry is very often written in strict form too, but these message-led selections, often underlining an editorial resistance to what is all too easily seen as old-fashioned and ostentatiously literary – the world of High Table and belles-lettres – particularly celebrate the emotional and serious capacities of free verse.

By the Eighties young poets were also being encouraged to

circumvent traditional forms by the sheer amount of high-quality poetry in often free-verse translation being published, predominantly by independents like Anvil Press (which had been founded in 1968 by Peter Jay). In the Sixties, Al Alvarez's *Penguin Modern European Poets* series, and the magazine *Modern Poetry in Translation* founded by Ted Hughes and Daniel Weissbort in 1965, had reminded post-Movement generations that, if you were less cantankerously insular than Philip Larkin, that self-styled 'mild xenophobe who never goes abroad if he can help it', you might well want to explore the majority world of poetry beyond the English Channel. The geopolitics of the Seventies and Eighties encouraged such internationalism. The Cold War was showing no signs of thaw, the 1962 Cuban Missile Crisis was still relatively recent, and US intervention in the affairs of South America was encouraging anglophone interest in Latin American writing. The decades after the Second World War were a heyday of PEN. Founded in London in 1921, the organization ran international congresses and lobbied on behalf of imprisoned writers, as it still does. It almost seemed as if every international poet must be a dissident hero: an impression also nurtured, after 1953, by the CIA-funded *Encounter* magazine, whose founder editor – until he resigned when the source of its funding was revealed in 1967 – was the jet-setting poet-translator Stephen Spender. Meanwhile, the stultifying effects of pre-war translations in inferior rhyme were being shaken off, not least by many fine American poet-translators. Those who led the way included Robert Hass, who worked with Czesław Miłosz, W.S. Merwin, who published several volumes of translations of Federico Garcia Lorca and Pablo Neruda, and C.K. Williams, who translated important work by Adam Zagajewski and Euripides.

A fourth element in the flowering of free verse into the poetic norm was the influence of rock, reggae and dub on urban youth culture's belief that it was entitled to verse. (Dub, a predecessor of rap, grew out of the speaking that MCs do over reggae tracks. Linton Kwesi Johnson (*b.* 1952) would coin the phrase 'dub poetry' in the mid-Seventies.) Ironically, it was the Three White Men of Liverpool – the

Mersey Beat poets Roger McGough, Brian Patten and Adrian Henri riding the slipstream of Beatlemania into cultural celebrity in the late Sixties and Seventies – who made room for Linton Kwesi Johnson and his successor, Benjamin Zephaniah.

Both have laid down important mainstream markers for British Afro-Caribbean culture through their virtuoso verbal performances. Interviewed by Mervyn Morris in 1982, Kwesi Johnson was aware how important it was for Black culture that poets writing dub be able to move into other forms where they wanted to:

> My only caution is that I think people should remember that poetry is much wider than dub poetry. To talk dub poetry alone or to call yourself a dub poet is a limitation, you know, it's putting yourself in a bag and it's a dangerous business.

At that time Black British poetry was moving freely between page and microphone in a way that today's young Black performance poets are not greatly encouraged to do. *Dread Beat an' Blood* was the title of both Kwesi Johnson's second collection (in 1975) and his first LP (in 1978). His ballads about the Brixton riots and knife crime are part of a literary political tradition that goes back to John Milton's *Areopagitica*, Thomas Paine's *The Rights of Man* or Percy Bysshe Shelley's campaigning *The Mask of Anarchy*, though they perhaps have most in common with each author's early tracts or pamphlets, and the wider, often anonymous, tradition of pamphlet ballads. Like theirs, Kwesi Johnson's work may be part witness statement, but it retains the writerly concepts both of authorship and of linguistic pleasure. The textual influences he cites in the Morris interview include the library of the Black Panther youth movement, the Bible, reggae and language itself: 'From the moment I began to write in the Jamaican language music entered the poetry.' Kwesi Johnson's experiments with form were personal technical advances, as well as speaking for a community:

> madness . . . madness . . .
> madness tight on the heads of the rebels;
> the bitterness erupts like a hot-blast.
>   broke glass.
>
>   ('Five Nights of Bleeding' I)

He stands for a model in which the author has a responsibility within history, to act as a witness. 'Bass Culture' is:

>   . . . a whole heappa
> passion a gather
> like a frightful form
> like a righteous harm
> giving off wild like is madness.

Taking a different path, Benjamin Zephaniah has, since the millennium, become a general ambassador for Black culture, advising on the National Curriculum and receiving a raft of honorary doctorates. He no longer works regularly in adult poetry itself, though he publishes work for children, and he doesn't directly mentor younger poets through the traditional routes: teaching, editing, curating or MC-ing. It has been left to an older generation, like veteran James Berry, and Kwesi Johnson's near-contemporaries the fine communitarian lyric poet John Agard and his wife Grace Nichols, to continue a tradition in which writing can both claim strong vernacular roots and make its mark on the page.

Among this group, Grace Nichols (*b.* 1950) is particularly noteworthy. A headmaster's daughter from Guyana, she moved to Britain with Agard in 1977. Her first book, *I is a Long-Memoried Woman*, won the Commonwealth Poetry Prize in 1983. For the rest of the Eighties her work appeared from a trade publisher of women's writing, rather than a specialist poetry press; this gave a wider general readership access to her work. Those two Virago collections, *The Fat Black Woman's Poems* (1984) and what was something of a follow-up, *Lazy Thoughts of a Lazy Woman* (1989), were – like her novel *Whole of a Morning Sky* (1986) – consciously political and directly addressed Caribbean women's experiences. In her first three collections Nichols creates personae to let this community speak for itself, arguably for the first time in European (though not in North American) literature. Hitherto, these experiences had been traduced by European women ('the madwoman in the attic' in Charlotte Bronte's *Jane Eyre*), or appropriated by men: James Berry's *Lucy's Letter* (1975), does something similar to *The Fat Black Woman's Poems*, but his delightful Lucy is a male invention: unconflicted, single-note, and more emotional than thoughtful . . .

Nichols's poems are more concerned with the Caribbean than with their author's British experience. In part this might be because the poet didn't move to the UK until she was twenty-five. (Kwesi Johnson went through secondary school in London.) But there's much more to these influential early books than simple autobiography. They are the product of a decade in which the women's movement in particular – and to a lesser extent that generation of British socialist intellectuals who had been influenced by the Marxist literary theorist Raymond Williams, and his student Terry Eagleton – sought to change patterns of discursive power: of who could speak, and about what. Nichols's narrator is not the educated, ambitious young woman the poet herself was – and as she might have portrayed herself under the old conservative contract with exceptionalism, which takes its lead from what the gifted outlier rather than the typical citizen can achieve – but an Everywoman. Yet that in turn is a liberal humanist fantasy, for women are created by individual circumstance just as men are. So Nichols creates a located, culturally specific Everywoman who is not simply generically Black, but has a specific heritage and, above all, a personal history.

Any such persona entails the 'long memory' of double migration: 'the pain and suffering that her ancestors had gone through in that crossing from Africa to the New World', as Nichols says in her 1989 essay 'Home Truths'. It's no coincidence that her 'long-memoried', and later 'fat black', woman is a kind of motherly repository of something close to, yet also much larger than, family stories. This cleverly naturalizes the speaker's role: and reminds us that storytelling takes place not only in libraries but over garden fences and at children's bedtimes. In other words, the technique enlarges rather than subverts the narrative canon: which meant that this wise-cracking, sexy narrator could join the literary high table straight away, rather than give decades to literary radicalism in the hope of overturning it:

> Give her honour
> Give her honour, you fools,
> Give her honour.
>
> ('Because She Has Come')

Nichols's poems are less reliant on patois than Kwesi Johnson's. In her 'Without Song' we hear an echo of Aimé Césaire's *négritude*, the poetics of the francophone Caribbean, which veered away from vernacular and contemporary European traditions – though it borrowed from both – to make a new, consciously literary language. *Négritude* is loosely indebted to modernism and not afraid to pack symbols with affect and freight:

> The faces of the children
> are small and stricken and black
>
> . . .
>
> They have fallen
> into mourning
> moving to the shrouds
> of tares
>
> ('Without Song', from *I is a Long-Memoried Woman*)

But the secret of Nichols's impact has to do as much with directness of diction as with political stance. In 'Tropical Death':

> The fat black woman want
> a brilliant tropical death
> not a cold sojourn
> in some North Europe far/forlorn

The fat black woman want
some heat/hibiscus at her feet
blue sea dress
to wrap her neat

. . .

In the heart
of her mother's sweetbreast
In the shade
of the sun leaf's cool bless
In the bloom
of her people's bloodrest

the fat black woman want
a brilliant tropical death yes

Despite its serious subject matter – exile and death – there are echoes of the playground in the way this characteristically affirmative poem slips in and out of rhyme; and it's no surprise that Nichols was quickly taken up as a children's writer. Her anthology of Black poetry, *Poetry Jump Up* (1988), remains a classroom classic.

One of Grace Nichols's poetic heirs is the fellow-Guyanese writer Fred D'Aguiar (*b.* 1950), whose *Mama Dot* (1985) portrays an island matriarch with quasi-mystical feminine powers of emotional intelligence, healing and cultural memory. Unlike Berry's *Lucy*, *Mama Dot* is not generally spoken *for*, but admired and observed. D'Aguiar's second collection *Airy Hall* (1989), also thematic, is named for the village in which it is largely set. But D'Aguiar is ten years younger than Nichols and, though he started publishing poetry only a couple of years after her, belongs to another poetic generation. Although his first collections used personae and borrowed from oral tradition, they were already moving away from this kind of writing. There is a conspicuous richness to the language and line, and a return to metaphor, which identifies D'Aguiar as a consciously literary writer:

> . . . Marriages
> Under the one roof are an upward
> Curve. . . .
> Go back to another age, one
> Sewn up inside the pitch a gas-lamp,
> Signing arms and voices map.
>
> . . .
>
> So many fictions has the wood spongy,
> A feel you double-take every time.
>
> ('Airy Hall's Dynasty')

D'Aguiar is a serious presence, producing prose, poetry and plays which have received wide critical acclaim; but, alas, he is no longer doing so in Britain. In the mid-Nineties he moved to the US, where he teaches at Virginia Tech. He has written about the campus killings there in poems collected in *Continental Shelf* (2009). A thoughtful, cosmopolitan writer, his work has most in common with that of the late E.A. Markham, the influential Montserrat-born poet, editor and latterly professor of creative writing.

The specifically Caribbean tradition within British writing has been an exceptionally potent carrier of free verse. The musical forms it brings with it – reggae, dub, calypso rhythms – break up the building blocks of blank verse, that formal default mode, confronting both the iambic beat and pentameter's count to five. But free verse isn't only useful for framing new cultural material. It leaves growing space for all kinds of new, organic, forms. Born in 1946, Ruth Padel came to intellectual maturity during Seventies feminism and cannot be entirely divorced from this context. While Grace Nichols's response to that challenge is overt, schematic – and even staged, through the 'characters' she creates – Padel has more in common with the 'transgressive' writing that French feminists like Hélène Cixous would make famous, which has inflected women's radical poetics internationally and which will reappear, later in this book, among the expanded lyricists. However her work is much more a spontaneous example of, than a position taken up on, the way some women writers use effusion and surplus – what in the nineteenth century would have been called 'enthusiasm' – to break through to an arguably more authentic kind of writing.

Padel specializes in a plenitude of images. But she is too intelligent a writer, one foot always on the grammatical ground, to lose either her way – or her reader. 'Heatwave', from *Rembrandt Would Have Loved You* (1998), evokes 'that weird relief' of sex. Or is it of:

> . . . seeing bees swarm in your own apple trees
> And a helical slipstream of woodpigeons bend
> > In a clear domestic fashion
> Down the mountain, home.

Apart from the characteristic science-talk ('helical'), there's nothing particularly hard-won about this. Like Sarah Maguire (for whom she has a touching poem, on the death of fathers, in 2002's *Voodoo Shop*), Ruth Padel has a tendency to use images that seem, at first sight, to work as touchstones. A glance at *Rembrandt*'s contents page reveals the sorts of tropes she scoops up for her evocative metaphors: 'Misty', 'Pharaoh's Cup', 'Still Life with Loaves, Seaweed and Wren', 'The Horse Whisperer'. However, none of these stick around long enough to become part of a personal poetic universe. In Padel's poetry, crea-tures from the natural world and items from the furnished interiors of London lives are all equally a part of our collective imagination: the register that film-makers and advertisers, as much as poets, know how to work to gain our emotional agreement. The metaphor of phospho-rescence, in 'That sudden dash of sea-fire / When a sleeping wave rolls over in the harbour // In the night' may be doubled (it represents a lover's body, too). But it is also collectively metonymic, standing in for all our memories and associations of phosphorescence.

Rather than being repeated touchstones then, Padel's images generate a kind of metaphorical evocation, which allows her to range over wide imaginative common ground. Her trio of middle-period collections,

Rembrandt, *Voodoo Shop* and *The Soho Leopard*, are thematically dominated by the story of a love affair. Or rather: not exactly a story, since Padel seems most at ease with the happy ending. It's almost as if she feels that finding happiness is the transformative duty of the poem. So we have poems that record a lover's unreliability, and experiences of vulnerability or jealousy, but only from beyond the moment of resolution, when all is forgiven or understood. European cities are visited, confidences exchanged, the couple make love: all on a note of unremitting joy – that single-handed, willed positivity which is the true voice of a mistress. If Jean Rhys was the first to acknowledge the Other Woman's anguished loneliness, Padel records like no one else the face she turns towards her man.

Another way of saying this might be that, just as an affair is so busily bound up with simply happening that the relationship can rarely contain anything beyond itself, so Padel's poetry from this period seems, in retrospect, to have been waiting to get beyond that theme. Her way out has been through a kind of richly morphological nature-writing. The lover who is portrayed as a range of natural forces – 'the secret ocean ridges of your skin', 'Your mouth, // Tasting of the breath / Of greenhouses', 'She was a lightning photographer / Handed the secret of storms' – becomes at length 'the Soho Leopard'. Padel's crossover book, the beautifully written prose travel volume *Tigers in Red Weather* (2005), opens with a declaration of authorial intent. The poet is going tiger-hunting to cure a broken heart. It has been followed by *Where the Serpent Lives* (2010), a novel that includes close observations of cobras, and *The Mara Crossing* (2012), a hybrid prose/poetry meditation on migration both natural and human; links reinforced by feminine personifications:

> Cell summons her treasurer,
> hoarder of energy, Adenosine
> triphosphate, to break the welded rungs
> and separate the partners
> in the hydrogen-bond pavane.

Got to be done. Like snapping a bone
to reset it . . .

                                        ('Breaking the Bond')

At the mid-point of this development, in 2009, Padel published *Darwin: A Life in Poems*. That rare thing, a biography in verse, it's a study of her great-great-grandfather that not only speaks for him, but does so using some of his actual writing. This makes Charles Darwin come alive; it also draws out the similarities between his nineteenth-century prose and her twenty-first century verse. Both are storehouses of names and things. Each has a kind of cheerful richness that veers towards superabundance:

Pure volcano. A mantle of hot bare rock. 'Nothing could be less
        inviting. A broken field of black basaltic lava
        thrown into most rugged waves and crossed
by fissures.' Lava tubes, tuff cones and bright,
        red-orange crabs. A land iguana! One saffron
        leathery elbow, powdery as lichen, sticking out

like a man doing press-ups while leering at the sand.
                ('On Not Thinking about Variation in Tortoiseshell')

A vivid burst of naming from the scientist's notebook bleeds into the narrator's whirling phrasal observations; as if she is as carried away as he is. This similarity of diction reminds us that to evoke any set of resonances – including dressing the set of a narrative located in the nineteenth century – is to make a conservative gesture. Such conservatism is something the book acknowledges, playing with old-fashioned marginalia and discursive titles in the nineteenth-century style.

If we place this conceptual conservatism alongside the idea of a women's poetry characterized by celerity and plenitude, we notice the extent to which Padel is part of a tradition. The gracefulness of such images from the book as 'The dog-rose, / starry on August hedges along the white-dust road' ('A Desperate Way to Avoid Paying your Tailor'), or – applied as simile – 'Reticence descends on the house / like an ostrich on its nest: a belljar of black feathers' ('The Devil's Chaplain') allows her to smuggle the particular exuberance that is the secret handshake of much gendered writing past those critics who look for 'muscularity' and 'control'. Cunningly, when she articulates this *ars poetica* she ascribes it to Darwin: 'He's in a rush – audacious – dangerous. / Boundaries drop away.'

Speedy and prolific, Padel is also that rare bird, a British critic capable of giving us the view from the female poet's world. Her readerly, anti-polemical critical style might suggest she is primarily reactive, both to the given text and to the grip of her own poetic sensibility. But it would be a lazy reader who tried to define her work in this way. On the contrary, Padel's training as a Classicist (something she shares with the fine Canadian poet Anne Carson) has left her with an exacting eye – and ear – for detail. Classical texts, relatively unsupported by contemporary contextual material, their 'dead' languages finally non-negotiable, call for undivided attention to what is on the page; and *The Poem and the Journey* (2007) and her Newcastle Lectures, *Silent Letters of the Alphabet* (2010), undertake the complex task of reading poems by their vowel sounds. However, Padel's critical writing first gained a high profile when for three years she wrote the 'Sunday Poem' column, in the *Independent on Sunday* that became *52 Ways of Looking at a Poem* (2002). Her writing here reaches over the shoulder of the poetry professional – indeed, even of readers with an amateur or emerging interest in poetry – to the general reader. Energetic, and as 'audacious – dangerous' as her ancestor, Padel has made a highly public practice of poetry.

Seventeen years younger than Padel, but also first published in the late-Eighties, Simon Armitage is another undeniably public poet. Long a feature of GCSE syllabuses, he is the Nation's Favourite for commissions which have ranged from the thousand-line Millennium Poem *Killing Time* to poems from the Yorkshire Sculpture Park. He has also collaborated extensively with his wife, the BBC producer Sue Roberts, on radio work that includes documentaries and a set of verse plays from Homer's *Odyssey*.

Now, in mid-career, he ranges between very fine translations of the Middle English *Gawain and the Green Knight* (2007) and *The Death of King Arthur* (2011), and promotions like 2010's *Walking Home* in which he 'sang for his supper' by walking the Pennine Way giving pre-booked readings in return for board. A self-declared wannabe rock star sporting a Beatles haircut, Armitage has always been careful to position his work among the cheerful ephemera of the late twentieth and twenty-first centuries. From his 1989 debut *Zoom*, through the almost-manic early productivity of *Kid* and *Xanadu*, both published in 1992, and *The Book of Matches* (1993), right up to *Tyrannosaurus Rex versus the Corduroy Kid* (2006) and *Seeing Stars* (2010), his titles make common cause with comic-book shorthand and slangy iconography. Yet the verse itself has staying power. If Simon Armitage is the Nigel Kennedy of contemporary British poetry: well, there is no denying that Kennedy can play (and indeed 'descends', violinistically, from the finest Establishment musicians). It is just that he retains, in middle age, a wunderkind's impatience with stuffy formalities. And underlying all Armitage's activity is a parallel sense that fluency and ease are crucial for poetry. He simply isn't trying for John Fuller's traditional resonance, Glyn Maxwell's intellectual flamboyance or Ruth Fainlight's overt technical control. He isn't even particularly interested in form, despite *Seeing Stars*'s controversial prose poems – so loose they can be hard to grasp – written as a homage to the playful American James Tate.

Insofar as he has been influenced by poetry, rather than wider cultural forms from pop lyric to comic, Armitage's influences are predominantly North American. The long tradition of speech rhythm in US poetry recruits partners as unlikely as Robert Frost and Walt Whitman, Gary Snyder and William Carlos Williams. Like these predecessors, Armitage has experimented with such rhythms, and with repetition as a structuring device. In 'You're Beautiful' (2006), for example, a chiming accumulation of 'You're beautiful because . . . / I'm ugly because . . .' tilts the poem from simplistic love lyric into apparent irony – and back again. Its examples seem guileless, led more by playful stream of consciousness than by a sense of escalation or dramatic logic (or indeed logic of any other kind: mysteriously, while 'You're beautiful because you're classically trained', 'I'm ugly because I remember . . . the year Schubert was born'). After a while we recognize Armitage's source, characteristically in pop culture: this is his *Men are from Mars, Women are from Venus* poem.

In *The Book of Matches* each poem mimics the imagined strike of a match that is then held up to 'illuminate' a person, relationship or scene for the roughly twenty seconds match – and poem – take to burn down. This idea of illumination is a metaphor through which Armitage steps in much the same way as a Central European poet like Wisława Szymborska, the late Polish Nobel Laureate. Szymborska is known as an Aesopian fabulist, but her excursions into the dream hinterland of metaphor don't lead to a concluding proverb or indeed conclusion in general. Instead they enter into the metaphor, seeming to ask, *If this were true, what would follow?* In 'Hatred', for example:

> Only hatred has just what it takes.
>
> Gifted, diligent, hard-working.
> Need we mention all the songs it has composed?
> All the pages it has added to our history books?
> All the human carpets it has spread
> over countless cities and football fields?
>
> Let's face it:
> it knows how to make beauty.
> The splendid fire-glow in midnight skies.
> Magnificent bursting bombs in rosy dawns.
> You can't deny the inspiring pathos of ruins
> and a certain bawdy humour to be found
> in the sturdy columns jutting from their midst.
>
> (*trans.* Stanisław Barańczak and Clare Cavanagh)

A similar resolute playfulness informs Armitage's poetry. It aligns him with the playful troubadour in Michael Donaghy, that key poet of Nineties Britain – and a sometime Irish American folk musician. A popular and unifying figure, Donaghy settled in London in 1985, and died aged fifty-one in 2004. His light but sure-footed approach to technique, and the extent to which his professional life was spent, typically for the Eighties and Nineties, on the road between readings and workshops, rather than – as might have been the case had he lived – in a university creative writing department, helped him to personify the anti-intellectual, ear-led approach which has been so powerful an element in recent British poetry. In fact, Donaghy's finely judged metrical verse belongs among the antecedents not of today's free verse but of the new formalists.

His writing was more narrative, emotional and indeed confessional than Armitage's half-abstracted characters, who seem not quite archetypes but are certainly exemplars. Yet there *is* an affinity between the two poets, and it's located in the song-like elements of their work. Donaghy's dark tales from a recognizably real life (like the ambivalent, complex 'Black Ice and Rain') share with Armitage's ironic, iconic narratives the unclotted quality that suggests song lyric rather than literary text.

In 'The Patent', Armitage's elegy for Donaghy:

> A man works late
> perfecting light,
>
> his hand cupped like some secretive priest
> of the ancient past
>
> protecting a flame in the night.

It's a piece that sees poetry – and so, also, itself – as going beyond the everyday. The explicit beauty of the central image belongs right in the lyric mainstream, and has the resonant clarity that we say 'sings'. Here, but also elsewhere in his work, Armitage recreates this song principle from a kind of ease, and from images that speak immediately and out of a world which is ready to hand for the reader. Sometimes this technique seems to produce almost wilfully democratic verse. The clear image-grammar, and his use of repetition in particular, can echo the over-simplification of a cartoon. But when Armitage relaxes and lets his native pentameter loose in either rhymed or blank verse, the line has an intact grace:

> Slow on the uptake, slow to take a hint,
> I'm still at a loss as to what was meant
> by the pair that swept past the window frame
> in the same split-second of bated breath
> in which the presenter, announcing his death,
> forgot then remembered the poet's name.
>
> ('Pheasants, iii: Brace', *Tyrannosaurus Rex. . .*)

Pentameter might be the heightened diction of formal verse, but it is also, as his fellow Yorkshireman Tony Harrison has claimed, the native speech-rhythm of this Huddersfield-born poet.

Armitage claims a further birthright, an English dialect shared with the *Gawain* poet, in his edition of that Middle English poem: 'The linguistic epicentre of the poem has been located in the area of the Cheshire-Staffordshire-Derbyshire border.' Elsewhere in his introduction Armitage says that 'to me, alliteration is the warp and weft of the poem, without which it is just so many fine threads. In some very elemental way, the story and the sense of the poem is directly located within its sound. The percussive patterning of the words serves to reinforce their meaning and to countersink them within the memory.' He's writing about *Gawain,* but he could be talking about his own poetry in general. The ideas are close to those Don Paterson expresses in his essay 'The Lyric Principle', about the non-arbitrary connections sounds make within a poem. For Armitage is no outlier but a poet who is, in many ways typical of his poetic generation: *Electroplating the*

Baby, the name of Jo Shapcott's debut, isn't a million miles from Armitage's trademark grunge titles.

He was, though, born ten years later than Shapcott, and his precocity itself provided the grounds for rapid early promotion (along with his near-contemporary, that very different poet, Glyn Maxwell). Lacking the time and space to develop more organically, and along more private, literary lines, Armitage has become a highly visible challenger to less flamboyant poetics and schools. His cool yet playful verse seems to urge us that it is our duty to have some kind of fun. For example, in his translations of the Wakefield Mystery Plays, for the Yorkshire Sculpture Park:

> So up swans some swain who is peacock proud,
> who must borrow my wain and also my plough,
> and with no gainsaying I must grant him out loud
> or I live in pain and anger and woe.

This is both faithful versioning and writing that is sheerly pleasurable on tongue and ear. It is also clearly not free verse. Yet in crucial ways – tonally, and in the hands-in-trouser-pockets charm and swagger of each – Armitage's formal and free verse are of a piece. Their neighbourly virtuosity reminds us just how important a role tone plays in free verse, and how that importance trumps metre and music to make us listen afresh.

6

THE ANECDOTALISTS

Free verse is a way of writing that seems to take a step backwards, leaving the foreground to what's being said, and who says it. The Estonian poet Jaan Kaplinski, well-known for his free-verse meditations on the natural world and the human condition but originally a formalist, calls strict verse 'word-bound'. Others avoid this kind of negative definition. In his influential 1950 essay 'Projective Verse', the American Charles Olson wrote that the poet needs to go 'down through the workings of his own throat to that place where breath comes from, where breath has its beginnings, where drama has come from'. In fact, the idea of 'free verse' simply isn't all that fleshed out. It indicates nothing more than the absence of strict metre. It does not mean that the sound of the poem has to be disconnected from its content or that its form is unimportant. Free verse isn't necessarily confessional or self-expressive, and it doesn't automatically replace regular metre with speech rhythms. It can be enriched by technical control and it almost always employs strategies such as assonantal coherence, internal rhyme or even mimesis through form.

Nevertheless, one particular style of free verse, disciplined and anti-indulgent, has gradually emerged from the dandified cool of the Nineties. It has been promulgated widely through workshops and in particular by two influential poet-editors: Robin Robertson at Cape and his own editor Don Paterson at Picador. This kind of writing represents a second moment in British free verse. In the first, as the last chapter suggested, poetry more straightforwardly frees itself from what came before: from whatever seemed inauthentic and lacking some sort of internal poetic necessity. That gesture is capacious, various and revolutionary. By contrast, at the second stage free verse acknowledges *itself* as a form, and starts to develop techniques and conventions of its own. The poets who embrace this second moment are indebted to those who pioneered the first, not necessarily personally – as students or mentees – or even consciously, but because until old rules had been broken new forms could not develop. Yet this shift doesn't take place everywhere simultaneously, but rather within an individual writer's sense of the available forms and of what can be done with them. Significant architects of this second moment – among them Carol Ann Duffy, Jackie Kay, Neil Rollinson and Paul Farley – have emerged over a period of roughly two decades. Their development is parallel and analogous; yet they differ markedly from each other.

In the years since *Standing Female Nude* (1985), her first, astonishingly polished, full collection, Carol Ann Duffy (*b.* 1955) has become the best known of this quartet. Appointed Poet Laureate in 2009, she also features on the GCSE syllabuses. When Dennis O'Driscoll talked in *Poetry Review* about Duffy's 'perfect pitch', he put his finger on something which is key to both what she says and how she says it: Duffy has a fine sense for what is exactly enough. The poems in *Mean Time*, her fourth collection, which in 1993 swept the Forward, Whitbread and Scottish Arts Council Prizes, are as adept as a BBC mini-series in their evocation of time and place. 'The Captain of the 1964 *Top of the Form* Team' is full of convincing detail:

> . . . Gargling
> with Vimto. The clever smell of my satchel. Convent girls.
> I pulled my hair forward with a steel comb that I blew
> like Mick, my lips numb as a two-hour snog.

This is eager stuff, and its evocation of both the Sixties and adolescence is beautifully judged: the selective list, the lovely transferred epithet

'clever smell'. It refuses to be tempted by risky or expansive explana-
tion. (*What about* convent girls? the reader wants to ask, Are they
anything more than smutty cliché, ciphers for unfulfilled male adolescence?) Instead, the poem moves as if on rails towards its destination,
disappointed middle-age: '. . . The keeny. I say to my stale wife / *Six
hits by Dusty Springfield* . . . / My thick kids wince. *Name the Prime Minister
of Rhodesia.'* There's a quality of preconception to this which is not a
million miles from Movement poetry; a resolved or at least contained
complexity that is fiercely controlled.

And it's of a piece with this containment that Duffy's tone is elegiac.
As Chapter Three suggested, it is the instinct for preservation – a kind
of memorializing – that separates elegy from lament. Preservation
keeps elegy in the drawing room of English literature, and lament as
a violent vernacular underbelly. Lament is inelegant, so out of control
that it can seem involuntary: it bubbles up as confessional stream-of-
consciousness in teenage diaries, verse by prisoners and, as all carers
know, the writing of people with long-term mental health problems.
Elegy regrets the rift in the fabric: it wants things repaired and can't
accept that loss or change has occurred. Lament acknowledges that
loss, and grieves it. Noisy lament is left to foreigners, from Federico
Garcia Lorca to Yannis Ritsos. Since the Georgian poets, elegy has
been the English tone. So, although Carol Ann Duffy first made her
name with poetry that was sassy, sophisticated and memorable, hers is
a conscious gesture towards this prevailing literary note. She resembles
an airy Philip Larkin; one who hasn't been trapped by unusual, even
controversial, conclusions like his ('and don't have any kids yourself',
'Home is so sad', 'It becomes still more difficult to find / Words at
once true and kind, / Or not untrue and not unkind').

Elegy's prepaid tune leads to conclusions which can be as predictable as a depressive's: Larkin himself often sidesteps these with a launch
into transcendence: 'Somewhere becoming rain', 'What remains of us
is love'. But Duffy has a strong claim to be the Movement's true heir.
Here she is, at only thirty-eight:

One chair to sit in,
a greasy dusk wrong side of the tracks,
and watch the lodgers' lights come on in other rooms.

('Room')

sounding like the elder Larkin of 'Aubade', which had appeared sixteen
years earlier, in 1977:

Slowly light strengthens, and the room takes shape.
It stands plain as a wardrobe, what we know,
Have always known, know that we can't escape

This borrows Thomas Hardy's technique of using images from a society
that has only just disappeared, so that they will be familiar and resonant
– but not still-lived and contested. Elsewhere the 'distant Latin chanting
of a train' in 'Prayer' is a long way down the line from most state
education since the early Sixties. One reason that she seems 'older in
poetry' than others of her generation is that Duffy was a precocious
debutant. But this most literary writer also seems 'older' because she
has stayed close to the traditional insight that formal control can
enhance a poem's message. That's no less true when the message itself
has to do with limits, such as those of disappointing lives. A 'lodger
looking out across / a Midlands town' is a symbolic figure, not an
individual character; part Mr Bleaney, he could also be out of John
Betjeman by way of J. Alfred Prufrock.

   Mean Time's most anthologized piece is its closing 'Prayer', for which
the immediately preceding poems – the 'Room' for rent at '£90pw',
and 'Disgrace' with its 'Inconsolable vowels from the next room' – are
a rehearsal. 'Prayer', though, offers a redemptive view of the suburbs.
It suggests that their particular version of the quotidian, evoked as a
child practising scales and the shipping forecast on the radio, could
offer transcendence. This packed-tight sonnet is every bit as full of
Duffy's characteristic examples, rather than the argumentation that
usually structures sonnet form, as 'The Captain of the 1964 . . .', or

indeed the colourful, celebratory poems from 2011's *The Bees*, including 'Oxfam', 'Rings' and 'Passing-Bells'.

'Prayer' is the call-sign of Middle England, and it's easy to see why Duffy is an ideal candidate for a Laureateship in the inclusive mould of Betjeman, who held the post from 1972 to 1984. His note, too, is a wry tenderness towards all things English, and he had a similar light touch with his own technical mastery. 'Business Girls' is readily memorizable stuff that moves along swiftly and enjoyably:

> From the geyser ventilators
>   Autumn winds are blowing down
> On a thousand business women
>   Having baths in Camden Town.
>
> Waste pipes chuckle into runnels,
>   Steam's escaping here and there,
> Morning trains through Camden cutting
>   Shake the Crescent and the Square.

However, that very celerity can give an impression of skating over surfaces. Duffy is steadier and more faithful to actual lived experience. Despite the success of 'Prayer', it is the volume's penultimate piece that is *Mean Time*'s title poem. This perfectly judged set of four quatrains is in ballad metre. Between their second and fourth lines, rhyme gradually coheres: *life/love, streets/mistakes, day/say, light/nights*, pairings which under the gentle cover of form bring together all human life in a poem about the end of British Summer Time. Once again the context is unremarkable; but within it something remarkable happens, as the poem swells towards first death, and then sex:

> But we will be dead, as we know,
>   beyond all light.
> These are the shortened days
>   and the endless nights.

Mean Time was followed, in 1999, by *The World's Wife*, a collection of comic verse monologues spoken by the wives of famous characters real and imagined, from Noah to Sigmund Freud. Such use of personae entails narrative. In each of the *World's Wife* poems it is a character with a specific personal history who is speaking; a whole scenario is brought into the work. Perhaps, therefore, it was only a matter of time before 'Carol Ann Duffy' herself appeared with confessional first person on the page. *Rapture* (2005), a book of love poems, was Duffy's next volume to win a major award, and her first with a trade publisher. Until that point she had remained loyal to Anvil, the small press that discovered her: this, and the fact that she lives and works outside London, may have helped sustain her independence from any particular generation or school.

Rapture glances towards ballad in a series of love lyrics, ordered to tell the story of a recognizably writerly affair from the outset – 'We text, text, text / our significant words' ('Text') – to the end where 'love exhausts itself, longs / for the sleep of words' ('The Love Poem'). It's a sequence that belongs in the song-lyric tradition; Duffy performed from it with the musician Eliana Tomkins. And it is in this volume that we hear most clearly the influence of Duffy's early mentor and partner, Adrian Henri. He was one of the Liverpool poets, whose interest in performance forms prefigured dub and Slam and came out of the Fifties fashion for poetry and jazz – and, within poetry itself, out of the Beat movement. Yet the torch Duffy would hand on to Jackie Kay, with whom she lived and worked for many years, is much more than simply a musical tradition. It is Duffy's measured, apparently straightforward but never artless, sensibility that finds its most distinct echoes in the younger poet's work.

Jackie Kay, a charismatic Glaswegian, burst onto the British poetry scene in 1991 with *The Adoption Papers*, an autobiographical collection whose examination of cross-race adoption spills over from its title sequence to colour the whole book. Since then, she has published five further volumes, as well as four for young people. It is a rare, and brave, poet whose verse for youngsters and adults makes such common cause that it not only achieves coherence, but serves to illustrate her true strengths. However, Jackie Kay, like Grace Nichols, belongs to that small group whose children's writing, rather than gainsaying their primary poetic project, enriches it by pointing in the same direction.

This is what happens at the opening of 'My Face is a Map', from children's book *Red, Cherry Red* (2007):

> I was born with a map of Australia on my face;
> it was beautiful, my mother told me,
> there was nobody like me in the whole wide world
> who could trace the edges of down under
> on the raised and grafted song lines of her face.

The poem seems to be about facial deformity. But Kay's verse works both down and across; its smooth surface is deceptive. In fact, it is a sugar coating that helps strong medicine slip down. Some of what makes 'My Face is a Map' so immediately and characteristically Kay's is its theme. Her defining preoccupations are place; the degree to which we incarnate it, whether through ethnicity or in our behaviour and language; and the trope of redemptive recognition by a female principle: 'it was beautiful, my mother told me'. These concerns inform her work right up to the new love poems of *Darling* (2007), frequently criss-crossing and blending with each other, so it's hard to tell which predominates. In 'Stars, Sea', 'Winter Heart' and 'First Light', for example, the lover's body isn't merely located 'not so far from Cardigan Bay', 'in the room', 'In the morning', but itself becomes a place to arrive at, 'As if every lover we had ever loved / Was here, or coming in.'

At times this iteration comes within a hair's breadth of seeming self-referential; in the punningly titled *Off Colour* (1998), for example. In a distinguished parallel prose career that includes novels and short stories, Kay has also written a memoir, *Red Dust Road* (2010), which tells the story of tracing her natural father. But, as befits an adoptive daughter of peace marchers 'at George Square where the banners /

waved at each other like old friends, flapping, / where they'd met for so many marches over their years' ('George Square'), she is a writer for whom the personal is always political. The famous 'Adoption Papers' sequence, with its three narrators – birth mother, adoptive mother, daughter – is a clear homage to Sylvia Plath's poem set on a maternity ward, 'Three Women: A Poem for Three Voices'. But while Plath's is a complex, inflected exploration of individual sensibilities, Kay turns outwards to the surrounding chorus of teachers, school friends and neighbours: she is enough of her socialist parents' daughter to locate meaning in the interpersonal, social realm.

In a poem about domestic violence from *Other Lovers* (1993):

> There is something the matter with my eyes.
> They are weeping like drains and changing colour.
> *What could you have done, what could you?*
> I talk to myself in this baby-voice
> I used to use for my son, *tell Mum.*
>
> ('Condemned Property')

Kay's strong ear for speech pattern allows accent and dialect to sharpen characterization. Much of her work is written in personae, allowing her to cover material we might speculatively call literary biography – the poet's adoption, her ethnicity, sexuality and even her own parenting – in narrative rather than confessional form. In 'Maw Broon Visits a Therapist', from *Off Colour*, the brow-beaten housewife confesses, 'When it comes tae talking aboot me, / well, A' jist clam up. Canny think whit / tae say.' Enjambment gives us the back-and-for of the narrator's uncertainty: she is uncertain because she's unconfident. But this is more than clever ventriloquism: it shifts the language to record a culture and a psyche. Like many poets before her, Kay embraces the linguistic music of childhood. W.H. Auden and George Mackay Brown, A.E. Housman and Rudyard Kipling are all audible behind her 'Twelve Bar Bessie' blues in *Other Lovers* (1993): 'See that day, Lord, did you hear what happened then. / A nine o'clock shadow always chases the sun. / And in the thick heavy air came the Ku Klux Klan / To the tent where the Queen was about to sing her song.' But an old music, ballad and folksong, can be heard in the clapping/skipping sing-song which haunts *Life Mask* (2005): 'We two sleeping like spoons, / under the bowl of the moon, / gone soon, gone soon, / quine and loon.'

While the Scottish lilt to all this resembles Kay's own musically Glaswegian accent, Bradford-born Neil Rollinson's free-verse narrative has a more level-pegging inflection, significantly close to his own speech rhythms. In his *The Deregulated Muse* (1998), Sean O'Brien made a forceful case for regionalism. Poetry was, he felt then, at long last escaping its traditionally metropolitan, upper-middle-class norms. Born and bred a Hull poet, O'Brien was not overlooking those, like Hull's own Philip Larkin, who had already been living and working outside London since the war. On the contrary, he himself remains part of the tradition of Northern modernism that includes Basil Bunting, and Roy Fisher who grew up in Birmingham. He was, though, making the point that, while decision-makers from Stephen Spender to Ian Hamilton had remained largely Oxford-educated and London-based, by the Eighties centres of poetic vitality had opened up in the regions.

One cause of this shift towards a regional confidence and aesthetics must have been the emergence of the baby boomers. By then in their late twenties and thirties, they were the first generation for whom Higher Education had been a realistic aspiration, regardless of parental income. All four poets in this chapter write proudly about working-class roots. Though Jackie Kay and Paul Farley (*b.* 1965) are, strictly speaking, members of Generation X, they too form part of this historical trend. Carol Ann Duffy read Philosophy, and Jackie Kay English, at university, while both Neil Rollinson (*b.* 1960) and Paul Farley went to art college. As aspiration became what turns out to have been a temporary normality, this was also the generation for whom, in the subsequent professional world, what in John Braine's generation had been a hard-earned *Room at the Top* would require no complex process of selling-out or camouflage. The working-class kids who began to make their way through Higher Education in the Seventies brought their regional accents and dialects in from the cold. After all, dialect isn't like street style or music: the kind of social formation that doesn't really start until the early teens. Language is an almost inseparable part of the individual's development.

When it renounces received diction, poetry stops aspiring to be middle class. This can't help but shift what a poem has to say: simply, the way it faces. It's in this context that the anecdote poem offers its semantic economy; a distrust of pretension and frills. The sense is that everything involved in the telling is earned. There's no indulgence. An anecdote poem has no difficulty establishing what it's all about. It is 'about' the story that it tells. If that story turns out to be a metaphor, parable or symbol, and to offer the reader a possible second meaning, so much the better value.

The poem itself, though, may act guileless about such possibilities. In Neil Rollinson's 'Hubris' (from *Demolition*, 2007), the poet recalls his teenaged self boasting, to a girl he's 'desperate for', that he hates his father – only for Rollinson senior to appear:

> and though I'm sure
> he could never
> have heard what I said,
> I'm troubled
> by an uncharacteristic smile,
> boy-like yet full
> of worldly suffering
> as he nods his head
> at the two of us
> and wanders through.

This is the entire second half of a slim, twenty-line poem, whose brevity seems designed not to outweigh the incident it describes. And that sense of not wanting to oversell itself forms part of the tactful, tactical sensibility that constructs this piece. The poem stops when the action stops. This coda-less verse pretends not to give itself or its subject a second thought.

It's a trick, of course. Simply by never ending with a description, contextualization or metaphor, but always including action of some kind in his closing lines, Rollinson, as if whistling and looking the other way, manages to suggest, 'What, me, come the poet?' But tricks, naturally, are really techniques; and this clever way of closing without announcement is also a way of *containing* something in the poem. The comparisons or conclusions another poet might feel compelled to finish with have already been made. In other typical Rollinson endings, also from *Demolition*:

> tomorrow I'll be out of here, heading south.
> ('Away with the Mixer')

> a bullet waits in its chamber.
> ('Chaos Theory at the 4.20 Handicap Chase
> at Haydock Park')

> dream of your supper, and weep.
> ('Onions')

Even the negative is active:

> . . . It's like nothing
> was there: like nothing had happened.
> ('Demolition')

This flourish of an ending uses 'like' to mean 'but *not* this', and creates a double negative with 'nothing' – to indicate that something *has* happened. Most succinctly of all, in 'Waiting for the Man', the icon in the Japanese pedestrian light that 'glows in his bubble of red glass, / mid-stride', ends in continuing action: '/floating'.

But if Rollinson is a poet of the active case, that does not make him either unreflecting or purely narrative. 'Head-shot' is taken from a 2010 sequence, 'Talking Dead', in which the murdered remember their violent deaths. In the first stanza:

> It didn't hurt a bit, in fact
> I felt ecstatic. I could see the bullet,
> bright as a star. I could trace
> its parabola over the field,
> like fishing wire, a pencil line
> drawn on paper.

No one could claim nothing is happening in these lines. After all, someone is being shot through the head (more than happens in the whole of, say, Vikram Seth's triumphant, delightful verse novel of manners, *Golden Gate*). Yet what we immediately experience is a kind of heightened luminosity; a stilling. Indeed, the next stanza opens, 'I was, for a moment, a visionary.' Distilled and momentary, this 'anecdote' is clearly not trivial. But it is *short*. In anecdote poems, the *thing that happens* is working as a metaphor, or a symbol, in the way that a *thing* usually does. The action has become the object of description, and that object functions in the poem in just the same way as a landscape, weather or roses in a window that looks out on snow. Paradoxically, the grammar of metaphor turns sentence grammar inside out, as these verb objects *act upon* the poem's subject/topic.

Rollinson's scenes of violent death act upon his human Subject, and also upon his topic. This is something richer and more indirect, as is so often the case with metaphor, than simple mortality, or the need to celebrate life in the face of death. In another poem from 'Talking Dead', 'At first I thought it was pain / but it was just / the beginning of bliss' ('In Bed'). The sense of the link between pain and pleasure is repeated by the speaker of 'The Good Old Days':

> The first few minutes were awesome.
> I didn't know I could scream like that,

but nothing lasts forever,
soon the adrenaline kicks in and you're high

as a kite . . .

On the one hand that 'awesome' is laconic, demotic; on the other, it
denotes *awe* at the way pain and pleasure are proximate, especially in
extremis. If this sounds a little pious, more suited to a tea towel than
to workaday literary endeavour, the lapse isn't Rollinson's. He is perfectly
aware of piety's true history and character: 'In the dark ages they took
their time. / They knew about pain / and butchered you slowly, whistling / as they went. It was God's work.' He doesn't prettify indignity:
'I went down like a sack of spuds, / sat on my arse in the shit.' There's
no quietism in the view of 'The Wall' against which his narrator is to
be shot:

There was a scent of marjoram.
The sea was blue, and a single ferry
sailed out of the harbour.

The stillness this passage evokes is a piece of purely literary integration.
Strong, contradictory emotions and wilfully differentiated elements –
peaceful summertime and murder, Roman history and the ecosystem
of the sea-bed – are brought together by voice: that nebulous element
composed partly of characterization and partly of diction.

The narrative presence in these poems is a slant kind of poetic persona,
not characterized but full of characteristics. Something akin to a sleep-
walker, it concentrates on the moment itself, as if neither past nor
future exist. This is not to say that Rollinson's narrator claims to be in
and of that moment. Rather the opposite: a key Rollinson trope is the
differentiating 'when'. Not all his poems start with the actual word,
but it is – whether stated or not – the transitional mechanism by which
we enter nearly every one. We step into the time machine, and 'when'
transports us through either time or place to where a particular thing

can happen; like a 'Once upon a time'. This sidesteps the reflexive stutter, those *perhaps*/*it seems*/*I remember*/*I imagine* devices, with which poems often try to keep their verse-worlds real. Decluttering the diction, it also releases the poem from any responsibility to be dramatic. Although Rollinson frequently adopts the first person, the poem doesn't have to stage the narrator's *having* the experience right now. Unlike confessional poetry, whose heightened images indicate not so much what's happening but how strongly the narrator *feels* about it – and despite this poet's own reputation for fine poems about food and sex – his first person has room to distance himself: becoming almost, though not quite, omniscient. 'The Wall' starts with a *when*, 'It was a day like any other', which seems omniscient, but is swiftly modified by 'us', 'when they came for us'; the poem oscillates between engagement and estrangement.

Rollinson trained as a print-maker, and his poetry has a kind of line-led naturalness – an unforced quality. Ex-painter Paul Farley produces immaculate, no-nonsense verse. Farley was thirty-three at the time of his 1998 debut, *The Boy from the Chemist is Here to See You*, which perhaps accounts for the astonishing maturity of its polish:

> The moon we know from dreams or celluloid
> is high tonight. A dried-up fountain bed
> gawps back, a baroque radio telescope
> the race has left behind, always on the up,
> defying gravity.
>
> ('Eaux D'Artifice')

This careful poet has published just three collections in fourteen years: *The Atlantic Tunnel*, his 2010 Selected poems, includes only seven new poems – and a couple of pieces from his collected radio work, *Field Recordings* (2009) – written since 2006's *Tramp in Flames*. Those that make it through what must presumably be a strenuous editorial process read with the ease that fully accomplished writing guarantees. One of the pleasures of such prosody is that the resulting on-the-nail clarity reads as certainty, which in turn sounds like authority. In 'The Sea in the Seventeenth Century':

> God's foot upon the treadle of the loom,
> the sea goes about its business.
> The photogenic reefs of the Pacific
> can build for an eternity before
> the cameras come . . .

This is deft, learned and straight in to its material. There's no throat-clearing. And yet Farley is a curiously evasive poet; his refusal to make bald points so constant that it becomes the motor of his work.

'Civic', from *Tramp in Flames*, is a long, numerically organized poem (in twenty-one seven-line stanzas): its rough schema of syllabics just close – and loose – enough to provoke the reader into counting and re-counting as she goes. Most of these stanzas' opening lines are thirteen syllables long; but not all. Most, but not all, have seven feet; and the feet are a tutti-frutti of metres – as most language is. This irregularity makes the poem's 'speaking voice' seem curiously sincere. Here, the narrator invites us to drink fresh water:

> and taste the great nothing that comes before pipes
> pass on their trace of lead, before fonts
> leech their peck of limestone,
> before public baths
> annihilate with chlorine.

The repeated *before* is a rhythmic pivot that reveals Farley's metrical variations at work: each time it appears, the rhythmic context differs. First, it makes the following 'pipes' unstressed; next, it turns 'font' into a feminine ending, though a first glance would have guessed a stressed syllable; its third appearance seems to want us to alter the stress pattern in the word itself, or else to use nip-and-tuck anapests to frame it. Gradually denatured, this 'before' makes a rhythmic pleat in the poem and by degrees becomes conspicuous. Though lightly disguised as purely formal, such repetition has an odour of polemic, even of politicking, to it: after all, 'Civic' is a title that suggests social and political responsibilities.

But what, actually, is this poem about? The opening seems a straight-forward anecdote about 'making my way down to the shore / of the reservoir in the dark'. But unseen, or low-lying, urban water is one of Farley's repeated themes: this collection also includes 'The Westbourne at Sloane Square', about one of London's buried rivers. Its author is a Liverpudlian and it's perhaps no surprise that the sea, and even fish, feature in many of his poems. In his previous collection, *The Ice Age* (2002), the setting and image for a close family member's dementia is a 'Landing Stage'; a tenderly evoked 'floating world' of sensuous memory. Farley deploys several other recurring tropes – one is the moon, another destruction by fire. So his readers understand that 'Civic's nocturnal reservoir is not incidental, but deep in Farley terri-tory. It forms the backdrop to the poem; it may not be what this particular poem is *about*. Still, 'I've read the reports / of the city engi-neers, done my homework' and 'all at once . . . I've found Manchester / at source'. And yet . . . *This isn't a study of cities but of water*, we think as we follow Farley through 'mysteries of pipe-work', 'Two miles per hour; a hundred miles' and back, to reflect on 'how water too / needs to introspect'. As this poem itself appears to do, until a blackbird's alarm call, dawn, and a 'Water Board van' on the opposite shore bring the narrator back to his 'civic duty', which is 'peeing quietly into the supply'. Or is it? The act will have no consequences, and so 'it will only really occur in the mind's eye'; which means that existentially, like Schrödinger's Cat, 'I wasn't here'.

This conclusion unspools the whole poem, which is no longer about being in that particular spot, nor about water; though it might after all be about the cities that Farley, or his narrator, needs as witnesses to his existence. This story is a thought-sequence, not a trip to the reservoir. But Farley belongs among the anecdotalists in part because there's a kind of affectlessness to his work, for all its beauty and use of recurring symbol, that's clearly related to Rollinson's, Kay's and Duffy's. It's not register, but what gets told, that distills feeling into these poems, each of which sustains an unbroken skim of tone.

Though Paul Farley's speaking-pace lines are often loosely five-stressed cousins of blank verse, they don't have the more insistent echo of authority that characterizes the iambic legislators. He does, though, make a bridge between the heirs of the free-verse revolution and poets who are reviving strict form. Perhaps this is because his early mentor, and editor at Picador, is the leading formalist Don Paterson. Paterson himself has been working this gap as editor, with a sequence of 'hits' – from elegant poets like John Stammers, Jacob Polley and Frances Leviston – engineered to strike this note of disciplined clarity. But Paul Farley's is the real, organic thing, because an economy so fast-moving that it is transformational – one thing shape-shifts into the next – is intrinsic to his verse.

In 'A Minute's Silence', from his first collection:

> Sooner or later silence reaches the coast
> and stops just short of getting its feet wet.

The steely, tensile strength of this mid-poem couplet comes from its matched vowel and consonantal sounds: *er/er/re/ge/we, Sooner/or/coast/ stops/short, oast/ort/eet/et*. The transformation of an aural event (the silence) into a visible, tactile one (a tide) provides a bracing set of cross-supports. More strength is supplied by the way a description has been transmuted into something happening; 'reaching the coast', the adjectival clause a weaker poet might be tempted by, is turned into active verbs. A similar technique appears in 'The Heron' (from *Tramp in Flames*), really pure description of how the bird takes off, which is transformed into a series of events. When the active case needs strengthening, Farley brings in the narrator's own acts of observation: 'I watched . . .'.

Paul Farley is associated with contemporary, urban life through his freight of quotidian reference, from school dinner ladies to 'supermarket shiraz'. But his poems (and prose) admit he's also a birder, and some of his symbols – moon, water, fire – are archetypal. Directed to city or country, the conscious or the unconscious, his vivid focus is on making sense in and of a world which is recognizably daily: 'Some similes act like heat shields for re-entry / to reality.' ('Tramp in Flames'). This lapidary slipperiness shows us how what seems fixed – the bare bones of a narrative – can slide sideways entire. The anecdote poem doesn't evoke the transitoriness of meaning, as poets like John Burnside do; it simply transfers meaning from person to community, from necessity to insight, and from writer to reader. And it does all this without the apparatus of drama, or prose fiction's capacious scale.

It looks easy – but it is not. The anecdotalists remind me of nothing so much as secret agents in a black-and-white movie. Hanging about in cafés or on street corners, lighting up cigarettes and acting the casual bystander, they're secretly engaged in missions of pitch and moment. Their register may be the opposite of the one adopted by the poets in the next chapter. But their strategies with narrative metaphors are markedly similar.

7

MYTHOPOESIS

Some ways of writing aren't team projects, but emerge on what seems to be a idiosyncratic private trajectory from within a poet's development; prompted by an individual imagination, character, reading and sense of what poetry is for. The dandy instinct for the baroque appears independently of its immediate context, and so does mythopoesis. Today, five highly individual British poets have developed a particular correspondence between poetry and myth. Neither Robin Robertson nor Pauline Stainer, perhaps the two most temperamentally-differentiated of these, rushed into print. Robertson was already a distinguished literary editor, responsible for such stars of the Scottish Renaissance as Irvine Welsh and A.L. Kennedy, before he published his first collection at the age of forty-one. Pauline Stainer followed a conventional gendered path, becoming a GP's wife and a mother after Oxford. *The Honeycomb*, her first full collection, appeared in 1989, when she was nearly fifty. By contrast David Harsent and Alice Oswald, the first and the latest of these poets to emerge, were first published in their twenties. Both appeared from Oxford University Press, that maverick list which, by the time it closed in 1999, embraced not only Penny Shuttle's sophisticated naivety and Jamie McKendrick's and Stephen Romer's donnish dreaminess, but the mandarin Peter Porter, and Elaine Feinstein's thoughtful realism. The quintet of mythopoets is completed by Michael Symmons Roberts, formerly the BBC's Head of Development for Religion and Ethics, published since he was thirty by Robin Robertson at Cape.

Uniting all five is an almost three-dimensional sense of the resources of verse. In their hands, the poem isn't only concerned with a particular diction or mood, but opens up an entire conceptual and tonal world of its own. True, each uses a language that operates like a cleaned lens, avoiding technical clutter. But however linear or fluently musical it may be, we don't engage with this verse *primarily* by following the phrasal line. Its resources work in predominantly vertical, rather than horizontal, ways; through symbol, fable and image, rather than the 'and then . . . and then' of anecdote, or even distinctive formal rhythm. Music remains, however. Pauline Stainer writes with pitch and poise. Robin Robertson offers the chime of disciplined sounds. And, while Alice Oswald's verse feels propelled by a dramatic speaking voice, both David Harsent, with ten collections the most widely published member of this group, and Michael Symmons Roberts, are also librettists.

David Harsent's professional musicianship can be heard in the way rhyme assumes a role as the secret instigator of form and through that movement, especially in his later verse. It remains latent in his 1969 debut, *A Violent Country*: an astonishing book for a twenty-six year-old, not least because it marks out the territory that Harsent continues to explore. The title says it all. Frequently, in Harsent country, violence – in particular, symbolic violence perpetrated upon a female principle – is combined with a gritty portrait of the kind of rural existence last widely seen in Britain in the Seventies, before Margaret Thatcher's first wave of second-home owners. At the time of *A Violent Country* it was still possible to live cheaply in the English provinces. Those rural traditions that remained were tougher, more ethnographic affairs than their contemporary prettification as tourist kitsch suggests: closer, in fact, to the settings and figures of Harsent's 1984 collection *Mr Punch*. In this anti-pastoral spirit his female principle – the poet's anima – often becomes a countrywoman or a hare, and his 'violent country' remains profoundly, and traditionally, English (though it can stretch to encompass urban dreamscapes and actual war zones).

A Violent Country, After Dark, Dreams of the Dead, Mr Punch, News from the Front, *A Bird's Idea of Flight*, *Legion*, *Night*: Harsent's collection titles braid these recurring themes. The eponymous 'front' from which 1993's *News* comes is at least partly emotional and romantic; themes the poet returns to in *Marriage* (2002), a series of meditations on 'the mysteries of domesticity'. If the title of 2011's *Night* echoes 1973's *After Dark*, however, this indicates no poetic or tonal reprise. *After Dark* clearly bears the marks of Ian Hamilton's influence. That vulnerable stage in a poet's development, the second collection, its glimpses of a perhaps-fictive emotional life borrow the older poet's affectless tone.

Charismatic and influential, Hamilton had discovered Harsent in the slush pile at either the *Review* or the *TLS*, on both of which he was then working as an editor; he not only published Harsent but was part of the panel that awarded him the 1968 Cheltenham Festival Prize – with the result that *A Violent Country* was optioned by Jon Stallworthy at OUP. Much more the poet's own, this debut displays a clenched economy that owes something to early Hughes and something to the Eugène Guillevic of *Carnac*. Yet the sounds are unique:

> There is nothing here
> for the birds
> clattering in the hedgerow.
>
> Their bald eyes swivelling,
> they riffle their feathers
> in the sallow light.

('Dawn Walk')

The imagery recalls Graham Sutherland's bird-grotesques, or Picasso sketches: this is what happens when modernism encounters the British countryside. An equivalent sensibility informs Harsent's cult classic *Mr Punch* (1984). Appearing when Harrison Birtwistle's opera *Punch and Judy* had just been premiered, the collection introduced these long-time collaborators to one another. Their work since includes the operas *Gawain* (1991) and *The Minotaur* (2008).

For both artists, Punch is a Grand Guignol who personifies all that is horrifying and horrified in heterosexual masculinity. A rapist, at least in his nightmares:

> . . . He showed

> one boy his girlfriend, spread
> in a vineyard, slammed across
> a rock, her back

> broken by rabid passion;
>> ('Punch in the Ancient World: Patmos')

he is also abjected by his own desire:

> She enjoyed and enjoyed and enjoyed. Punch gibbered;
> he stood alongside and howled
>> ('Punch's Nightmares 6')

This is thematically powerful stuff. But do themes truly belong on the map of poetic strategies? They can be an alibi that weaker writing resorts to: as the late Peter Porter pointed out, death is always a trump card in poetry's reception. (Recently, two consecutive 'cancer collections', Christopher Reid's *A Scattering* and Jo Shapcott's *Of Mutability*, have been Costa Book of the Year.) The answer is that Harsent's theme is not the painted puppet himself. It is not even the dark narrative content of each nightmare scenario. Instead, his stories and their characters are themselves symbols. These are *narrative metaphors* and, just like Imagism with its objects or modernism with allusion, mythopoesis uses them as the tropes *through which* its true themes are explored.

Mr Punch employs a compacted but not accelerated diction. In other words, the poems don't break the storytelling contract. It's easy to follow what's going on. Though Harsent doesn't use a great deal of rhyme in this book, he exploits conventional stanza forms. 'Bonnard: Breakfast', from a rogues' 'Punch's Gallery' of ekphrastic poems, all of them revisiting artists' representations of sexualized violence, is a set of eight paired couplets whose second lines slant-rhyme:

> He has posed her there, but can't make her descend,
> or smile, or speak. He wonders, was it rash
>
> to have picked that dress, to have left her feet unshod?
> The welt on her cheek comes and goes like a blush.

Pierre Bonnard's repeated studies of his wife Marthe – those domestic interiors in which she is nearly always washing or bathing naked – would become the starting point for 2002's *Marriage*. This collection's title-sequence adopts a narrative that faces in the opposite direction from *Punch*, towards domestic harmony and intimacy. Yet it explores the same territory of risk, trust and, ultimately, the existential boundaries which both protect and isolate the individual. Among the poet's most full-voiced writing to date, these pieces glow with colour that is both described, and located within the language itself. Gleaming, rationed vowel sounds characterize and unify phrase and stanza, as in the rapt *a-i-a-o* of this passage of aural as well as visual reflections:

> The lamplight falls bang in the middle
> of the almost-oval mirror on your grandmama's armoire

Legion (2005), possibly the poet's best-known book to date, does something similar with war, taking it not as a theme but as equipment with which to explore Harsent's underlying, universal existential territory. This collection represented a new high-spot in a process of clarification, a movement into rhythmic certainty, worked out through *News from the Front* (1993) and *A Bird's Idea of Flight* (1998) into *Marriage*. It is as if some deferential turning-down of the sheer shine of his talent had until then muted his diction, the clarity of his gaze and his own sense of what he could do. Truly significant poets write like no one else, and this can be both a boon and a burden.

Night takes over where *Legion* left off. For the reader accustomed to the English lyric convention that moves from the close-at-hand to whatever can be wrung from it, fabular technique remains surprising, even shocking; and it is particularly marked in these fables, set more clearly than ever before in an archetypal, hyper-real landscape. Harsent has been called our most European poet; but these dream-scapes are profoundly British, from 'The Hut in Question', which finds Edward Thomas's writing hut full of telling local detail – 'Weather-worn, half-hidden by gorse / in full fire, it being that time of year; the window / thick with cobwebs, clarty candyfloss' – to the '*terra incognita*' of suburban gardens whose extra-mural life is presided over by 'The Garden Goddess'. An in-every-sense filthy presence who belongs with the archetypal British tricksters Sheelagh-na-Gig and Jack in the Green, she speaks to our disgusted fascination with what might lie beyond cosy belonging: 'how the dark of her eye / can bring you on, or the wet of her lip, how the dab of cuckoo-spit / that fell to her thigh from some dead-head or seed-pod / has left a trickle of glisten'.

A septet of 'Garden' poems, like the 'Blood' lyrics that are spaced through the first half of this collection of nearly a hundred pages, revisit and integrate the rural badlands with urban anomie, that City of Dreadful Night where *Night*'s title poem is set: 'A quarter-moon, livid like a burn-scar. An airbus drops / into the Heathrow corridor. A vixen yips with pleasure-pain.' Exceptionally a writer for whom both city and country are sensuous and immediate realities, Harsent reduces neither to the image through a view-finder. Instead, the poems turn outdoors, as if this radically anti-confessional poet intends to resist any private meaning or experience, and instead return us to communal territory. That's also the territory of the vernacular, and Harsent has acknowledged his poetic roots in ballad – *Night* includes one – and the

Baptist hymnal, which surely informs a version of 'The Death of Cain'.

Rather than merely cite these traditions, the collection seems to pass through them to their origins in psycho-drama and rite, not least in the sixty-three extraordinarily sustained septets of 'Elsewhere', a poem of escape that whips from scene to scene, its momentum supplied by characteristic half-line phrases:

> . . . and a poke of silver coin

> to buy their way out of hell, most with an eye on each other,
> but one with an eye on me, or so it seems . . .

These half-line units switch shifts and open action out of action. But the verse is at work on every level at once, unified by rhyme, and such variants as alliterative chime, which in 'Abstracts: Red' fill the mouth and beg to be read aloud: 'The skim on the surface of your soup, or the cut on your plate / in the Café des Anges.'

Pauline Stainer (*b.* 1941) is an altogether quieter talent. Her brilliantly clear, distilled verse, published in nine collections to date, most resembles cloisonné or the painted miniatures of Indian traditions. Rather than foreshortening perspective or reducing colour, this scale acts as a formal intensifier. Here is the whole of 'Keats on Iona', from her sixth collection *The Wound-dresser's Dream* (1996):

> Did he hear
> the four beasts
> saying *Amen*
> in the tall rain

> did he see
> Ezekiel
> white-blind a moment
> in the magnesium flare

did he taste the salt
on Salomé's neck,
a bubble of blood
rising in his throat

as the pearls
expire on her flesh?

The poem uses few words and takes the understated form of a question, but it is neither yielding nor fragile. Like much of Stainer's work, it uses myth – here Christian – as a kind of resonating chamber. It borrows religious iconography; but as it's not written from within that iconography, it doesn't suffer from the inertia that could accompany a closed or given symbolic system. As this use of the interrogative mode makes clear, Stainer's turn to Biblical repertory – the beasts of the Evangelists, the prophet Ezekiel and Salomé's responsibility for the death of John the Baptist – is absolutely no act of faith.

But it is *knowing*. The figures she squeezes together are taken from each of the three 'stages' of the Christian Bible: the Old Testament prophets, Christ's lifetime and the evangelizing that followed his death. This 'folding over onto' is a characteristic Stainer transformation. If the poet-physician in 'Keats on Iona' were to 'taste the salt / on Salomé's neck', that would surely be a sexual gesture. Sweat and blood both taste salty; the the poet's own consumptive blood must taste as salty as Salomé's neck, where the blood ringing the neck of her victim, John the Baptist, is folded onto her own sweat. The temptress has been performing the Dance of the Seven Veils, after all, and those beads of sweat are something she wears, perhaps like a trophy or perhaps in the absence of much else, like 'pearls' which '*expire on her flesh*'. (Perhaps this is even an echo of Carol Ann Duffy's much-anthologized 'Warming the Pearls', in which the necklace is a principle of life, love and loss.) As blood and sweat evaporate, so John – John the Baptist or John Keats – dies. To expire is also more specifically to breathe out; to be out of breath, as was the consumptive Keats. 'Dying' is the old word for a

sexual climax: now these salty beads become an ejaculate. And if a
man dies in her arms in either sense, the proxy murderess and sexy
stripper Salomé becomes the Pietà.

Such 'pleating' of senses together works through exactitude. This
sequence of semantic equivalences is not lazy conflation, in which
roughly similar things suggest each other, but a concertina of deep
correspondences. Juxtaposed, Stainer's symbols construct hinterlands
for each other. They aren't chains of metaphor, one leading to the
next as they do for a poet like Ruth Padel or Pascale Petit. Instead
they work in both directions and all at once. John Keats, the real
historical human being – no symbol – here deepens our understanding
that the human Baptist, too, must have been terrified and suffered,
however strong his faith. Because this symbolic grammar is exact,
Stainer's alignments sharpen her message. Unlike other poets who use
a large number of cultural referents in their writing – from Peter Porter
to Ian Duhig – she is not simply speaking from a well-stocked mind,
leaving it up to us whether we explore a poem by looking up its allusions. But neither is she doing the opposite, and allowing a vague,
remembered resonance do all the work of the poem.

By 2008's *Crossing the Snowline*, the iconography has largely shifted
from religious symbols to artistic *representations of* those symbols. St
Francis's stigmata and the Pietà have been replaced by the work of
painters ('After Vermeer', 'After Cimabue', 'Mantegna's Hares'), poets
('John Donne in the Azores', 'Dante at the Three Gorges') and musicians ('Mozart at the Falconry Lodge, 1763'). These allow Stainer to
trace the *action* of symbol at the same time as she exhibits it. 'Dowland
at Elsinore', for example, uses synaethesia to evoke what the composer's
music does: 'his passionate pavanes / absorbing all light / except blue'.
Blue isn't the only colour to feature in her symbolic registry, but it is
arguably the most important. Acknowledging it as the Marian colour
– Stainer titled her Selected Poems *The Lady and the Hare* (2003) – she
also separates it from this context, using it as a touchstone. Studies of
the colour also enrich her Orkney collection *Parable Island* (1999). She
notices blue – in 'The Borrowdyke', fen water is 'blocks of raw glass /

running bright-blue' – and *adopts* its evocative powers. In 'Voltage' blue is both literally and metaphorically 'electric': 'Wet streets, / shining slates, / indigo on a tremble / . . . // as when Mary / in electric blue / before the angel . . .' Elsewhere, she simply *reflects* upon the colour: 'They say that blue / slows the passage of time' ('Herman Melville jumps ship'). This revisiting imparts a textural cross-hatching to her writing.

It's a way of working that seems linked to 'Christ the colourist' ('Song without voices'); although Stainer does not *explain* herself. She's no essayist, either in or outside her verse. The nearest she comes to exposition of any kind is probably her pamphlet sequence *Little Egypt* (1987), a series of stories about Sutton Hoo later which was illustrated by the Brotherhood of Ruralists. The glancing blow of a one-line *ars poetica* in 'Sourin' (from *Parable Island*) sums up this way of working: 'The poetry is not firstly in the words.' And it is true that her verse is not much shaped by the satisfactions of sound. 'Keats on Iona', for example, thickens up just before the mid-point, after 'Ezekiel', suggesting neither beat nor syllable-count can be allowed to control a poem which seems shaped by its own necessity – as if that were prior to language. Formal poems like 'Dancing the Mysteries', an elegy sequence for Father Peter Elers of Thaxted which draws on the 'Dancing Day' carol, with its circling repetition of a round-dance, are exceptional.

As everything about this strategy demonstrates, it would be ludicrous to accuse Pauline Stainer of inauthenticity because she was not herself a witness at the Crucifixion or a Quattrocento painter. Yet this kind of accusation is levelled at both David Harsent and Robin Robertson, who was the next of these fabular poets to emerge, with *A Painted Field* (1997). Like Harsent, Robertson is unabashed by the savagery of the natural world and what that implies for a speaker who, as a living being, is essentially a part of it. Also like Harsent, he explores the resources of this intimate interrelatedness between world and individual as a way of explaining or symbolizing the psyche. While Harsent diversifies into domestic interiors and the urban, however, Robertson's world has grown increasingly distinct. It is primarily rural and has become a landscape

of the far north and of 'Sea-Fret', 'Where broken and eroded stones
/ still reef the headland's brow'.

'Sea-Fret' appears in 2006's *Swithering*, published in the same year
as *The Deleted World*, Robertson's versions of fifteen poems by Tomas
Tranströmer. His Tranströmer is not the more familiar, emotionally
intelligent Laureate of interiors, the psychologist who meditates on the
human heart while playing Haydn to relax after a day at the clinic. In
Robertson's volume he is primarily a conjuror of rocky, often snow-
bound, landscapes not dissimilar to Robertson's native north-east
Scotland:

> A hidden tuning-fork
> in the great cold
> throws out its shivering tone.
>
> I stand under the starry sky
> and feel the world thrill
> through me, like the pulse
> of ants in an anthill.
>
> ('Winter's Code' III)

This isn't descriptive postcard verse; nor the kind of writing about
place and community, like Elizabeth Bishop's, that transcribes long
understanding. Instead, it is poetry which changes affect around: is
Tranströmer's vibrating tuning fork a metaphorical description of a
winter's night, or is the night scene a metaphor for a certain way of
feeling?

Robertson's own verse shifts affect in similar ways. In 'Kalighat',
from *The Wrecking Light* (2010), the poet watches a goat being sacrificed:

> The last thing I notice is a red petal
> still in his mouth, and another,
> six inches away, in his throat.

This 'small black goat' has been conducting a sacrifice of its own, 'nosing a red hibiscus flower onto its back / and nibbling the petals'. 'The last thing I notice' offers us a pathetic last glimpse of this vegetarian option: until that final 'throat' turns the image back to a 'red petal' of blood – or else doesn't, since what the goat last ate is also visible in the throat's severed stump. Flower or blood, this spot of red conducts powerfully in both directions.

John Ruskin disparaged the idea of a mutual emotional field between subject and object as the 'pathetic fallacy'; but it is no fallacy that we have moments in which we connect our feelings and our surroundings as one single experience. Entering a 'scary' dark cave, or watching a 'beautiful' sunset, we convert our own reactions into qualities of the world we encounter. The consistent image register which results from such an affective double-bind is in fact more scrutable than scatter-gun imagery, and Robertson's preference for symbolic consistency is also apparent in the poets he edits. From John Burnside's haunted disappearing act, Paul Farley's fire and water and Neil Rollinson's world of bodily appetites to Vicki Feaver's gendered, bleeding body or Michael Symmons Roberts's Christian sensibility, image-worlds generate the tone, register and colour of their work.

Pre-eminent in Robertson's own writing is the horizontal charge between a tough, even brutal, natural landscape and the forces that mark a psyche. In *A Painted Field*, a first collection unusual for its beauty and sense of range, the north has not yet been identified as the dominant tone-world. Birds, trees, Irish landscape and history fill the poems: a more furnished horizon than that of *Swithering* or *The Wrecking Light*. First books are often busier with experiment and display than later books; a trademark stillness already distinguishes this collection. In 'At Dusk':

> Walking through the woods
> I saw these things:
> a cat, lying, looking at me;

> a red hut I could not enter;
> the white grin of the snared fox

The list structure and the way the lineation preserves the individuation of every item allow each of 'these things' to hang in the air; and this placing and pacing of 'things' as if they are conceptually side by side is highly disciplined, yet manages to suggest artlessness. Each detail might have a story behind it; or it might not. But then the poem coheres into a still-fragmentary narrative:

> a fire, still warm, and a bone
> the length of my arm, my name
> carved on it, mis-spelt.

This mysterious image invokes sympathetic magic; while the 'spell' creeping inside 'mis-spelt' suggests the kind of list the whole poem might be. Despite the accumulating rhyme *warm/arm/name*, its sound is primarily built by rhythm. Though the verse accelerates at this point, commas and lineation continue to separate the 'things' the narrator perceives; mimicking the way they're observed one after another. This throws us into complicity. We 'see' with the poem's speaker, and the effect, like the camera's slow reveal of a scene in a horror movie, is to produce a dawning chill of recognition. What this poem might *mean* is both literal and metaphorical; these elements are united, not alternative, as they are in, for example, Stainer's work. No punning vocabulary or cultural references add flourishes of information or resonance. In a blockish, almost monumental way, the poem means simply and entirely itself. For Robertson, a 'Pibroch' is a pibroch is a pibroch.

Block-like: but subtle. The refinement is all in the specificity and selection. Stripped back, elemental symbol suits the landscape these poems increasingly explore, and provides apt colouration for the increasingly hard-bitten scenes from mid-life which characterize both *Swithering* ('Wormwood', 'Strindberg in Paris') and *The Wrecking Light* ('Tulips' and 'My Girls', a poem of rare multiplicity about betraying both daughters and lovers). Robertson's later work does occasionally pun, but these puns, as clear-struck as every other note, are too loud for pleasure. Maintaining register, they trip over from happy giggle to furious shout. In a poem of ageing, 'About Time', the narrator finds 'this heart going / like there's no tomorrow', while in 'Wonderland' the geisha-trained 'Alice' will 'drink me / under the table'.

If high-decibel writing and austere northern landscapes create a furious containment, Robertson's use of myth is darkly resonant. All of his collections include vivid versions and retellings of Ovid, and of stories from folk traditions and superstition. This use of traditional material underlines the link his diction makes with the mid-twentieth-century Scottish tradition: in particular, with work by George Mackay Brown and, to some extent, Norman MacCaig. Though the rage in Robertson's poems might at first glance suggest he is the heir of the stormy modernist didact Hugh MacDiarmid, they stand at some distance from MacDiarmid's argumentation. A radical progressive, whose nationalism came from a desire for Scotland to stop itself being exploited, MacDiarmid's is the talky, vigorous verse of a political utopian: at the least, a communitarian idealist. In their desire to distil what they saw as still existing in highland and island life, Mackay Brown and the pacifist MacCaig were engaged in an altogether more lyric, and also *culturally* conservative, project. Their Scottish Pastoral turns for identity, aesthetic order and even purpose to traditional forms and ways of life.

Robertson is marked by no such nostalgia. Like Harsent he is borrowing a diction to explore existential topics. Folk traditional forms, such as sea shanties and ballads, compress danger and complexity into a willed simplicity. This simplicity replaces the resolution that fear and grief long for, but which is inherently impossible (revenge, the resurrection of a lost love, virginity regained) with one that is purely aesthetic. Consolation is to be provided by pattern. But the darkness remains. Robertson's chilling 'At Roane Head' is the story of a triangle gone wrong. A woman has four sons by her selkie lover:

> and each one wrong. All born blind, they say,
> slack-jawed and simple, web-footed,
> rickety as sticks. Beautiful faces, I'm told,
> though blank as air.
>   . . .
>
>
> Her husband left her: said
> they couldn't be his, they were more
> fish than human,
> said they were beglamoured

One drunken night the husband returns and goes 'along the line /
relaxing them / one after another / with a small knife'. And still the
shocks aren't over. In the final reveal, the selkie turns out to have been
closer than we thought all along, and unmasks himself as the poem's
narrator.

The classical strand in Robertson's work is still more visceral: literally so when Ovid makes his first appearance, in *A Painted Field*'s 'The
Flaying of Marsyas'. In this version 'two apprentices, one butcher'
provide a commentary. 'Tickle does it? Fucking bastard, / coming
down here with your dirty ways . . . / Jesus. You fucking stink, you
do./ . . . / That's your inside leg done: / no more rutting for you,
cunt.' This ear-led accuracy sets one foot firmly in the contemporary
world. The poem's third section is an extended set of ways of looking
at the flayed human body: 'unsheathed', a 'map' or a 'shambles'; and
the piece is balanced in the immediate present, somewhere between
bodily dread and pride, as much as it is a historical story from
Metamorphoses. As he will repeatedly, here Robertson uses Ovid to create
a tripod structure, a new synthesis with one foot in contemporary
experience, one in the original myth and one in the dramatic territory
of the psyche.

In *Swithering*, Robertson revisits another violent scene from the
Metamorphoses. Though one sequence, 'The Death of Actaeon', is relatively faithful to Ovid, it is matched in the collection's second half by

'Actaeon: The Early Years', in which the themes of the original recur repeatedly: female power cruelly misused; the costs of inadvertently witnessing a woman's body. The poem is a sequence of sixteen unrhymed sestets, each one a scene of violence suffered in childhood. In one the boy-narrator, climbing a monkey puzzle tree, finds himself overlooking the family bathroom and his mother in it, in a scene which mirrors the moment when Actaeon the hunter stumbles upon the goddess Diana bathing naked. Earlier:

> . . . – a four-year-old
> admiring her growing bulge. 'Look, Mummy,'
> he said, 'now you have two bumps,'
> meaning her breasts and her pregnancy.
> She turned and knocked him to the floor.

Robertson doesn't rely on traditional verse form, yet here as elsewhere his poetry is shaped by deep form; the 'good bones' of a poetics that moves outwards from a deeply integrated symbolic and grammatical logic rather than polishing a surface which searches downwards for resonance.

Michael Symmons Roberts is by his own account a Catholic poet and, though his verse doesn't generally rely on specifically Christian iconography, he frequently addresses the themes with which that faith engages. This is clearly no kind of artistic limitation – most great Western art was for centuries produced from within Christian tradition – and Roberts isn't concerned with either testing or prescribing limits. His work is characterized by gestures towards possible forms of thought, rather than thumping statement, as if echoing the ways in which faith is more often a series of states of hopefulness than an absolute experience. Roberts's writing becomes most brightly coloured and has most in common with the other poetry this chapter examines when he surrenders to dream logic in the stunning short poem sets 'Carnivorous' and 'Food for Risen Bodies', which have been sliced through *Corpus* (2004). Christ is a 'cook' in the first of these sequences, where stacked creatures (a

lamb inside a sow, the 'shell-less snail, fattened on milk' 'stuck' in a
salmon's throat) follow the logic of the food chain rather than any
traditional iconography. This strategy deals with an absolute – the Christ
– by the sequence's sideways logic.

In 'Ascension Day', at the '*Blue Lobster Café* backyard' ideas are nicely
located in things:

> Sex and death are in the air
> this May morning: pollen and spent
> blossom on an aimless breeze;

along with the smells of fish detritus in 'sun-baked bin-sacks'. But the
poet's relationship with symbols, whether of life or death, works differently from other mythopoetics because it is non-transformative. Roberts
isn't taking religious symbolism apart or turning it to his own ends.
For the poet-believer the Ascension, for example, is part of the real,
the given world within which his poems move. His own images are
simply similes or metaphors for the great Christian tropes. This given
world is already idea- and resonance-laden; already a great collective
psychodrama. There is no need for additional meanings. Rather the
opposite: lyric understatement, recognizably cousin to that deployed
by his close contemporaries Paul Farley and Don Paterson, allows him
to move *within* this complex territory, as it were without touching its
edges. The symbols of faith remain a distant thunder: they are held
back, just on the edge of focus, where a slight fuzziness makes them
the more resonant. Jacob, wrestling his angel through 'Choreography'
in the prize-winning *Corpus*, is never named. The twenty-three sections
of 'Anatomy of a Perfect Dive' both are and are not the stations of a
death and resurrection, or the leap of faith.

By contrast, radical rearrangement is Alice Oswald's secret art. At
first glance her poetry seems to be faithful to, rather than to disturb,
the natural world. But it is impossible to avoid the feeling that this
world matters to her so much, is so freighted with significance, that it
offers her the same kind of primary symbolic currency it does Roberts.

In *A Sleepwalk on the Severn* (2009) the narrator is surrounded by the nightlife of an estuary. The creatures around her seem more like totems than living specimens:

> there goes that dunlin up to her chin in
> the simmering dish of mush and
> all night that seeping feeding sound
> of moistness digesting smallness

This same sense of forces and presences that are much more serious than mere whimsy has Oswald anthropomorphize plants in the illustrated sequence *Weeds and Wildflowers*, a collaboration with Jessica Greenman that was published in the same year.

Something similar was apparent even in her debut *The Thing in the Gap Stone Stile* (1996), in which both the moon and the sea adopt the lyric first person and humans assume mythic dimensions:

> When a man went to fight a stone,
> he clenched his knuckle-stones, he lifted his foot-stones,
> he upheld himself like the last megalith,
> he kissed his lady like a white, abandoned sea-pebble,
> he felt as justified as a set slate.
>
> ('When a Stone Was Wrecking His Country')

The estrangement seems bold. But it is less structurally radical than it appears; on closer examination it proves to be as purely a descriptive strategy as Martianism was. The book is full of such vivid re-imaginings, which equally suggest the Classical tradition of kennings. For this poet, the identity of a thing resides in its qualities. Thus, 'The sea is made of ponds – a cairn of rain' ('Sea Sonnet'), while 'The glass house is a hole in the rain' ('The Glass House'). Oswald is a natural phenomenologist. As the first myths must have, her qualitative poetics emerges from observation.

An Oxford classicist, Oswald is a hair-raising performer of her own

work. She speaks *Memorial* (2011), her cumulatively incantatory monologue after Homer, entirely from memory. And, like David Harsent,
she sees the natural world not as picturesque but as a stage; the one
on which, *and why,* everything happens. Here too there is a sense that
the elect know that we belong in the natural world and choose to be
celebrants of that giddy fact:

> They began to sway, rubbing their hands together,
> they moved cautiously to the brink of one glance and back.
>
> At each turn, morning was more there
>
> ('For Many Hours there's been an Old Couple Standing
> at that Window')

Oswald's distinctive gifts include a tough, substantial Hughesian
diction. In Ted Hughes's 'Widdop', from the mid-career *Remains of Elmet*:

> Where there was nothing
> Somebody put a frightened lake.
>
> Where there was nothing
> Stony shoulders
> Broadened to support it.
>
> A wind from between the stars
> Swam down to sniff at the trembling.

'Field', from *Woods etc.* (2005), echoes with several of Hughes's poems
at once: not only the well-known 'Full Moon and Little Frieda' but the
children's verse of *What is the Truth* as well as much of *Elmet*:

> Easternight, the mind's midwinter
>
> I stood in the big field behind the house
> at the centre of all visible darkness
>
> a brick of earth, a block of sky,
> there lay the world, wedged
> between its premise and its conclusion

Also like Hughes, Oswald refuses to accept conventional boundaries, both between the human and non-human and more specifically between the individual thinking self and the place in which that finds itself. It's not just that there's no category difference between the human, animal and vegetable worlds: something which means human psychodrama can be staged in those worlds. It is that the human psyche *forms part* of each of them. For Oswald, distinction between these worlds is the superstition, not the old traditions that treat them as coterminous: 'Dart Dart wants a heart.' As her introductory note to *Dart* (2002) says, 'There are indications in the margin where one voice changes into another. These do not refer to real people or even fixed fictions. All voices should be read as the river's mutterings':

> whose voice is this who's talking in my larynx
> who's in my privacy under my stone tent
>
> . . .
>
> under the bent body of an echo are these your
> fingers in my roof are these your splashes

In this passage the young river itself is speaking from one of the places where it runs underground. Yet this speech erupts suddenly, in the middle of an 'eel-watcher' passage. It almost seems to be testing how much we will accept before we think that the man has been over-identified with the river. Or is that questioning 'whose' just a licence for radical indeterminacy? Once a symbol slips its boundaries, its powers – and usefulness – become more or less unlimited.

A similar challenging, or effusive, instability haunts *Woods etc*: in the repetitive versicles and responses that make up 'Walking Past a Rose this June Morning', and other 'games' including the list poem 'Various Portents', the double alphabet 'Tree Ghosts' (described as 'a ballad with footnotes'), and 'Three Portraits of a Radio Audience'. The third section of this poem opens with an echo of William Shakespeare's 'Who is Sylvia? What is she, / That all our swains commend her' from *The Two Gentlemen of Verona*, used to unhomely, exciting purpose:

> Who is Rachel. What is she. Not she.
> Not what she says she is . . .

The passage starts as pentameter, but Oswald's lineation and stanzification obey an internal necessity which laps given forms. Sometimes that necessity calls for musical phrase and thought to be aligned, as in the meditative spaces of 'Ideogram for Green':

> In the invisible places
> Where the first leaves start
>
>   Green breathes growth
>
> Simultaneously dreaming into position what impinges on its
>   edges
> So that grasses of different kinds should appear in the world
>
>   Green hides roots, lights flowers

At other times, as in the nervy state evoked by 'Poem for Carrying a Baby out of Hospital', mimetic line breaks themselves 'burst out / suddenly in a shock of cracks'. There are pages of prose poetry in both *Dart* and *Sleepwalk*. But Oswald's first collection, though coherent with the rest of her work in terms of its thematic and symbolic strategy, is more strongly characterized by traditional forms than were many collections, and certainly most debuts, of the Nineties. As well as sonnets and a ballad, it includes a rhyming version of 'The Pilchard-Curing

Song' in alternating pentameter and tetrameter, and an eleven-page blank verse 'folk narrative', 'The Three Wise Men of Gotham Who Set Out to Catch the Moon in a Net'.

Dart, successor to *The Thing in the Gap Stone Stile*, seems to have liberated Oswald's poetic forms. Perhaps some of this has to do with the book's scale – its forty-eight pages make one continuous poem – and oral character. It is every bit as much a 'play for voices' as *Under Milk Wood*, that much earlier, lyrical radio verse drama. In both, each character is simply an aspect of the whole. This applies even more dramatically to *Memorial*, a performance piece about and for the casualties of Homer's *Odyssey*, which lists the dead of that book and employs haunting, wholesale repetition of what seems to be Choruses.

Superficially, such formal risk-taking might suggest Oswald belongs with the expanded lyricists of Chapter Twelve. Yet it is symbol formation, rather than diction and versification, that makes her work radical. Her take on 'Solomon Grundy' is a distant cousin to Ted Hughes's *Crow*, by way of W.H. Auden and Benjamin Britten's folk lumberjack *Paul Bunyan*:

> He rolled on Wednesday, rolled his whole body
> full of immense salt spaces, slowly
> from one horizon to the other.
>
> And on Thursday, trembling, crippled,
> broke beyond his given strength and crawled.

David Harsent's *Mr Punch* acquires characterization from particular imagined landscapes and stories. But Alice Oswald's Solomon Grundy (who was, of course, also set by Britten) is a grotesque Everyman in the folk tradition. He represents all of us and he pulls us in, forcing us to engage with him. It's a kind of catharsis by symbol. If we 'put on' identification, we become implicated in the story, or its logic.

Mythopoetry is not a movement, but a primary poetic strategy shared by an important group of contemporary poets. Instead of the isolate, illustrative images within verse that most images and metaphors become, narrative symbols structure a poem's entire logic and direction. This precedence given to the symbolic means that mythopoetics deals in what Sigmund Freud called the *Unheimlich*: unhomely experiences that go beyond what we think we know, or can encounter in daily life. Each poet deploys this strategy through a technique developed more or less in isolation. While David Harsent's narratives are evocative parables of unconscious emotional life, Pauline Stainer aligns symbols to create a newly ramifying whole. Robin Robertson uses myth and archetypal natural symbol almost like touchstones; while Christian iconography forms a kind of iconostasis in the work of Michael Symmons Roberts. Alice Oswald raids the symbolic register of the natural world, but peels the boundaries from what she finds there, so that neither symbol nor reader is left to its, or his, own devices. The range, resonance and sheer originality of these writers raises the stakes for what poetry is doing in Britain today in ways that are confirmed, not challenged, by the answering authority of another kind of deep form, working at the level of diction rather than of idea. In the next chapter, we turn to the Iambic Legislators.

8

THE IAMBIC LEGISLATORS

In Eighties and Nineties Britain, iambic pentameter seemed to speak with a Northern accent. It rang with the gritty, steady-as-you go intonation of Nonconformist preachers, union leaders and town hall officials. Pentameter was full of echoes of applied rhetoric: language set to work and grainy with conscience. Ideas, for example about social justice, seemed to fit its measured gait, as if a rhythm could be inherently serious. In the closing scene of Tony Harrison's coruscating 'The Railway Heroides', 'Leeds City Station, and a black man sweeps / Cartons and papers into tidy heaps.'

Perhaps some of the reasons for this were historical. After all, iambic pentameter is one of the foundations of canonical British poetry. From the blank verse of William Shakespeare's plays to Lord Byron's ottava rima, from John Milton's *Paradise Lost* to Elizabeth Barrett Browning's *Sonnets from the Portuguese*, it is the metre that English verse has most regularly adopted. A mixed marriage between the English language and a Classical metre, it is so familiar that it seems almost natural. But is that long cohabitation a matter of nature or nurture? Does iambic pentameter fit existing English-language speech rhythms with a particular intimacy, or have our ears simply got so used to it that this is one of the first sounds a poet has to hand?

Adopted in the late fourteenth century by Geoffrey Chaucer in *The Legend of Good Women*, iambic pentameter emerged as what we might call the English Form in the same post-Mediaeval moment that modern

English was being developed as a literary language. It's no coincidence that by the sixteenth century the language's capacities were being explored and extended by a cohort of poets – including Sir Thomas Wyatt, Edmund Spenser and Sir Philip Sidney – who were also developing the English sonnet form. The four-beat tetrameter had been usual in earlier carol, lyric and ballad, and there's an intuitive link between the longer lines of pentameter and the reflective and reflexive processes associated with the newer, more literary, 'indoor' writing. This introduced forms of deferral and working-out, including the symbolic 'parallelism' of extended metaphor or paradox that sonnets resolve with their calculated turn. Increased reflectiveness was associated with the emergence of new European ideas about personhood and the importance of individual meaning-making in early modern Europe: legacy of the sixteenth century's Protestant Reformation. In poetry, this new assertion of individuality was also apparent in the narrator's more developed persona. The speaker, whether of words of love or prayer, was no longer a universal, indistinguishable Lover or Praying Figure, like that of William Dunbar's meditation on mortality, 'Lament for the Makers', or John Skelton's mock-requiem 'Philip Sparrow'. Instead, for the first time we encounter both the confessional poet-narrator and the character, a *particular* individual who loves or prays in a *particular* set of circumstances, in Sir Philip Sidney's 'The Bargain' ('My true love hath my heart, and I have his') or Sir Walter Raleigh's 'The Passionate Man's Pilgrimage: Supposed to be written by One at the Point of Death'.

This internal link between iambic pentameter and the credibility of a poem's narrator remains even today. Our ear associates pentameter with a speaker who *stays with* what's said. This *staying with* seems to prevent him or her from disappearing among the symbols or in a 'dying fall'; allowing what's said to be understood clearly, rather than trumped by poetry's music. Iambic pentameter sounds explicatory and so, although historically a literate rather than a vernacular form, it can seem curiously informal. (Slav languages which stress the pen-pen-ultimate syllable are closer to the dactylic and anapestic 'triplet' rhythms.) In sounding closer to speech, the metre *appears* to move further away from the decorative functions of form, despite remaining formally worked, and so creates the illusion of its own necessity.

Pentameter is also the regular metre most widely expected to stand alone, un-reinforced by rhyme or stanzaic form. As blank verse, it creates aural unity while appearing to suggest that it does no such thing: implying, in other words, that the shapes of images and ideas somehow *match*, and that it has simply revealed a secret harmony between them. This makes it a terrific resource for marshalling unwieldy material, especially argument or narrative. It's not surprising that it has traditionally been used for long poems and verse novels, from *Paradise Lost* to *Childe Harold*. Twentieth-century verse novels in iambic pentameter range from Les Murray's *Fredy Neptune* to Vikram Seth's *Golden Gate* or Derek Walcott's *Omeros* and – with a Northern British accent – from Douglas Dunn's *The Donkey's Ears* to Tony Harrison's *V.*

In the Eighties these last two poets appeared to be the major national proponents of iambic pentameter. Douglas Dunn, born in Inchinnan in Renfrewshire in 1942, and Tony Harrison, who was born in Leeds in 1937, both write with a strongly socio-historical sense of experience as something largely man-made. Their theme *is* living within human society. The title sequence of Douglas Dunn's 1969 debut *Terry Street*, for example, tells the stories of life in the 'concrete yards' and terraced houses of a city street in Hull; while his *The Donkey's Ears* (2000) translates a Russian Flag Engineer's letters home into verse, in order to tell the true story of the flagship *Kniaz Suvorov*, sunk during the battle of Tsushima in 1905.

For Tony Harrison, social oppression and war create *The School of Eloquence*: an umbrella title for many of his poems, which identifies the source of his poetry with his background and politics. His longer poem *V* is an elegy for his father, and for his father's lost way of life in a Leeds that has since changed so much that his parents' gravestone has been defaced. Harrison's film- and theatre-poems include the anti-feminist *Medea: A sex-war opera*; the *Phaedra* retold as a fable of British colonialism; *A Maybe Day in Kazakhstan* and *The Shadow of Hiroshima*; and

The Gaze of the Gorgon, in which the fate of a statue of the Jewish German Romantic poet Heinrich Heine stands for the destiny of a whole people. *The Gaze of the Gorgon* was also the title of a 1992 collection of the 'war poems' for which Harrison is widely celebrated: in 1995 the *Guardian* sent him to Bosnia from where, like a traditional war artist, he produced poem-dispatches for its news pages. The volume includes 'Sonnets for August 1945' and 'A Cold Coming', a long poem which gives imagined voice to an Iraqi soldier killed by Allies bombing the Iraqi retreat in the 1992 Gulf War.

Tony Harrison's use of pentameter in what used to be called verse plays creates an unavoidable link with Shakespearean drama. It's appropriate that he himself uses the terms 'film-poems' and 'theatre-poems', for there's nothing pastiche in his use of the form. It is also a million miles away from the playful experiments of, say, Peter Oswald or even Glyn Maxwell. Here, iambic pentameter is simply concentrated natural speech. In a 2001 BBC interview Harrison said, 'You find iambic pentameter on the lips of people the whole time. And I love listening on trains to people speaking unconsciously in the metre that's natural to English speech.'

As robustly urban as it is literary, *The Blasphemers' Banquet* (1989) is set with allusive cunning in the '*Int. Omar Khayyam Restaurant, Bradford*':

> It's perfect for tonight's blasphemers' meeting,
> this place renowned in Bradford for good eating
> that used to be a church and gets its name
> from the poet who loves *this* life, however fleeting

But Harrison takes on, and takes over, country life and pastoral in similar ways. In 'Loving Memory', an earlier reflection on Thomas Gray's 'Elegy Written in a Country Church-Yard', 'They're muffling the bells for Stanley Hall'. The recognizably local proper name – one that so clearly belongs to the generation born near the start of the twentieth century – fits a line that is even more full of chiming *l*s than the original, 'tolls the knell', which it replaces.

Naturalized as concentrated speech, pentameter faces two ways at once. It's the Everyman accent of a regional inflection, not too educated to fit in; a kind of camouflage. Yet at the same time it's a privileged, heightened metre that takes itself seriously. After all, the first part of 'Loving Memory' does explicitly measure itself against Gray's 'Elegy': 'in spite of creeping yuppies Breamore's still / the sort of churchyard known to Thomas Gray'. That stanza about the local curry house from *The Blasphemers' Banquet* is preceded by one somewhat more hubristic:

> The blasphemers' banquet table: there
> on mirrored cushions will sit Voltaire,
> me, Molière, Omar Khayyam, Lord Byron
> and that, that's Salman Rushdie's chair.

Distinguished literary company indeed. Yet the result is not confusing duality, but an experience of compression. It's as if two worlds – the corner restaurant and the literary pantheon; the local cemetery and the Romantic canon – have been squeezed together. A recognizably similar compression underlies Harrison's retellings of *Prometheus* (set partly at the collapse of the British coal industry, partly in post-revolutionary Romania and Bulgaria), of *The Oresteia* and, in *The Trackers of Oxyrhynchus*, of Sophocles.

Though it is a dominant note, not all of Harrison's work uses iambic pentameter. His folkloric material, such as *Yan Tan Tethera* or the translated libretto of *The Bartered Bride*, tends to coalesce around balladic tetrameter. This vernacular form is in some ways the People's Voice; an anti-literary, even pre-literate, street and pub oral tradition. But literature, for Tony Harrison, is always in solidarity with the political contemporary. His writing crowds traditional verse forms with non-traditional, urban, working-class material. When his first work appeared in the Seventies, this kind of cultural transfusion had yet to be normalized, as it has been today by poets such as Ian Duhig and Paul Farley. The sixteen-line rhyming poems of *The School of Eloquence* – poems which refuse to be sonnets, though they tend to use the sonnet turn

– are apparently unremarkable scenes from daily life: remembered youth, or parents ageing. (The parents speak a broader dialect than the poet-narrator's.) What made this writing revolutionary then was the interpolation of reported speech: in dialect, moreover. Still, his poems never simply stop at this trope in the way that, forty years on, Daljit Nagra displays the broken English of his parents' generation. In Harrison's long sonnets – residually love poems, as that form must always be – reported speech leads to conceptual dialogue. The poet-speaker is cheek by jowl with each family member, not standing apart as an omniscient narrator:

> *Say bye-bye, our Tony, that's enough!*
> *We've got to buy some liver for dad's tea,*
>
> . . .
>
> Sensing her four year old's about to cry
> she buys me a postcard with the dodo on it.
> 43 years on this filial sonnet
> lets the tears she staunched then out: Bye-bye!
>
> ('Bye-Byes')

'Confessional Poetry' confirms this equality between spoken and written language. It insists that deliberate speech is as formed, and can be as aurally satisfying, as poetic scansion:

> *But your father was a simple working man,*
> they'll say, *and didn't speak in those full rhymes.*
> *His words* when *they came would scarcely scan.*
>
> Mi dad's did scan, like yours do, many times!

The poem makes its concerns at once personal and political, as it puns on writerly responsibility and class survivor's guilt: 'I'm guilty, and the way I make it up's / in poetry'.

Compression is a form of acceleration; and his rich mix of

unexpected conjunctions can sometimes make Tony Harrison feel hard
to keep up with. Douglas Dunn proceeds differently. His starting point
isn't speech, but iambic pentameter's reasoning ability. In *Dante's
Drum-kit* (1993) several long poems use it to address the reader directly.
Dramatic monologues, they lack the pacey cut-and-thrust of Harrison's
encounters; instead letting the reader sink into the argument's own
tone, texture and geography: 'I had my moments in the disrepair /
Time rippled into on a Firth-side hill.'

This couplet comes from the collection's key, the long poem
'Disenchantments', which takes terza rima, the eponymous 'thirteenth-
century beat, // Dante's drum-kit, a metronomic tick', as its form.
Dunn's own extended mid-life reflection questions where to go with
verse as well as in life, and this entire volume has an allusive, intelligent
manner. 'Audenesques for 1960' portrays that great poet as:

> . . . fantasy's ear
> Attentive as I twaddled half-baked poetical opinions
> Walking to work in Renfrew County Library.

This isn't pentameter, of course, any more than the rollocking ballad
'Kabla Khun' (*sic*):

> The Person from Porlock was cooking his tea
> When Coleridge rapped on his door.
> 'Remember? You once did the same thing to me,
> Pimpled, Porlockian bore!'

But in their unashamed proximity to literary subject matter, as well as
regular form, these poems are relatively easy to decode. Dunn writes
from small town, provincial experience and was formed as a young
poet by that most liminal of British cities, Hull, where he studied, and
then worked at the university library with Philip Larkin. Marginally
situated maybe, but these poems haul themselves up by wise, witty use
of form to join the literary mainstream.

Dunn's early writing was admired for its fresh, light touch with a kind of post-blank verse; often not pentameter, but built from lines of roughly matching length and metre. Like Tony Harrison's, his earlier books – including 1969's *Terry Street* and 1985's *Elegies* – reported on scenes from a 'real' life in what is still a very contemporary lyric tone. Although the quietly tender *Elegies* record his first wife's death from cancer, even here bookishness is in evidence. In 'Re-reading Katherine Mansfield's *Bliss and Other Stories*', a mnemonic of their first meeting, a dead fly and a bus ticket bookmark trapped together in a volume of short stories symbolize how life imitates art: 'These stories must have been inside my head / That day, falling in love, preparing this / Good life.'

Despite this richness, neither Tony Harrison nor Douglas Dunn alone represents 'true North' for the late twentieth-century revival in iambic pentameter. As Dunn's own 'Audenesques' suggests, that compass points to W.H. Auden. Nevertheless, for this audacious, witty master, iambic pentameter was just one in an armoury of techniques. Even his long poems are not necessarily written in the form. *New Year Letter* (1940) is in tetrameter; though, as befits a sort of interior verse drama, *The Age of Anxiety*, composed in 1947, does use the blank verse long regarded as 'poetic speech'. In general, too, Auden's iambic pentameter is oddly constricted, filled with the ghosts of half-line breaks and assonantal repetition that suggest pre-modern verse. Paradoxically it is the languid, looping writing of his verse in other metres, like *In Praise of Limestone*, that has more influenced today's British pentameter, giving it permission to decompress, and to discuss even large political ideas with informal stylishness:

> They were right, my dear, all those voices were right
> And still are; this land is not the sweet home that it looks,
>   Nor its peace the historical calm of a site
> Where something was settled once and for all: A backward
>   And dilapidated province, connected
> To the big busy world by a tunnel, with a certain
>   Seedy appeal, is that all it is now?

It is the late Peter Porter who is the missing link between iambic pentameter's association with the metaphorical limestone of Auden's lyrics, and its return as millstone grit in Northern British verse. In 2001 Porter returned to a suggestion he had made 'twenty years or so' earlier, 'that a new school of poetry was emerging which would take up the baton from Auden's Thirties generation and bring back intellectualism and populism'. He did so in order to contextualize the work of Sean O'Brien (of which more shortly). But Porter's innocent coupling of 'intellectualism and populism' encapsulates his own writing, and evokes its uneasy situation within British poetry. Brainy and self-taught, Porter was an Australian émigré who moved to London in the Fifties and whose resolutely metropolitan existence included stints in bookselling, advertising and as Poetry Critic of the *Observer*. The people he met in these milieux *were* both worldly and intelligent and rightly saw no conflict between being moved by a lost cat ('Max is Missing'), rueing 'Sex and the Over-Forties' (and, in due course, 'Sex and the Over-Seventies'), or writing an exquisitely powerful elegy – while at the same time loving bel canto opera ('Homage to Gaetano Donizetti') and Leopardi ('To Himself').

Porter's iambic pentameter, like Douglas Dunn's and Tony Harrison's, enjoys the resonance of traditional continuities. But it leans back on that resonance, allowing itself the space to be discursive, even gossipy:

> Where do we go to live? We're born ticking
> on the page and from the first disclosure on
> we sense that time is useless without fear.
>
> > ('Throw the Book at Them')

Porter's heirs have been encouraged to 'talk' in their verse. Today, poets using iambic pentameter belong among those most likely to work out an idea in a poem, demonstrating the accretion and incompletion of a thought: 'I fold my paper, turn it in my hands / Like a petitioner, and wait, and stare', as Sean O'Brien's 'Sunday in a Station of the Metro' has it. Some of this discursiveness comes from the characteristically Australian, ruminative style that can also be heard in Antipodean poets as intelligent and as various as Chris Wallace-Crabbe, Martin Harrison and even, at times, Les Murray. (Antipodeans fall, alas, off this book's map, but it would be impossible to ignore Murray's influence, in particular on British poetry of the Eighties and Nineties. He thoroughly revised the art of seeing; forcing language to recognize the immediacy of the natural and, more generally, the physical world.)

Porter's primary heir is indeed Sean O'Brien (*b*. 1952). Although he grew up in Hull and often writes about the urban, post-industrial North, Sean O'Brien enters this landscape more as a light-on-his-feet thinker-aloud than as a Northern polemicist. Even *November* (2011), a volume that addresses both personal bereavement and the collective loss of post-war social values, is lyric first and only secondly idea-led. Every phrase earns its own musical keep; the verse is loosely blank. O'Brien doesn't always write in pentameter, yet it remains a centrifugal presence even in lines of four or seven stresses. A walking, talking metre creates space for a thoughtful exploration that isn't mere monologue:

> We fear that the fields of blue air at the world's end
> Will be the only court we face.
> We fear that when we reach the gate alone
> There will be neither words nor deeds
> To answer with . . .

('The Citizens')

This plural pronoun is both a sign that something more than simple confession is going on and a call to collective responsibility: we, the you-and-I of writer and reader, are 'The Citizens'.

O'Brien becomes a citizen poet through, not in spite of, this often-beautiful phrase-making. In the same collection, a dystopic 'On the Toon' prophesies the dismantling of the Welfare State and the closure of its public libraries: 'It takes / Less than a lifetime to renew the ignorance / This public mind was built here to dispel.' The writing's conscience remains above all poetic: kennings, like 'public mind' for 'library', have deep roots in British poetry's Anglo-Saxon past. This kind of formal borrowing is a modernist gesture. Modernist, too, is the crunch of thought and reference within each striking phrase: 'seeking and selling the flesh of the earth . . . We cannot be other than real' ('Europeans'). O'Brien studs poems including 'Bruges-la-Morte' and 'The Island' with allusions, from James McNeill Whistler to Eric Ravilious, B-movies to Russian revolutionaries. A central passage of *November* is a sequence of elegies and homages to fellow poets, including a version of Rimbaud's '*Le Bateau ivre*' and poems addressing Michael Donaghy, Derek Mahon, E.A. Markham and Peter Porter. In each, O'Brien's diction turns towards that of the poet saluted – Donaghy's whimsical song, Markham's high-table phrasing – but this virtuosity is subsumed by tenderness.

In a 'Leavetaking' for Porter, the narrator admires fire's 'crimson speech / As though like alcohol it were / A kind of poetry'; the rapid set of transformations – flame into word, colour and alcohol into poetry – exemplifies the loving familiarity with which O'Brien handles the material world. Elegy's conservative note can all too easily lead to facile verse, but these poems aren't pre-tuned. Instead they create a new, anti-metropolitan, symbolic reality out of railway cuttings and foggy suburbs. Excellence of the spirit, they suggest, is close-at-hand and refuses glib individual transcendence: 'Work is good, like love and company'. *November*'s centre of gravity is an 'Elegy' for O'Brien's mother, and the accompanying poem 'Novembrists'. Both are moved, and move us, by their recollection of the values of the talented woman who 'taught the children of the poor for forty years / Because it was the decent thing to do'.

'Work is good'. A centrepiece in Sean O'Brien's own critical practice to date has been his remarkable *The Deregulated Muse* (1998): a survey of contemporary British poetry which manages to combine authority with a committed, even militant, tone. It's a pretty much irresistible combination, not only because the *Muse* is testament to the body of knowledge which accrues to 'a public literary critic devoted to poetry and able to speak authoritatively to the scholar and the general reader alike' (this is, in fact, how O'Brien characterizes Tom Paulin); but because its sense of passion, even necessity, speaks to the poetic auto-didact each of us secretly believes ourselves to be. The book's introduction presents a rousing picture of 'a previous age of cultural coherence' whose influence persists 'for all its baggage of class- and self-interest' and arrives at a call to arms: '[poetry] risks losing its essential nature if it does not maintain a vigilant regard for its own interests as an art made of language'.

An accompanying anthology, *The Fire Box*, has an ambiguous title. Should we imagine stoves or Olympian fire? Is poetry itself (always) a fire box, or is *this* canon the fire box of poetry? Such transfers of power are the work of metaphor – and of discursive sleight of hand. A similar passing-along of power takes place in many of the poems of O'Brien's 2001 collection *Downriver*. 'Piers Powerbook's Prologue', 'Lines on Mr Porter's Birthday': epigraph, acknowledgement and dedication, cultural allusion and quotation, map a web of influence. It's true (*pace* Harold Bloom) that all poetry is a poetry of influence. But here the prose poem 'The Railway Sleeper' also explicitly visualizes the *material* conditions in which the dream of a poem might get translated by the secretary to some anthropomorphized steam engine: 'Our barmy old party is writing everything down, amanuensis to an abolished god with wings of fire, a surveyor's telescope and a black top hat.'

This mythopoeia of the railway has travelled a long way past John Betjeman's gentle forays into *Metroland*. Part notebook as artwork, 'The Railway Sleeper' is built not on allusion or the kind of simple appropriation that Marcel Duchamp staged with his urinal, but on a poetics of situatedness. 'We are entering *L'Angleterre profonde*, which does not exist', the poem opens. But it does: 'Yonder lies Ferrybridge, Lies Castleford.' This authentic England is 'the sunset pang as the lines divide at York, or the much-abridged viaducts of Leeds, or the vast white elephant of Liverpool Edge Hill – that sexual warehouse and car park.' *L'Angleterre profonde* is in the eye of the beholder and in the beholder; it *is* the observant child sent upstairs to a summer bedroom overlooking a railway line, who becomes a poet, a dreamer, even the eponymous Railway Sleeper: 'The mouth of the sleeper opens silently. There is the faintest breath like the suspicion of a train entering the far end of a long tunnel . . .'

While poetry avoids what's too casually generic in favour of the resonant specific, it nevertheless aims to echo as universally as possible. The paradox is that a poet must rely on his or her own sensibility to test that resonance. In 'Ryan's Farewell' from *The Frighteners* (1987), published when O'Brien was thirty-five, 'Tonight the summer opened like a park / Seen distantly, a blue-green reservation,' and while the idea of summer 'opening' is shamelessly seductive, the choice of a 'park' is so frankly suburban it immediately places the reader within a particular, located sensibility. The whole collection selects this perspective: politically informed, but *felt*. Where O'Brien does give us open countryside, in a poem pertinently called 'Trespass', it opens with 'The downlands, private under drizzle': the line makes its social point without seeming to.

It's a trick of local, concrete implication that O'Brien never loses, and which makes his poems sensuous as well as thinky; both particular and involving big ideas. The effect works in both directions. We might not care so much about the 'me with my headache and choc-ice' of childhood in 'A Matinee' were we not also contemplating the march of time in every life. And this marriage is rhythmic as well as intellectual. What creates clarity and ventilation is O'Brien's use of *measure*; both in the musical sense of metre – one thing after another – and in careful calibration of tone: specifically, of 'input'. An O'Brien poem is never overcrowded: one image, whether concrete or metaphorical, leads to another in due course, in a *rhythmic deployment* that resists both over- and under- writing. Particularity means focus and accuracy. 1995's 'A Rarity', set in a provincial hotel, avoids the coy tricks of Anthony Thwaite's 'Mr Cooper' or even Philip Larkin's 'Mr Bleaney', poems whose narrators always seems one step ahead of the neighbours they observe:

Polish your shoes, climb into bed
And breathe in the sweetness of nylon and Bass.
The girls are done up to the nines,
Like raccoons with affective disorders,
Rehearsing three steps round their handbags
And speaking in smoke-rings, a code
Meaning *Fuck off and die* or *Be older*,
Knowing it's to you the management reserves
The right to do pre-emptive violence.

('A Rarity')

This rhythmic tone, with its meat-and-two-veg phrasal line breaks –
'The girls are done up to the nines, / Like raccoons with affective
disorders, / Rehearsing three steps round their handbags' – resists too
much pliancy. Like some Northern lad rolling his sleeves up in mid-
winter, it signals a tough, man's world. *The Frighteners* also includes
ballads ('London Road', 'Unregistered') and uses strict metre to tell
stories of mental illness ('Young Howard') or how the '*ancien régime* gets
away scot-free ('The Mechnical Toy Museum').

But *The Drowned Book* (2007) is the most crisply rhythmic of O'Brien's
first three collections of the new millennium. A short poem about
Nazism ends:

Look now: the tanks are massing on your desk;
The gods must be garrotted or adored.

('The Them')

while a twelve-line reflection on a 'Blue Night' closes:

They have no time for pity or belief,
The heavens, in their triumph of technique.

In this widely admired volume (which made O'Brien the most garlanded
contemporary British poet), European history increasingly takes its

place alongside British class- and labour-relations, and the decay of Western industrialized societies, as a topic that the verse inhabits with genuine sensory engagement. That engagement now also reflects social anxiety, sometimes using concrete symbol to produce a greater sense of historical proximity. In the opening and close of 'Blizzard': 'The snow will bring the world indoors . . . the world is not a place / But an occasion, first of sin and then the wish / That such self-knowledge may be gratified, / While snow continues falling, till we learn / There will be neither punishment nor grace.' These are surprising terms for an *ars poetica*, but such they are. O'Brien's 'places' are in fact the 'occasions' to learn or think about something, spread out by a loose pentameter's relative ranginess into conceptual spaces, rather than condensed as framed snapshots.

The imaginative forces that mustered in *The Drowned Book* and kept it forceful and surprising were loosened somewhat by *November*'s personal, elegiac note. They had been looser still in *Downriver*. In some ways the source book for *The Drowned Book*, this collection prickles with invention. Though occupying familiar O'Brien territory, it seems to turn its back on the 'look no hands' decency of earlier reportage. Three sets of songs, the fruits of collaborations with other poets, musicians and a film-maker, compose the 'The Underwater Songbook'. Pablo Picasso, ballad form, counting-songs, the brainy self-referentiality of W.H. Auden's chatter, the blues and even T.S. Eliot's *The Waste Land* – 'Time on yer beer / Time on yer beer / Time on yer beer now PLEASE' – are synthesized with joyful energy. The 'Lines on Mr Porter's Birthday' are furious but also funny. They make the reader wonder how O'Brien has been allowed to get away with his own intelligent 'poems regarding the past and future as if they were real':

> Some are driven to spasms of spittle-flecked rage
> By poems with bits of Italian or German left in,
> And made to feel
> Anxious and sweaty and dim
> By poems regarding the past and future as if they were real.

Gwyneth Lewis (*b.* 1959) is another Peter Porter protégé. Her first adult collection, published in 1990, was a volume of sonnets in Welsh. Wrenching together the language and a form foreign to it, the project was neo-modernist in its interest in both textual structure and cultural 'progress'. *Sonedau Redsa a Cherddi Eraill* were controversial because they were seen in some places as compromising a living tradition, central to national identity, by diluting it with 'English' forms. In contrast, her 1995 debut in English, *Parables and Faxes*, was an eminently fashionable blend of irony with inventive allusions to contemporary culture: there are 'mercury thieves', golf courses and drunks in lay-bys. If this was a vein opened in 1988 by Jo Shapcott with her *Electroplating the Baby*, however, Gwyneth Lewis is no fellow dandy. Her poetry is altogether more level-pegging than Shapcott's; largely because of the way pentameter – used in both pure and lightly corrupted forms – slows down the diction. Its effect is to balance youthful high spirits and high technique with the *sound* of authority:

> So this is the man you dreamt I had betrayed.
> I couldn't have saved him if I'd stayed,
>
> He's old as his language. On his bony knees
> his hands are buckled like wind-blown trees
>
> that were straight in his youth . . .
>
> ('Welsh Espionage' XI)

This reads like something written by R.S. Thomas's more temperate older sister. And certainly, for all her revolutionary reputation in Welsh, Lewis is a poet who synthesizes influences. If Seamus Heaney's limpid diction seems a presence in poems like that key early sequence 'Welsh Espionage' or indeed the 'Birder' lyrics in 2011's *Sparrow Tree*, Joseph Brodsky's explicit, construction-kit style is audible in another poem from Lewis's debut, 'A Golf-Course Resurrection':

Mid morning, above the main road's roar
the fairway's splendid – eighteen holes
high on a mountain, which should be all slope,
too steep for a stretch of evenness or poise.

Yet she also channels the sensible irreverence of Stevie Smith or Frances Cornford, especially in the quietly furious *A Hospital Odyssey* (2010). As all these influences suggest, there is something in the practical way Lewis locates her writing – in the US on a Harkness Fellowship, she studied with Joseph Brodsky, Seamus Heaney and Derek Walcott – that is tied up with an idea of poetic authority. We could conjecture that, for this Welsh writer, poetry remains the language of distinction and prestige: the poet is still the *Bardd*. So it's not surprising that her second collection in English, *Zero Gravity* (1998), takes on the 'big topics' of space travel and science. Like *Parables and Faxes*, it does so with the aid of exemplary anecdotes. The concrete world is Lewis's living (or, sometimes, inanimate) proof.

Sometimes, this evidential world is so closely recorded that the eye of the poem seems almost Martian:

The Boeing dreams its boarding passengers
which are poured, like poison, through its weeping ear.

('Illinois Idylls' I)

But here iambic pentameter ('which are' read as anapest) muffles the vivid imagery. The Martian flâneur and the iambic legislator walk to differing rhythms:

The guidebook directed us to a nunnery
where no one spoke English.
Nearby, a quarry
was blasting for granite

('The Soul Mine')

This passage reads as if, having fallen short of pentameter in line two (after an opening line not exactly marked by rhythmic exactitude), the rest of the poem smuggles that metre forward in slightly shame-faced disguise, lines three and four combining to make one whole pentameter. But Lewis brings the levelling rhythmic attributes of 'Dante's drumbeat' to bear tellingly in *A Hospital Odyssey*, a mythologized verse-memoir of her husband's treatment for cancer. Though it ends with a homecoming, and many creatures are encountered along the way, this is as much a Purgatory as an Odyssey. Echoing the structure of Dante's epic poem, each chapter is a new circle of suffering.

Lewis's *Odyssey* uses five-line rhyming stanzas, which retain the notion of *five* but don't stick closely to iambic pentameter. This far from confessional poem is written in the third person: Maris is married to Hardy, the cancer patient, and this is the story of her experiences with her psychopomps – the greyhound Wilson; Ichabod; and Ludlow, a Knight Templar – as she meets a New Age 'healer' and a snaky 'Administrator' and parties with the viruses. The cruel cliché of the 'cancer journey' is stolen and attested to by the book's entire project. But the stanza form adds air to the mixture, and rhyme keeps it moving:

> . . . Good doctors co-ordinate
> the body's rhythms, orchestrate,
>
> a place to live. For we perform
> our health, like music, in ensembles,
> within the limit of our genome.

Like bubbles in a baking mixture, this whipped-in air also brings to life the collection that follows. The poems of *Sparrow Tree* feel accelerated; their native braininess and play is revealed by shortened lines. In 'Remission Sevillanas':

> Now that you're with me, back from the dead
> (I didn't turn round! I didn't

Turn round!) I'm losing my mind.
No loss, you say. Outside
Oranges ripen in cold
For bitter marmalade.

As its title makes clear, the big topics are still here. Elsewhere, the book includes a twelve-part sequence on childlessness. Europe and death are both still part of the poetic vision. But the post-iambic tramp has been replaced by the spring and give of a dance step.

Lewis may be concerned with forms of poetic authority, but she modernizes them through a characteristic mixture of play and emotion. In *Fortinbras at the Fishhouses* (2010) the avowed European George Szirtes stakes his claims for 'historical consciousness in poetry, or, if that sounds a little too grandly ambitious, the sense, that plays about some poems, of being informed by more than the personal or the local or the immediate present.' History, in this analysis, is told as much slant as straight; and it may be more than coincidence that Szirtes himself (*b*. 1948) has been preoccupied with the slanting action of form since his first appearance in Faber's *Poetry Introduction 4* (1978). Which is not to say that the early poems – and those from the first three collections, including *Short Wave* (1984) – are undifferentiatedly formal. Short-bite lyrics, they bespeak many of the usual Seventies influences, from Miroslav Holub, to Alan Brownjohn's or Herbert Lomas's vocative anecdotalism, and the jaunty dandyism of Gavin Ewart or Peter Porter, the latter an early mentor who particularly haunts 1984's 'Kissing Place' sequence.

Regular metre did not come to dominate Szirtes's work until 1986's *The Photographer in Winter*. Szirtes is never short of words however, and by the time we get to *The Burning of the Books and Other Poems* (2009), bulky suites are interleaved with six *canzone*, themselves a sort of rich man's sestina. Their twelve-line stanzas, each built round the same five rhymes, make a pattern of reinforcement but also of self-absorption. As 'Canzone: Architecture' has it, 'Our fame is inward: it is a private frame / for which we must create an architecture / of outwardness . . .'

Szirtes's poems offer up recognizably Mittel-European tropes that come close to pastiche: 'To eat books is to have a stomach full of corners, / Because the word is angular and has sharp edges.' We might not be sure exactly what such an image means – is language tougher than experience itself? Surely the stomach should then be full of holes, not corners? – but its cultural referents are unmistakable, and work a little like shortcuts to colouration. *In the Face of History*, which responds to a series of well-known Second World War photographs, is essentially ekphrastic. In 'Sudek: Tree', for example, 'The visionary moment comes / just as it is raining, just as bombs / are falling, just as atoms // burst like a sneeze in a city park / and enter the dark / as if it were a waiting ark.' Yet even these lines give the impression of waiting on their end rhymes. A tautological 'laughing, its sides splitting' (in 'Kertész: Latrine') is only there to make the metre up, and 'just as it is raining, just as . . . just as . . .' has an ambulatory pace at odds with the drama it's evoking. This lengthiness in the line, a metre less vivid, visceral *Dante's Drumbeat* than forced march, is surely traceable in part to Szirtes's Hungarian ear. It calls up not only relatively uninflected Hungarian speech rhythm, but the extended deadpan of novelists like László Krasznahorkai and Sándor Márai – both of whom Szirtes has translated.

Carol Rumens, born in 1944 and Szirtes's near-contemporary, is another poet writing in iambic pentameter whose seriousness sometimes seems to go by way of Europe before returning to twenty-first-century Britain; but her syntheses are authentic, individual and worked. The title sequence of *De Chirico's Threads* (2010), a 'verse-drama with soundscape', explores the Greek-born painter's artistic motivation. As befits her subject, it is a post-Classical piece in twenty-one scenes; with a populous cast including Ariadne and the Minotaur, André Breton, Guillaume Apollinaire and Giorgio de Chirico's colleagues, as well as more intimate psychic presences – the artist's family, 'forgers', an 'expert' and the Press. There's richness and risk in this cast alone, and Rumens is alert to its possibilities. She handles some with humour – naming them 'CHANGE-IT, a newspaper editor. CHANCE-IT, a columnist.

ANONYMOUS POET, a loser' – and ventriloquizes others, for example in a virtuoso pastiche of an article by Breton ('Here, the tower dominates the arcades / And the male force is supreme'). Yet she's unafraid to let her speakers articulate moments of emotional intensity, as when De Chirico's ghostly sister asks, 'But was it the truth that once, / When the autumn light was clear / And the shadows long in the square, / Shook you with pity and terror?'

This mixture of registers creates an experience of simultaneity and busyness, appropriate for a portrait of surrealism. Philosophical ideas are tightly characterized. When, in his salon at 'the Café Kubik, Paris', Apollinaire asks, 'Do you bring salvation / Or sal volatile? A mutilation, a muse, or a two-headed monster?' Chance-it comments, in jangling headline-ese, 'Giorgio was eating pizza while reading Nietzsche in the Piazza', while Mama's off-stage injunction adopts the homely quatrameter of ballad and proverb: 'Take care – you'll have indigestion. / Never mix lunch with a philosophical question!' Rumens's attempt to make emotional sense of this least confessional of artistic movements is full of intelligent play. Like Lewis and above all O'Brien, she has pressed the guaranteed decency of iambic pentameter into her own service. Her authority comes from a characteristic balance between idiosyncratic observation and musical, often strictly metrical, control. In 'East Ending', for example, Wilton's Music Hall is 'fresh-bathed and tremulous, // Her tits like pearly scandals and her ankles / Barley-sugar.' This is lovely, exact imagery that doesn't stop where a lazier poet might, with a personification of the theatre, but goes two steps further, imagining the call girl in bodily detail that is, in turn, metaphorically transformed. None of which prevents the poem from clicking shut with a rhyme that carries off its big idea with grace: 'Our mobiles wink from gallery to pit, / To catch the past, show ourselves in it.'

The same loosened pentameter lends dignity to 'The Concentration-Camp Poplars Remember their First Gardeners', where more personification creates a 'slant' perspective from which to break the taboo of poetry after Auschwitz. Rumens earns the right to do so by

the sustained integrity of her threnody. Enjambment evokes the
contained movement of the trees. It evokes, too, the movement of
emotion against a grid of statement:

> Because they had to be slaves before they died,
> their hands were used, their feet were used, their spines
> were bent and used, their breath was pumped, pumped,
> pumped till the valves failed . . .

Elsewhere, a confident ear allows her to break up conventional lineation, as the pain of childbirth breaks up first composure and then
sense:

>   . . . rhyme it further
>   and harder   wider   harder   till wide nature
>   is satisfied   closes her golden eye
>
>   ('Dipthongs')

    Carol Rumens is an unusual, important figure: a lyric thinker who
happens to be a woman. Moreover, she exemplifies a third route to
contemporary iambic pentameter, one that parallels both the Northern
school and the Auden-Porter tradition. After all, pentameter is neither
essentially masculine nor residually patriarchal. Behind Rumens stands
another strongly independent woman poet and critic, Anne Stevenson,
born in England in 1933 to an American family. Stevenson's first book,
Living in America, was published in 1965, when she herself was already
moving between the US and Britain. But she has maintained a steady
presence here, as both poet and poet-critic, that makes her a role model
for poets, especially women poets, of Rumens's generation and younger.
(After all, a literary generation is only ten years.)

    A poet whose interest in formal music distinguishes her from her
contemporaries among the plain dealers, Stevenson has led a writing
life which has been a complicated plea for clarity united with form.
The daughter of an American philosopher, she had planned to be a

musician, but while still a student switched to poetry. She was an early biographer of fellow North Americans Elizabeth Bishop and Sylvia Plath, and this has helped her intellectual standing. But she is always primarily a literary rather than a critical writer. Her poetry's formal intelligence is incorporated, not ostentatious. In 'Utah', written like many of her metrical poems in sestrameter, the all-American diction is surprising for the British reader:

> Somewhere nowhere in Utah, a boy by the roadside,
> gun in his hand, and the rare dumb hard tears flowing.
> Beside him, a greyheaded man has let one arm slide
> awkwardly over his shoulders, is talking and pointing
> at whatever it is, dead, in the dust on the ground.

But it shouldn't be. That verbless first sentence mimics the tableau the poet wants us to see: a kind of 'American Gothic' by way of a coming-of-age road movie.

Stevenson is explicit in her belief that music, in poetry, means metre. In a letter to the author, she says that 'You can't get around the fact that a rhythmic pattern of stresses AND of long and short intonations (notes), AND of alliterative consonants plus assonantal vowels determine the "tune" of all the best poems in the English language.' Consistency is also a kind of musical form; and intelligence is something not to be rushed, but demonstrated by being thorough-going. Thoughtful, yet no intellectual name-dropper, this sensible poet can produce verse whose diction seems oddly trim because it is unencumbered by erudite reference:

> They belong here in their own quenched country.
> I had forgotten nice women could be so nice.
>
> ('By the Boat House, Oxford')

Here, of course, trimness is just the intention – despite the lines' flexible foot – as Stevenson balances her own depth of intellection against more simplistic narrative obligation. Elsewhere, though, a resolutely stitched quality, demure yet forceful, characterizes her writing, for example in 'Before Eden', from *Stone Milk*:

> A day opens, a day closes,
> Each day like every other day.
> No day is like another day.
>
> . . .
>
> A wall fits its belt to a hill
> As a mason fits stone to hand.
> No stone's like any other stone,
>
> And every stone has a like stone.
> Why should another spring surprise me?

This is luminously exact. In the same collection, Stevenson faces 'The Enigma':

> Falling to sleep last night in a deep crevasse
> between one rough dream and another, I seemed,
> still awake, to be stranded on a stony path,
> and there the familiar enigma presented itself
> in the shape of a little trembling lamb.

We guess this is the kind of pentameter Emily Dickinson might write. Ostensibly contained, in fact it obeys few limits, and is careless about iambic regularity. It is also absolutely clear-sighted. Iambic pentameter, that had seemed so much a masculine, Northern British voice, reveals itself in another guise. Stevenson's writerly sensibility combines something of the *Little House on the Prairie* (a much less cosy habitation than it might appear) with the bookishly British. Hers is a very Protestant, and unburnished, form of speech. Yet it is also elegant. Anne Stevenson is a witness of the modernizing force of tradition. She has made a diction of her own out of the most familiar poetic elements, and in doing so she demonstrates the enduring capacity of iambic pentameter to lend both itself and, particularly, an associated air of tradition, to a continually renewed poetics.

9

MODERNISM

Modernism is, of course, not postmodernism. Postmodernism succeeds modernism and positions itself in relation to it, establishing both itself, and thereby modernism, as cultural moments. Modernism, on the other hand, self-identifies as an attitude or project. As the term suggests, it has faith in progress; it follows that it holds some states of affairs and ways of doing things to be better than others. Postmodernism sees this kind of belief as superseded. It argues that the contemporary world demonstrates how nothing is more valuable than anything else, and that what we imagined was progress was merely change. Postmodernism is the cultural cousin of moral relativism; while modernism is associated with social conscience. Progress, after all, is a largely social enterprise, associated as it is with such collective phenomena as the introduction of the Welfare State, 'The Electrification of the Soviet Union', or the replacement of superstition by human and civil rights.

To suggest that the modernist idea of progress is optimistic, largely well-intentioned and collective in outlook is not, of course, to pretend that everything done in its name – such as the brutalist Sixties architecture that turned so many city centres into windy wastelands – now seems good or even moral. But it *is* to suggest the enormous gulf between modernism and a postmodern idea of play that is most manifest within culture as instability and change. In the arts, postmodernity is all about the maker's *process*: it is here that it locates conscientiousness, even responsibility. Modernism's concerns, on the other hand, are with the actual material *produced*, and its effects on a user community. The architect Le Corbusier may have been wrong when he thought that homes were 'machines for living', which could be located in 'radiant cities' in the sky, but he was certainly thinking about the people for whom his apartments and houses were designed.

This link with a principle of progress not tied to any particular time or place means that modernism is still available as a cultural strategy today. One can be a modernist even in the era of post-modernism. But then why postmodernity? Three things seem to have combined to produce this shift. First, modernism had succeeded *enough* – the average Westerner had become sufficiently affluent – for the urgency that fuels collective action to die away. Second, modernism itself includes forms of questioning. Traditional ways of taking things on trust – including, in literature, the realist novel and the reliable narrator – were questioned by modernist progressives. Arguably, this produced the very climate of cultural anxiety from which Post-modernism arose. Third, modernism was never as successful in Britain as in the rest of Europe, even in its most popular pre- and inter-war cultural forms. Out and proud, British philistinism remains uncomfort-able with the 'arty': if it must have pictures and stories, it prefers them naturalized as representation. Conceptual art, after all, is the *represen-tation* of an idea or pun; it devalues such modernist concerns as materiality and texture. So it's no surprise that, though Britain can claim two great modernist poets – the American-born, French-educated T.S. Eliot and the Welshman David Jones, whose 'European education' took place, by contrast, in the trenches – the trail of their successors seemed at first glance to go cold in the second half of the twentieth century.

It didn't, of course. Instead, Britain passed through a period of regional modernism. Basil Bunting (1900–85) demystified the High Anglican idea of the Beauty of Holiness which T.S. Eliot's *Four Quartets* had so perfectly pitched into English culture. In 1965 he published a long poem that replaces the Somerset churchyard of Eliot's *East Coker* with the eponymous Quaker Meeting House at *Briggflatts* in Cumbria, and Eliot's cosmopolitan range of educated allusion with writing that works away at its own geographical and cultural location:

> In Garsdale, dawn;
> at Hawes, tea from the can.
> Rain stops, sacks
> steam in the sun, they sit up.
> Copper-wire moustache,
> sea-reflecting eyes
> and Baltic plainsong speech
> declare: By such rocks
> men killed Bloodaxe.

Bunting's model is the formal containment of the Baroque sonata, rather than the exploded Classical forms that Eliot borrowed from Beethoven's late quartets. His River Rawthey constantly deepens its own groove. Unlike the anxiety associated with Eliot's 'words' that 'decay with imprecision, will not stay in place, will not stay still', his modernism is not millennial. It simply makes us aware of the material the poet is using. And its project is more than merely autobiographical: localism acutely sites general, existential questions in the immediate lives of particular communities.

Bunting severed modernism from the urbanity that is often seen as its correlative. His contemporary W.S. Graham went a step further. Though his writing has a tendency to a confessional note we might call expressionism – a kind of loud, chaotic overtone – it captures the grittiness of rural poverty in Cornwall. He does this without resorting to either simple realism or the didacticism of the great argufiers like Hugh MacDiarmid and Sorley Maclean (Somhairle MacGill-Eain). The occasional loud notes in Graham's key long poem, *The Nightfishing* (1955), are in part a legacy of the previous decade, spent largely in London, where he was identified as a New Apocalypse writer. His characteristic tone, captured in a poem like 'Malcolm Mooney's Land',

is somewhere between the bounce of *Briggflatts* and the mannered sigh
of T.S. Eliot's 'A Cold Coming':

> . . . Footprint on foot
> Print, word on word and each on a fool's errand.
> Malcolm Mooney's Land. Elizabeth
> Was in my thoughts all morning and the boy.
> Wherever I speak from or in what particular
> Voice, this is always a record of me in you.

Younger regional modernists include Derek Mahon (*b.* 1941), now
living in Co. Cork, who moved from a childhood spent in Northern
Ireland and off the map of this book to become a hugely significant
figure in poetry in the Irish Republic. His lapidary, intelligent, diction
helps counterbalance the touchstone lyricism that might otherwise have
overwhelmed Irish verse in the late twentieth century. Yet, as poems like
'Achill' demonstrate, his work is profoundly located in the particular texture
of local life. On the east coast of England, the Hull Poets of the Eighties,
who included Peter Didsbury, Douglas Houston and Sean O'Brien, saw
themselves as inheritors of a conscientious regionalism. (Though other
poetic nexuses sprang up in this decade – Huddersfield, Manchester –
they were less explicitly preoccupied with creating a regional *poetics*.)

However, regionalism isn't the only route by which modernism has
been passed down to contemporary poets. O'Brien's friend and mentor
Peter Porter, rather than being the survivor of a generation or coterie,
was a cultural epoch all to himself, with a lightly worn passion for
'What is fuel / for understanding'. That fuel famously included
Renaissance art, Martial and wryly observed pets. Who else would
start a touching elegy, 'The flower which gave Browning his worst
rhyme / lined my father's walk to his Paradise Garden / but he took
his time': thus giving us not only smiling literary knowingness and the
composer Frederick Delius, but an absolutely characteristic metaphorical sidestep? In nineteen collections Porter celebrated the well-
furnished mind:

> Much have I travelled in the realms of gold
> for which I thank the Paddington and Westminster
> Public Libraries . . .
>
> ('The Sanitized Sonnets 4')

and the importance of unpretentious fluency:

> What a clever moggie to tread only
>   in the keys of G Minor and D Minor,
> but then the gifted walk with care and flair
>   as if on hot bricks . . .
>
> ('Cat's Fugue')

His final three books, *Max is Missing* (2001), *Afterburner* (2004) and *Better Than God* (2009), form an ascending sequence of declared stakes and poetic achievement. Yet the early work revealed much of what was to come. A title like 'Death in the Pergola Tea-Rooms' may be clever kitsch, but the poem itself trumps the merely Larkinesque, or some tinted period photograph from the school of John Betjeman. Its protagonist, who chooses to keep 'stroking comfort on other fingers, / Patting the warm patch where the cat has been', speaks presciently to Porter's last poem, 'After Schiller': 'Where was I and what then happened to me / When half-light moved beyond eclipse? / Didn't I foresee the end, and you agree / Love is the clumsiest of partnerships?'

'What is it / Turns an atheist's mind to prayer in almost /Any church on a country visit?' the poet asks in 'An Angel in Blythburgh Church', from *The Cost of Seriousness* (1978). 'An Exequy', his elegy for his first wife, dominates that collection, in the title poem of which, 'Once more I come to the white page of art / to discover what I know / and what I presume I feel.' 'An Exequy' is composed of more than a hundred lines of rhyming quatrameter couplets which use the second person to address her: the case is relatively rare in Porter's poetry, although his work is never solipsistic. Conscientious in the modernist way, he frequently uses the first person plural of shared experience in poems addressing the state of the contemporary world or the human condition. 'An Exequy' arrests the reader, line by quotable line: 'the channels of our lives are blocked', 'And marriages are all opaque', 'the stars, / Most middle-aged of avatars'. But what makes this a major work is its immense feat of incorporation, a mere 'five months' after the loss of his wife. Janice Porter died in her own childhood attic bedroom, and the attic staircase itself becomes both a life and also a Calvary: 'each stair now will station me / a black responsibility.' The lost woman herself undergoes a series of transformations, from 'Dear Wife, lost beast, beleaguered child, / The stranded monster with the mild / Appearance' to confessor – 'I have no friend, or intercessor, / No psychopomp or true confessor / But only you who know my heart / In every cramped and devious part' – and, finally, Virgilian psycho-pomp: 'Oh guide me through the shoals of fear – / "Fürchte dich nicht, ich bin bei dir."'

As this suggests, Porter's sensibility is profoundly literate, and emerges elsewhere as a prodigal, throwaway and often punning wit. 'The Rest on the Flight' is about writing and drinking on board a 'Boeing'. His humour could also emerge as satire: of suburbia, in 1961's 'Made in Heaven', or in the cat parables of *Preaching to the Converted* (1972). Yet his poems are not homilies, but essays. Wondering and wry-spoken, the poet's worldly ease with moving between registers marks him out as W.H. Auden's heir:

> My vernacular was always bookish;
> somehow I missed the right Americans,
>
> I couldn't meld the High and Low –
> even my jokes aspired to footnotes –
>
> but I am open to Wordsworthian signs.
>
> ('Streetside Poppies')

Porter linked the satire and wit of the Soho generation (which included Gavin Ewart and Ian Hamilton) to its rediscovery by the Cool Britannia of middle-generation poets like Paul Farley and Don Paterson. By contrast, his British near-contemporary Charles Tomlinson, born in 1927, was a conduit for international modernism. A committed translator of Hispanic verse, notably of the Mexican Nobel laureate Octavio Paz, Tomlinson belongs to the generation who benefitted from the patronage of *Modern European Poets*, the series Al Alvarez edited for Penguin and which, in the Sixties and Seventies, brought many then-contemporary European greats to a mainstream British audience. Tomlinson himself also featured among Penguin's national *Modern Poets*. His chipped, often resolutely unmusical, verse displayed greater affinities with the craggy experimentation of Louis Zukofsky or the Peruvian modernist César Vallejo than with the more discursive British modernists. A relatively reclusive lifestyle in rural Gloucestershire lessened Tomlinson's influence on the British poetry scene; in this he somewhat resembled the craggily demanding Peter Reading (1946–2011), whose satirical and sometimes neo-Classical take on the world as Vanity Fair was written in Salopian seclusion. The widely translated critical reception abroad arguably exceeds Tomlinson's standing in Britain; a fact that is probably only partly explained by a British preference for the easy-reading lyric.

Tom Raworth (*b.* 1938) seems a touch less single-minded. An inveterate editor – first founding a little magazine in the Sixties, he set up the Goliard edition in 1965 – he was influenced by Ed Dorn, Charles Olson and other Black Mountain poets. Yet his 1966 debut, *The Relation Ship*, was admired by Donald Davie among others. Raworth, who is also a visual artist – largely of found art – has synthesized these influences with writing from Latin America to produce an idiosyncratic mix:

'Let us,' said one of the natives whose language we could speak, but imperfectly, 'build from the trees a thing we call a "ship" – from the wood remaining I will show you how to make "paper" – on this "paper" (once we set sail) I shall show you how to "write" (with a charred twig from the same tree) – and if your grand-mother is with you, here's how we suck eggs.'

('Logbook')

That Raworth is often grouped with the exploded lyricists reminds us how both modernism and postmodernism express their ideas about poetry in the very texture of the verse.

Unlike these three modernist contemporaries, a fourth, Geoffrey Hill (born in 1932) belongs securely in the Eliot tradition, not least through his High Anglicanism: if *Tenebrae* (1978) is his *East Coker*, the hagio-graphic *The Mystery of the Charity of Charles Péguy* (1983) is surely his equivalent to *Little Gidding*. But Hill is also a poet in whom several British traditions converge. Like Tomlinson, and in a different way Porter, he has become a kind of internationalist, spending more than two decades, from 1988, living and working in North America. However, he also belongs to the Welsh Borders, where he was brought up close to A.E. Housman's home town of Bromsgrove, and which have a poetic tradition of Anglican mysticism that precedes modernism. The histor-ical roots Eliot had to search out through his remote ancestor Launcelot Elyot were to-hand for Hill, a village- and grammar-school-boy who grew up with the local shades of the aristocratic George Herbert, born in Montgomery, but also of Thomas Traherne, from Hereford, and Henry Vaughan, who came from Llansantffraed near Brecon.

Geography is an accident of birth, but Geoffrey Hill's determination to make meaning out of place aligns him with Bunting and Graham. *Mercian Hymns* (1971), still arguably his most widely read collection, seems 'accessible' because it weaves together contemporary provincial life and the Anglo-Saxon kingdom that once occupied the same territory. In these prose poems, his characteristically transformative thought is slowed down sufficiently to make sense to a general reader. The local and historical knowledge of the well-known opening hymn to King Offa is exact, rather than impressionistic. But it is a matter of ordinary general knowledge rather than the arcana of specialist study; the eighteenth-century Iron Bridge at Ironbridge Gorge in Shropshire was a landmark of the Industrial Revolution and the Welsh Bridge is in Shrewsbury:

> King of the perennial holly-groves, the riven sand-
> stone: overlord of the M5: architect of the his-
> toric rampart and ditch, the citadel at Tamworth,
> the summer hermitage in Holy Cross: guardian of
> the Welsh Bridge and the Iron Bridge: contractor
> to the desirable new estates: saltmaster: money-
> changer: commissioner for oaths: martyrologist:
> the friend of Charlemagne.

In 1971, when this book was published, the first eight miles of the M5 had been open for only eight years, while 'the historic rampart and ditch' of Offa's Dyke had been in place for twelve centuries. Here juxtaposing these two eras – with the pleasing resonances of anachronism that this produces for both – is enough to produce Hillsian transformation.

But that provincial boast ('desirable new estates') also tips its hat to the modernist ideal of progress and, despite the High Church rhetoric and political nostalgia of much that he has written since, I find it hard to read Geoffrey Hill's development as absolutely separate from that of Raymond Williams, the Marxist political theorist, who also grew up in a village on the Welsh Borders. Williams's father was the local railwayman, as Hill senior was the village bobby; and Williams's *The Country and the City* (1973) acknowledges his debt to the experience of growing up in this liminal territory, echoing *Mercian Hymns* in the way it looks both backwards and to the future:

> When I was born [my father] was a signalman, in the box in the
> valley: part of a network reaching to known named places, Newport
> and Hereford, and beyond them London, but still a man in the
> village, with his garden and his bees, taking produce to market on
> a bicycle: a different network, but it was a bicycle he went on, to

a market where the farmers came in cars and the dealers in lorries: our own century. He had been born as much to the land as his own father, yet, like him, he could not live by it.

Is Williams senior's 'network' in this passage a way out or a safety net? It would be easy to see Hill's early developed love of patterning as another kind of net, holding the speaker of his poems in place. Certainly, allusions pattern his next book, *Tenebrae* (1978). Its 'Pavans' and 'Chorale-Preludes' borrow Renaissance and Baroque musical forms. Respectively a sixteenth-century dance, and a congregational church form much loved by J.S. Bach in the seventeenth century, both originally invited participation. These forms signal the importance of the collective; although the poet's diction is already, at this stage, erudite and apparently unyielding:

> Splendour of life so splendidly contained,
> brilliance made bearable. It is the east
> light's embodiment, fit to be caressed,
> the god Amor with his eyes of diamond,
>
> celestial worldiness
> . . .

> ('Lachrimae: 2 The Masque of Blackness')

Interweaving and alternating world-views, this passage wonderfully compresses those two great Mediterranean cultures, Classical civilization and Christianity, which in past centuries arrived in Britain from the 'east / light's embodiment' – towards which churches still face. It also touches upon how 'blackness' contains all the colours of the spectrum. And there's more. These *Lachrimae* share form, subtitle and some individual 'number' titles with John Dowland's 1604 suite of the same name. A set of seven religious meditations, they further suggest the *Seven Last Words from the Cross*; conventionally the basis for a sequence of seven Easter sermons but also wordlessly 'set' by Josef Haydn and others.

Tenebrae also explores Victoriana ('Apology for the Revival of Christian Architecture in England') and includes a fifteen-part homage to Federico Garcia Lorca, 'The Pentecost Castle', in which the Spanish poet both becomes and does not become the figure of the murdered Christ. But such rich borrowings are not, arguably, the most important aspect of Hill's modernism. Ever since 'Genesis', the opening poem of his 1959 debut *For the Unfallen*, Geoffrey Hill has been a poet of big ideas; at first predominantly spiritual and lately, in the collections from 1996's *Canaan* onwards, political. In fact, he seems to make little distinction between these twin concerns: perhaps one grows out of the other. Certainly, in his extraordinarily sure-footed early work he seems to build a civic argumentation from a spiritual one, as in the perhaps-a-shade-too-precocious 'Two Formal Elegies: For the Jews in Europe': 'At whose door does the sacrifice stand or start?'

Faced with challenging topics, Eliot sought authority in impersonality – and in the borrowed voices of history. Hill combines these impulses, replacing Eliot's human chorus with abstract, impersonal forms on loan from musical history. Instead of a speaker, his poetry gives us *that which is spoken*; but, as befits contemporary anxiety, what is spoken is framed as if by quotation marks. Such a distancing device is profoundly modernist. The title of 'Florentines' (from *Tenebrae*) awakens near-Proustian memories of those crystallized biscuits. But the entire poem itself reads:

> Horses, black-lidded mouths peeled back
> to white: well-groomed these warriors ride,
> their feuds forgotten, remembered, forgotten . . .
> a cavalcade passing, night not far-off;
> the stricken faces damnable and serene.

This interplay of sound and lighting effects, and the archaism of the central image, combine to outsmart the sheer Martian brilliance of the description: the horses' 'black-lidded mouths peeled back / to white', a countryman's precise sense of the light and time of day, and the brilliant characterization 'damnable and serene'. These descriptions act like slow fuses run through the poem. Sound makes them seem more pattern than image: what Gerard Manley Hopkins called the vowelling-on of 'white: well-groomed . . . warriors' pulls the 'white' of teeth towards the warriors themselves. Alternating changes ring through 'night not far-off'. Sound also frames the ambiguities that surround the first line: of course, there are the 'Horses' with their teeth bared in their bits. But the comma that follows them allows for the possibility that the human riders, too, are baring their teeth. Horse or human flesh peeled back to white is skeletal. These horses can serve as memento mori; the 'cavalcade' can also become, as do all armies on the move, the horsemen of the Apocalypse. Criss-crossed with cultural resonance, Hill's 'Florentines' carry Dante's famous anomie into the poem because they are from his city; that they are probably Paolo Uccello's curvetting Florentine warriors in *The Battle of San Romano* is almost incidental.

Modernism's expansiveness allows this kind of crowding-in of meanings. But the sense of 'crowding' is most apparent in Hill's later collections. *Canaan* appeared in 1996 and thereafter came, in short order, *Speech! Speech!* (2000), *The Orchards of Syon* (2002), *Scenes from Comus* (2005) and *Without Title* (2006) and *Clavics* (2011). Though *Clavics* returns us to the world of Baroque musicology in both title and form, this run of books explores the state of a nation that has abandoned its spiritual values – as the Israelites did in Canaan. Britain is summed up, in Hill's *Canaan*, as a series of East Anglian 'Dark-Lands' in which Margaret Thatcher's Grantham 'rises above itself' but Ely Cathedral, the ancient seats of learning at Cambridge, John Constable's Dedham, and the homes of the *Pilgrim* John Bunyan and of the proselytizing Wesleys all seem engulfed by the symbolic, hellish flames of stubble-burning.

The *Canaan* poems do not attempt a dance, Baroque or otherwise. After all, pleasure is not the point of such verse; form is merely instrumental. Their diction is mandarin – 'One sees again how it goes', 'Consider now the valley / of Hinnom' – but they read more easily, more intimately, than the hundred and twenty clipped, twelve-line, not-quite-syllabics of *Speech! Speech!*, which sometimes push condensation over the boundary into hermeticism. Still these packed, often non-linear, ruminations contemplate, for example, the nature of God:

> In re: radical powerlessness of God
> to be reconceived. Not for millennial
> doom-mood, nihilism's palindrome,
> but for what it ís and we áre: no use
> against backed-up inertia, ignorance,
> proclivity . . .
>
>   (97)

This blocky read has no truck with fashionable vagueness or New Age 'spirituality'. Like a late Cartesian, Hill is only certain about what he's certain of: the method of doubt is always really a desire for certainty.

The following year, a similarly dense argumentation would characterize *The Orchards of Syon*. Yet its collection of seventy-two twenty-four-line poems in approximate blank verse relaxes the forcibly public diction (*Speech! Speech!* indeed) into a kind of daybook in this most English of metres:

> Downhill to go, then up the long curve of field.
> December chastens the stream bed; frosted mist
> hangs in autumn's leasowe; the far slope
> burns hazy yellow where it is spring . . .
>
>   (XXXVI)

Any contemporary British poem which opens 'Downhill . . .', and employs the first person, pays homage to Edward Thomas's 'The Owl', that epitome of his renovation of the part played by symbolic landscape in the English lyric tradition. 'Downhill I came, hungry, and yet not starved,' Thomas's piteous and prophetic war poem opens; and as the narrator rests in a pub he hears an owl's cry:

And salted was my food, and my repose,
Salted and sobered, too, by the bird's voice
Speaking for all who lay under the stars,
Soldiers and poor, unable to rejoice.

The modernist relationship to its material is conscious and conscientious. Even what appears involuntary should not be read as either oversight or an expression of the poet's 'authentic self': the modernist poem is 'authentic' to itself. Another example, the meaning smudges in that first couplet of *Speech! Speech!* 97: 'radical powerlessness of God / to be reconceived.' Is God simply powerless to be reconceived, or is it God's more general powerlessness that must be reconceived? And how much is this about the impossibility of a 'second coming'? But the double meaning is advertent: it alerts us to the doubled nature of incarnation, hinted at again in line four's 'what it ís and we áre'. In *Syon*, Hill uses the five-stress line of blank verse, but 'naturalizes' or interiorizes it by resisting the regular iambic stress. This isn't a failure of technique, but a cunning theft of the resources of a form whose discursivity and relative spaciousness allow it to present a very British kind of 'balance'. The formal 'keys' of *Clavics* are even more mischievous, relying as they often do on justified type and syllable count (even numbers only) to create thirty-two concrete-poetic 'keys': more than the twenty-four Preludes and Fugues of *The Well-Tempered Clavier*.

Geoffrey Hill's belief in a public role for poetry, however mischievously he executes it, is echoed in the work of Ian Duhig (*b.* 1954). Another Peter Porter protégé, Duhig is that rare thing in contemporary British verse, a working-class poet: in the particular sense that class-consciousness plays an important role in his writing. Such consciousness means thinking through experience *as* a member of a class, and is particularly significant for disempowered positions since it makes conscious to the individual the body of knowledge he or she does have – for example as a worker or someone subject to exploitation – and the authority that comes from those experiences. British poetry of class consciousness includes a fertile vernacular tradition: ballads, fishermen's shanties and work songs from industrial communities such as mining, as well as older songs about conscript soldiers and ruined servant girls. Alongside these are protest songs, from 'When Adam delved and Eve span / Who was then the gentleman?', traceable to the 1381 Peasants' Revolt, to the eighteenth century 'The Diggers' Song', an expression of that ruthlessly suppressed revolutionary movement. All these examples share an anti-descriptive, direct approach to telling. They also demonstrate the vernacular love of strict form: formal verse is not an effete bourgeois novelty. Metrical rhyming verse – with its heightened accessibility, its ease of memorizing and the straightforward pleasures of the sounds it makes – is anti-elitist. Its sound patterns are easily recognized and its authors, whether named or anonymous, reveal a craftsman's pride in the care and exactitude of their making: such crafty pride is central to much working-class consciousness.

Class-conscious poetry is inherently political; but not all political or protest poetry is class-conscious. Percy Bysshe Shelley, in 'The Mask of Anarchy' and 'England in 1819', is a revolutionary disgusted by the treatment meted out to ordinary working men and women; but he writes as an onlooker, his moral authority intellectual rather than derived from experience. Yet Romanticism did produce not only working-class celebrities like Robert Burns, but also poets who used their work to explore and avow an emerging class-consciousness. John Clare's poetry was a rural, William Blake's an urban, act of witness. It is as if Romanticism's stress on lived experience allowed them the first articulations of what Karl Marx would later turn into a systematic idea about the importance of self-realization. Recent British poets of class-consciousness have included Barry McSweeney, Ken Smith and Tony Harrison and – working a little earlier – Jon Silkin and Jack Clemo. Several Irish poets recall rural hard times but do so through wrong-end-of-the-telescope retrospect. It is a world they have escaped, usually through education; an exception is the working-class Galway poet Rita Ann Higgins. In North America, where segregation meant that race was an especially over-determining form of class, the legacy of class-consciousness in poets as various as Muriel Rukeyser and James Baldwin not only enabled the feminist poets of the Eighties and Nineties – Adrienne Rich, Maya Angelou, Maxine Kumin – but provided role models for British poets from backgrounds that were not traditionally literary.

Among today's fine mid-generation British poets who come from working-class backgrounds, however, only Ian Duhig takes this as his intellectual and conceptual standpoint. Although Paul Farley's lyric verse includes scenes from daily life, his poems do not *explore* class: which simply provides the characters and settings he uses. Don Paterson's early poem about his father's encounter with a patronizing shop assistant, 'An Elliptical Stylus', *is* class-conscious, but it is one poem within a body of work: 'I'd swing for him, and every other cunt / happy to let my father know his station, / which probably includes yourself. To be blunt.' John Burnside's prose memoirs are, of course, autobiographical, and much of his fiction has a post-industrial setting, as does much of Sean O'Brien's verse, which can be highly political and socially engaged; David Harsent adopts a general position of alienation. Women poets with a working-class background, like Kathleen Jamie and Sarah Maguire, often have other, related, concerns: Jamie's with the 'class' of gender, and Maguire's with ethnic, national and genetic identity.

Belief in social progress is a modernist idea and, writing from a life which has included fifteen years spent working with the homeless, Ian Duhig adopts neither an individualist confessional tone nor free verse, but usually metrical, often rhyming forms that draw from both past and present. 'Róisín Bán', from *Pandorama* (2010), seems at first glance to be a 'Lament for the Makers', the Irish navvies who built much of post-war Britain:

> The M1 laid, they laid us off;
> we stayed where it ran out in Leeds,
> a white rose town in love with roads,
> its Guinness smooth, its locals rough.

That Yorkshire 'white rose' and the proverbial alternation 'smooth'/ 'rough' are tropes as traditional as a bargee's painted roses. They lull the reader into a sense that this will be a bitter-sweet ballad of labouring life. But the poem turns out to be about the ascendancy of road-building over writing:

> Pulped books help asphalt stick to roads
> and cuts [*sic*] down traffic-sound as well . . .

This sleight of hand, the characteristic Duhig swerve that upsets our reader's sense of where the poem was taking us, gives the verse an almost jaunty edge.

In the title poem of *The Lammas Hireling* (2003) a farmer's loneliness turns the eponymous hired cowboy into a shape-shifter: at once a dream of his master's dead wife and a hare, the witchy beast of superstition. Perhaps Duhig's best-known poem to date, its lines have sometimes four, sometimes five stresses and it doesn't *quite* rhyme. But sonic and largely, though not exclusively, assonantal echoes mark the line-ends. For example, in the *heart/ cheap/ time/ cream/ company/ night* sequence of the first stanza:

> After the fair, I'd still a light heart
> And a heavy purse, he struck so cheap.
> And cattle doted on him: in his time
> Mine only dropped heifers, fat as cream.
> Yields doubled. I grew fond of company
> That knew when to shut up. Then one night,
>
> Disturbed . . .

In this poem, Duhig's swerve comes in the farmer's sexual confession, made using the terms of superstitions he would have had to hand:

> I knew him a warlock, a cow with leather horns.
> To go into the hare gets you muckle sorrow,

> The wisdom runs, muckle care . . .

The confession also uses homely, rural and tender similes – which their context of murder and magic transform into something brutal – to imagine that last shape-shift:

> I saw him fur over like a stone mossing.
> His lovely head thinned. His top lip gathered.
> His eyes rose like bread . . .

This powerfully characterized pragmatism, an imagination using what it has to hand, finely evokes the mindset of rural working life.

A deep thematic coherence characterizes Duhig's collections. *The Lammas Hireling*'s colour comes in part from its observation of cultural customs: it juxtaposes the local with the international, de-exoticizing what comes from further afield, and making strange what is traditional or local. *Pandorama* is unified by themes from construction: freemasonry, road-building and buildings themselves (sometimes appearing as boxes, as in the elegy for Michael Donaghy, and sometimes as towns). A deeper unity still characterises the book's long, reflective poems. 'Jericho Shandy', in blank verse, and 'Glass, Darkly', in rhymed iambic couplets, are cultural explorations so intricate they seem almost to create a hermetic mind-world. It can seem as if the rhythms, rather than its thinker, speak the poem:

> This Bradford route's a sideline to a sideline,
> sidelined now, reflecting on itself,
> he thinks, a black-silk-hatted parody,
> a *Soft Cell* synth man who only plays
> recessionals on his harmonium
> as doors close on the coffin and the flames.
>
>   ('Jericho Shandy')

Tim Liardet (*b.* 1949) is another mid-generation modernist who creates complete psychological worlds. *The Blood Choir* (2006) reconstructs a borstal and its mob mentality; his pamphlet *Priest Skear* (2010) the death of twenty-three Chinese cockle-pickers in Morecambe Bay in February 2004; and *The Storm House* (2011) the ramifications of a brother's mysterious death. As Duhig's brainy, foot-down writing is full of such literary and historical references as 'Glass, Darkly' – a homage to Vladimir Nabokov – so Liardet's is punctuated by allusions to visual art in particular. Sometimes these go beyond mere illustration and become structural devices: it's here that Liardet's modernism is most apparent. Frequently Futurist, occasionally chiaroscuro, his visual imagery can be jagged and anti-realist, almost cubist, as in 'A Futurist Looks at a Dog', from *To the God of Rain* (2003):

> I see instead every stride the dog has made
> in the last twenty metres at once,
> the sum of strides per second jumbled up
> on top of one another: its tail
>
> a cactus of wags, its rapid legs
> a sort of tailback of centipedes,
> a strobile of stunted steps, a carwash brush,
> two bleary propellers rotating

Liardet's early writing is often filmic. In *Competing with the Piano Tuner* (1998), his 'Mirror Angled at Sky' is:

>   . . . tilted as it is
> reflects every detail
> of onrushing sky – the gulfs of blue and weightless cumulus
>
> that drift like floes, that billow, fly, and break apart.

The glass may be static, 'dumped in the back of a Peugeot truck', but

seeing, in Liardet's poems, is always *looking*, an active search through
a multiplicity of images. This mirror 'reflects' not only 'every detail /
of onrushing sky', but also the slower movements of condensation on
and speckles within its own surface.

Doublings and reflections keep these poems in motion, often without
the need for narrative incident. But sometimes the camera holds still.
In 'Wormwood', a study of Welsh rain laden with radioactivity from
Chernobyl, Liardet holds the observer in place as the rainstorm comes
and goes, although an actual human witness would doubtless have
taken shelter from the weather that:

> Fuzzed in rainy farmsteads, then steadied,

> Then fuzzed again, then steadied, then vanished
> Into storm . . .

> The world drew near.

Liardet's descriptive doggedness echoes that of another modernist
forebear, D.H. Lawrence, whose verse observations of the natural world
refuse the old realist contract of simply naming things seen, and instead
try to *look at* them afresh, in overlapping, searching phraseology found
particularly in the creature poems from *Birds, Beasts and Flowers*.

Liardet's spatial imagination means that sometimes it's a virtual
microphone, rather than a camera, that he pans around a scene. He
is able to conceptualize time as space:

> Retracing a hesitant path where the steps were worn
> Uncle Henry for sixty years climbed the tower
> of a stammer, one step up, ten down, one up.
>
> ('Lumm's Tower')

But this preoccupation with artful observation changes, in 2006, with
the publication of *The Blood Choir*. Later, denser Liardet has

incorporated modernism's special effects, and they have become
psychological. The title sequence of *Priest Skear* – twelve poems of
nine couplets each – views the grotesque dance of drowning in close-
up: 'One filled-up glove is magnified / ten times its size; in two to
three minutes, the heads drop // and the hair sweeps up, beneath
an upstream of gas.'

Modernism is undergoing a revival. Some of the most exciting, and
very newest, poets emerging today seem to be searching for a poetic
resource capable of responding to the limp-on-the-page work of many
of today's performance poets. Toby Martinez de las Rivas, a trained
archaeologist born in 1978, practises a modernism of unashamed
'geological' density – piling allusion on allusion, the hieratic with the
historical. The effects are grand, but also, because of that density, gritty.
'Penitential Psalm' is clearly Hill-inspired in the way it recreates the
history of his native Somerset:

Fierce joy that is like retching, undo me. As a dead polity,

brick by brick, stitch by stitch, the squat, feudal tower at Langport,

or the drowned mole in this baptismal water, claws subtly demonstrative

of admonishment, supplication, *woefully arrayed.*   *My tender heartroot for thee brake:*

My tender heartroot for you in the brake of thorns,

                    and the desperate purchase of this falling metre, Laura.

Publishing his first full collection, *Confer* (2011), to critical acclaim
at only twenty-five, Ahren Warner (*b.* 1986) is, on the page at least, a
brainy flâneur who seems to have emerged fully formed. Already
fascinated by, and thinking through, broken poetic forms and continental philosophy when he was still in his teens, Warner is no scholarly
postmodernist mumbling to himself. His is an engaged, boulevardier's
voice. He may allude to philosophers and their ideas but, rather like
Peter Porter with his artists and composers, does so simply because this

material is within range of a well-stocked mind. His light touch with such material can be deliciously witty:

> **Between**
> the *barre* and the *grand battement en cloche,*
>   the *en dans*
> and the *en dehors* of last night's night-off
>   fuckathon –
>
> her room at the Grand hotel, the *première*
>   *danseuse*
> and me (mere *sujet*) grinding through first
>   to fifth
>
> and on to two positions in which she led,
>   never
> having studied – under or on top of –
>   J.G. Noverre
>
> <div align="right">(from <i>So</i>)</div>

A couple of years younger still is Chloe Stopa-Hunt (*b.* 1989), already publishing in periodicals as a fine critic and poet of striking promise. Her modernist approach to texture creates a colourist's scenography, with a floating, feminine inflection:

> It may be time, I said, to rise and go
> riverwards: to cease saying that the deer
> turning their heads as the car passes
> are a necessary comfort.
>   ('The Illustrated Compendium of Russian Fairy Tales')

With some of our youngest fine poets prepared to risk originality and flair in the face of dull conformity, the outlook for British verse in the next couple of decades is newly, and markedly, improved. But flair and originality come in many forms – as the playful virtuosos of the next chapter demonstrate.

10

POST-SURREALISM AND DEEP PLAY

Interviewed in *American Poetry Review*, the American poet Robert Bly talked about a 'new imagination . . . which allows the unconscious to come in with its various ignorances and brilliances'. He was identifying a particular kind of creative synthesis, one that goes further than mere description or even syllogism. In the kind of writing Bly is interested in, things are brought together according to a logic that seems incomprehensible until, once they have been juxtaposed, the links they make become vibrantly visible.

Not all poetry looks for quite this synthesis. Mythopoesis steps right across into the unconscious, using symbolic stories as entire metaphorical realms. Modernism simply doesn't take realism at face value. Surrealism probably comes closer than either of these to Bly's 'new imagination', because the 'various ignorances and brilliances' of the unconscious provide not just the poems' illustrations, but also their linking logic.

One obvious reason for bringing resonance into a poem is that the matter with which the poem deals may itself be resonant. The Belfast poet Medbh McGuckian's *The Book of the Angel*, for example, full of 'the agitation / of wingless angels throughout / the pathways of the world' ('Sagrario'), is an intense meditation on the mysterious nature of incarnation. McGuckian's humans, rather like those dreamed up by the radical novelist Elizabeth Smart in *By Grand Central Station I Sat Down and Wept*, are sometimes angelic; and her saints and angels are sometimes human:

The young saint is weeping

> at that view of the holy life
> in his mind, like brown wallpaper,
> and it is difficult to imagine
> how his body fits together
>
> in its heaviness and delicacy,
> the underlying silver
> of its conventional desire.
>
> ('Studies for a Running Angel: 2, A Chrisom Child')

Yet the angelic is also the unknowable and McGuckian's poetry reaches, repeatedly, towards that zone. She often uses the reasoned speech of step-by-step argumentation, but at the same time fills her verse with revelation's chaotic plenitude. 'Closed Bells', for example, has the rhythmic, grammatical balance of mid-period Seamus Heaney:

> they inspire
> devotion of a sort,
>
> using this world
> as if not
> using it to the full,
> a risky limbo.

But what opens this poem out is a sweep of onward connections, in which 'Frost hollows / small areas of leaf' become the poem's eponymous bells, which become the pulse in the human throat, which becomes love-making:

> movement towards
> a touch, with two
> five-nerved lips

> reflexed to form a star,
> or one indistinct nerve
> erect and desirable
> in your violet throat.

Yet each of these steps feels more associative than transformative. For McGuckian, mystery isn't found in metaphor's powers of change but in unexpected connections between what is recognizably local – the 'bronze-flesh-hook' of honeysuckle, a sunset, 'the stones pressed / on the fields' – and universal themes of birth, love, death. So it's no coincidence that she dwells on the Annunciation and the Resurrection, those moments that doctrine associates most closely with Christ's bodily incarnation. In 'Silva', among the trees – from which the Cross comes – wind is the 'self-reeling energy' of 'This graced world, / two thirds of the way out / on a spiral arm' ('The Saints of April'). Sensuous reality is amplified and becomes immanence: 'Saint Faith' laments that 'there were too many spires / and waves, more than my own footsteps.'

From the start an independent spirit, Medbh McGuckian (*b.* 1950) emerged in Belfast in the Seventies and Eighties, alongside her then-partner Ciaran Carson. Her first three books were published in England by Oxford University Press, but since the closure of that poetry list she has been published by the leading poetry publisher in the Irish Republic, Gallery Press. As this illustrates, for much of her working life the cultural and political position of Northern Irish poets has been complex, to say the least. And McGuckian's verse is deeply engaged, even as it refuses to simplify. Her writing wrestles the Catholic tradition it is infused by, for example, and does not override the questions of gender thrown up by that tradition.

The Marian shade of blue appears repeatedly in her work: it is the colour of mist, moon, 'the furrow of the graveyard', stones and angels, and can be seen in knitwear and marble alike. But her complex subject matter has not always been directly religious. In an interview with Shane Alcobia-Murphy and Richard Kirkland she says that:

a Christianity which is labelled or tattooed 'Roman Catholicism' . . . is fundamental to my work: it inhabits every poem. The births and deaths, the loves and relationships, all are viewed sacramentally, if I can. The idea of sin is never absent, nor the concern with salvation, nor the awareness of Christ's voice as poetry.

As this indicates, McGuckian's more than a dozen collections have also addressed family, womanhood, love and politics. But her trademark 'difficulty', whether or not it was developed in order to contain a complex relationship with complex beliefs, also stems in part from her layered borrowings. Sometimes she quotes 'the sources', the avid reading from which she systematically distills ideas, images and phrases almost directly. This imaginative pillaging echoes T.S. Eliot's 'raids on the inarticulate'. McGuckian's borrowings both raid the territory beyond poetry *for* the poem, and release the poem to go beyond itself. They allow her verse to conjure up a different kind of realism, one that portrays how complicated experience is. A similar sophistication operates in her view of gender. 'Turning the Moon into a Verb', the narrator admits, is:

> An image I have consciously
> Broken like a shoulder on your hearing,
> The inconstancy within constancy
> That is the price of a month.

'Inconstancy within constancy' is the doublespeak emotion adds to human thought; 'Turning the Moon . . .' an allusion to the menstrual cycle and its associated emotions.

Other poets use techniques related to surrealism primarily or solely to address questions of gender. Social authority can act like Plato's 'founding myth', legitimatizing and strengthening – or destabilizing and limiting – the speaker; as debate among Irish women writers about the public role of the poet, led by Eavan Boland in her groundbreaking essay collection *Object Lessons* (1995), points out. What happens, they ask, when that founding myth is destructive rather than supportive; for example when it places a speaker in a socially inferior position? Worse still, what if the individual poet's founding myth is something that cannot even be spoken of? Both Selima Hill's and Pascale Petit's serious playfulness seems to occur on some brink between certainty and existential uncertainty. Both have published work which suggests youthful experiences of sexual abuse. Founding myths define, and sometimes over-define, an individual's identity and self-consciousness. As if circling around what can and cannot be said, Hill and Petit have each developed a poetry led by fantastical, and fantastically juxtaposed, imagery.

But each does so in her own way. Petit is not surreal, as Hill can be. Instead, her imagery is striking for the intensity of its register, and its vividly sensuous qualities. In her childhood 'House of Darkness', obedience to a demanding mother is reimagined as service to a Mexican god:

> Silver bells painted on my cheeks
> so Mother could always find me,
> my hair cut, woven into hers.
> I polished the obsidian floor.
> The sweetness at the centre
> belonged to Tezcatlipoca –
> Aztec Smoking-Mirror god.

The pair also belong to different poetic generations. Pascale Petit (*b.* 1953) emerged fourteen years after Selima Hill (*b.* 1945), whose debut, *Saying Hello at the Station*, appeared in 1984. Yet they share a notable fervour; a kind of hyperbolic energy sharpens the edges of their imagery.

In a response to Frida Kahlo's 'Self-Portrait with Monkey' from Petit's ekphrastic collection *What the Water Gave Me* (2010), high-register verbs – *work*, *rustle*, *grip*, *yelp* – animate the verse:

> The bristles on my brushes work
> like furtive birds. Hours pass.
> When the painting starts to rustle,
> Fulang-Chang grips my neck,
> too frightened even to yelp.

This register is distinctive. None of the poets in this chapter writes the well-ordered, Aesopian fabulist poetry prevalent in communist Central Europe before 1989. Poets of the Cold War era, including Miroslav Holub, Wisława Szymborska and Zbigniew Herbert, were responding to their double-facing roles as 'unacknowledged legislators' within an over-regulated society. Compromised by censorship and oppression on the part of national regimes, yet aware of the importance their peers accorded to what they had to say, they wrote technically astute verse that could be read as parables about the state of the nation – or as about nothing at all. In Miroslav Holub's 'Brief Reflection on Cracks' (translated by Ian and Jarmina Milner), from *On the Contrary* (1982), 'Something cracks every moment because / everything cracks one day, an egg, / armour, a book's spine': is this a reflection on mortality, revolutionary sentiment or mere whimsical existentialism? By contrast, the wilfully scattergun British poetics of deep play embraces plurality and even a kind of artlessness. We might guess that this has something to do with a different kind of relationship with authority. Working under comparatively non-existent political restraints and yet surrounded by arguably greater social distrust of their role as poets, some British women writers seem locked in a self-doubt that's close to the obsessive self-questioning of postmodernism.

Deep play can release a fundamental rethink, and critique, of what goes on in verse. It's also often joyous, inclusive and highly energetic. In the Eighties and Nineties, when the poets featured in this chapter were emerging, Latin America was a breeding ground for the not-unrelated project of magical realism. In the American twentieth century the confessional poets – among them Robert Lowell, Anne Sexton and Sylvia Plath – presented stories of emotional experience as prior to logic. Their poetry makes sense: but the sense it makes is emotional. However, the roots of this writing go deeper than twentieth-century experiments in literature. An outlier exception to the Western European literary tradition of the male speaker is that cluster of mediaeval women mystics – from Julian of Norwich to Mechthild of Magdeburg – whose work was widely disseminated within their lifetime. Their use of a heightened, ecstatic register suggests that logic is a lesser truth than revelation.

Such affect-led writing, whether religious or emotional, carries the reader along by assent and feel. Its primary approach is not to build an argument or a progression; emotional momentum provides the forward movement. All guns already blazing from the first line, the poem operates a continuous state of intensity, rather than finding something out. The verse exists first of all to create its own tonal and emotional world. Everything depends on sustained register and vigorous imagery rather than formal patterning; the results can feel somehow simultaneous, even overwhelming. These strategies are borrowed by Selima Hill, Pascale Petit and Medbh McGuckian. Petit's 'The Mirror Orchid', from *The Huntress*, is as sustained in its intensity and the intensity of its observation as the rainforest bio-system it evokes. Its long-lined couplets overflow. Scale is also expanded and distorted by the child's-eye horror visualized from the opening line:

A megasaurian massif reared above our vineyard,
its reptile-scale thistles slowly opening and closing during siestas as if they
wanted to speak.

In the quarter-century since her debut, *Saying Hello at the Station* (1984), Selima Hill's equally intense voice has deepened and strength-ened; its subject matter widening from specific losses, such as bereave-ment or time spent in a psychiatric unit (*The Accumulation of Small Acts of Kindness* (1989)), to more general difficulties with romantic and family relationships and with the business of living. Despite these themes, she is funny and exuberant, juggling an outrageous symbolic lexicon as if there were nothing to it. *The Hat* (2010) offers the reader a set of gleaming miniatures, only two of which are more than ten lines long. Gold snails, 'be-jewelled' trout, horses, cows and cowboy country are among recurring tropes which, repeatedly rearranged, reveal a ceaselessly innovative imagination. For Hill, such rearrangement is metamorphosis. The same gold snails which rest 'deep within the glades of giant rhubarb leaves' in 'The Holy Brains of Snails' elsewhere 'encrust' a husband's body, and are used to 'grace the mouths of billionaires' in 'Aeroplanes'. Image pivots on description into another image, as if these transformations might continue indefinitely:

> Her heart is like a room full of roses
> that fall apart
> like dry white wounds;
> her heart is like a garden full of wounds
> that know that pain
> needs them and aches for them.

('Violence')

These rapid transitions make the verse a brilliant *moto perpetuo*; but consistency of register underlines the coherence of both thought and symbol. *The Hat*'s 'Goose Feathers', an explicit homage to Ovid's *Metamorphoses*, reminds us that the source of this coherence is the human emotional currency – the affect-value – of each symbol.

   Like the great Slovenian poet and former art theorist Tomaž Šalamun, whose work her own resembles, Selima Hill's starting point was visual art. Though she read Moral Sciences at Cambridge, she comes from a family of artists and writers, and married a painter. Also like Šalamun, she is a conscious surrealist (no paradox) who uses techniques of juxtaposition, interruption and symbolism – the whole dream vocabulary – to tell stories from the unconscious. These stories form universal, and universally recognizable, psychodramas. Hers is poetry of exacting emotional apprehension, lightly worn: 'Although she doesn't know what it is / she knows this isn't it / . . . Penetrative sex and housewifery / do not really interest her that much' ('Penetrative Sex and Housewifery');

'The man who burns her burns her all the time. / Why? / Because he loves her!' ('Turpentine'). It's important not to be distracted by the superficial flippancy that exclamation mark suggests. Like Stevie Smith, Selima Hill uses playfulness as a decoy while she smuggles in the 'blood and milk' of, as an apt title has it, 'Departing for Womanhood' (*The Accumulation of Small Acts of Kindness*). Like Smith's doodles, these apparently guileless lines are written in very dark ink. Hill's epigraph to *A Little Book of Meat* (1993) quotes what Flannery O'Connor's mother told her about femininity: 'If you need to ask, you'll never know'.

Such serious exploration is strengthened by characteristic use of book-length series of poems. 1997's *Violet* unpicks what has not yet been made conscious within a family, using action and emotion to stand for characterization. When 'My Sister Calls Me Darling', 'It isn't really me / she calls Darling / but another, better, sister / she's invented.' In 'Red Cows', 'I remember the day we got married. / Very nice. / Prettiness was all I thought about. / It never entered my head to think about *you*. / Who were you? / Were you there? / I can't think why.' *Portrait of my Lover as a Horse* (2002), with its chorus of 'Portrait' titles, is another book-length project. But Hill never repeats herself; here using the way that lovers see the entire world through their beloved in order to reconfigure that world with characteristic vividness. 'Portrait of my Lover as Hildegard of Bingen' imagines 'a constant supply / of uplifting musical instruments / shaped like intestines / made of beaten gold'. Far from being involuntary or baldly therapeutic, several of these poems draw on metaphysical tradition and address the 'lover' as 'Lord'; an approach echoed in the title of her Selected poems, *Gloria* (2008).

Despite this continual development and change, the extreme distinctiveness of Hill's technique runs the risk of making her work seem at first glance repetitive. Pascale Petit's poetry, which in storytelling reveals its emotion directly and explicitly, is a little less unusual. Perhaps this gives Petit more lateral room for manoeuvre, should she wish to take it. Her breakthrough came with her second collection, *The Zoo Father* (2001), a book of grief and fury about abuse by her father. But her first, much quieter volume, *Heart of a Deer*, published in 1998, starts a

sequence of volume titles which use images from the natural world. *Heart
of a Deer, The Zoo Father, The Huntress* (2005), *The Wounded Deer,* (2005)
The Treekeeper's Tale, (2008) *What the Water Gave Me.* Taken together, these
reveal a deep imaginative consistency (although the last collection takes
its title from one of Frida Kahlo's paintings). The violence and primacy
of the natural and creaturely world is Petit's 'muse'. It matches and
sometimes even trumps her personal subject matter, and seems to allow
her both a heightened register and an increased use of tonal colour.

The Huntress, a companion piece published four years after *The Zoo
Father*, addresses a difficult relationship with her mother. But Petit looks
beyond the family for female icons. In *What the Water Gave Me*, Frida
Kahlo seems to become a kind of persona, less role model than a
testing ground for ideas about the poet's self as damaged woman artist.
Petit's signature image-vocabulary is shared by the painter:

> When you came back to me –
>
> I painted a green day-hand and a brown night-hand
> holding up Mexico, her canyons and deserts,
>   her candelabra cacti.
>
>   ('The Love Embrace of the Universe, the Earth (Mexico),
>   Diego, Myself and Senor Xólotl')

The hands may have been painted by Kahlo, but the apprehension
that the cacti are like – or are – candelabra is Petit's. This ekphrastic
ventriloquism – one art form speaking through and for another – is
not a million miles from Medbh McGuckian's raids on her 'sources'.

Elsewhere, Petit adopts Kahlo's persona to explain how 'the visions
keep calving / like bergs of trolley-bus glass'. This is itself a 'calving'
image, in which things seen become icebergs become glass – and
specifically the broken glass of the trolley-bus accident in which Kahlo
was injured. The idea of 'calving' brilliantly symbolizes the way that,
in Petit's writing (as in Ruth Padel's), images seem to contain their own

similes already in embryo; and those similes, in turn, to contain others. This isn't a series of image relations like a set of Russian dolls, but something more asymmetrical. Each further simile has a relationship only to its immediate predecessor, and not to whatever that in turn was a simile for. Toppling chains of image-sense allow meaning to keep moving, rather than remain anchored and static. 'My Mother's Perfume', from *The Huntress*, offers a series of associations from the perfume the narrator's mother used to wear:

Even now, the scent of vanilla stings like a cane. But I can also smell
      roses and jasmine
in the bottle's top notes, my legs wading through the fragrant path,
      to the gloved hand emerging
from a black taxi at the gate of Grandmother's garden. And for a
      moment I think I am safe.
Then Maman turns to me with a smile like a dropped
      perfume bottle, her essence spilt.

These image-transformations are pushed into alignment by that final 'smile like a dropped perfume bottle': itself a simile which acts just like that dropped bottle, as everything spills backwards through the poem from it.

    The sequence tips to order to arrive at this point: the perfume's flower notes evoke the garden, which evokes the arrival of the mother, whose visit interrupts a period of safety with the grandmother, a happiness which evokes the fury of the mother, who is evoked by her remembered perfume. Writing like this must plan its trajectory some distance back, among resonances hidden within the original image. 'The Second Husband' performs a similar, if more joyous, trick. This almost-shamanistic poem enlarges the *felt* notion of a second chance at love being like something found under 'permafrost' into an image of a buried king who 'must have ridden . . . to heaven' – as lovers do, at least in metaphor – in a royal apparatus of beasts and a 'headdress with its gold foil frieze'. Petit's poetics operate not so much a symbolic shorthand as a symbolic longhand, building a highly distinctive world out of each nutshell.

Kathleen Jamie's poetry is marked by an equal force; even ferocity. In 'The Queen of Sheba', the title poem of her 1994 breakthrough collection, she doesn't so much play with, as seize on, a persona that will permit the kinds of greedy transgression women traditionally hope to disown. It is all cannily written in the third person. Or is the real presence here the crowd, that first person plural, which cheerfully disowns personal responsibility?

> Yes, we'd like to
>   clap the camels,
> to smell the spice,
> to admire her hairy legs and
> bonny wicked smile, we want to take
> PhDs in Persian, be vice
> to her president: we want
> to help her
>   ask some Difficult Questions

The verse is tight, rhythmic; almost jaunty. It announces that there will be no smudged notes in a narrative voice that hops in and out of accent: 'Stick in / with the homework and you'll be / cliver like yer faither / but no too cliver, no *above yersel.*' This use of dialect cannily implies the poem's not above itself, either, for all its wit. Nor is the even brainier 'The Way We Live', the title poem of Jamie's 1987 collection, with its speedy existentialism. 'Bash' and 'scary' give this a slangy, informal feel:

> Pass the tambourine, let me bash out praises
> to the Lord God of movement, to Absolute
> non-friction, flight and the scary side:
> death by avalanche, birth by failed contraception . . .

and gifted observation is hip to the small and larger details of everyday life:

. . . To overdrafts and grafting

and the fit slow pulse of wipers as you're
creeping over Rannoch, while the God of moorland
walks abroad with his entourage of freezing fog,
his bodyguard of snow.

Deeply playful poetry, because it disrupts logical argument, can be
over-associated by casual readers with confessions of emotion, or – far
worse – a lack of poetic control. But, like Medbh McGuckian with
her intricate evocations of mystery, Kathleen Jamie has a quite other
project. She allies fantastical, high-octane imagery with concentrated
diction to make clear that everything this speaker does is voluntary.
Description and vocabulary show her colouring-in her characters and
speakers, and their sometimes symbolic, sometimes realistic actions
and roles. The poetry repeatedly goes beyond mere reference to a full
realization, as if to help the reader discover that such lives matter.
Such writing is political, rather than simply an affair of the heart.
Unsurprisingly, Jamie has gone on to publish thoughtful, reflexively
political prose. Her account of travel in Pakistan, *Among Muslims:
Meetings at the Frontiers of Pakistan*, was revised and reissued in 2002. A
prose study of landscape closer to her own home, *Findings* (2005),
explores the exploited rural working communities of her native
Scotland; communities of whom her own family were part. She traces
the effects their labour has had on the environment, and those of the
landscape on them. *Sightlines*, her 2012 collection about place, has the
clarity and precision of her verse.

The precision of this concern with human interaction is equally, if
differently, apparent in 'The Galilean Moons', from her most recent
collection *The Overhaul* (2012):

Tell me, Galileo, is this
what we're working for?
The knowing that in just

> one Jovian year
> the children will be gone
> uncommonly far, their bodies
> aglow, grown, talented –
> mere bright voice-motes
> calling from the opposite
> side of the world.

This is replete with emotional intelligence, yet its gaze is never steadied but flickers – to the other side of the world, out into space, and back. Narrative presence is conjured by this movement; as it is elsewhere by other touching and tender poems of direct address. 'Materials' is both an out-for-the-day-together poem and nothing of the sort, full of existential risk pinned as a literal cliff edge:

And look at us! Out all day and damn all to show for it.
Bird-bones, rope-scraps, a cursory sketch – but a bit o' bruck's
all we need to get us started, all we'll leave behind us when we're gone.

For all that it's nested in human community, though, *The Overhaul* belongs to an older tradition than the lyric. Its slant titles – 'Fragment', 'The Dash', 'Five Tay Sonnets' – cannot disguise the fact that the body of the book is a *Bestiary*, that mediaeval form of wisdom poetry which turns creatures into part-symbols of, part-natural neighbours to, the human place in the cosmos. So these poems of beautiful variegation are in fact a celebration of order:

> When we first emerged, we assumed
> what we'd entered
> was the world,
> and we its only creatures.

('Swifts')

and:

. . . Already

the gulls shriek *Eagle!*
Eagle! – they know
more than you
what you'll become.

('Halfling')

With a characteristic transgressive spring, Jamie recruits plants – rose
and bluebell, a wood and 'some auld fairmer's / shelter belt' – to her
modern 'bestiary' too. The project's inexact: fluid and contemporary,
as good writing should be. And if some of its poetics seem to involve
an ecological witness which echoes Jamie's work in prose; well, the
ecosystem is perhaps our modern cosmogony.

Jamie's intelligence and discipline first made her an influential figure
as part of the New Generation. 'Ultrasound', from 1999's *Jizzen*, is
cross-hatched with allusion:

If Pandora
could have scanned
her dark box,
and kept it locked –
this ghoul's skull, punched eyes
is tiny Hope's,
hauled silver-quick
in a net of sound,
then, for pity's sake, lowered.

Most evidently, this hatching turns the womb into the original Pandora's
box. There's also the *et in arcadia ego* death's head that Jamie gives to
the image in the scan; that baby who, Christ-like and an infant
Everyman, is born to die. Also interlined here are quicksilver, images
of deep-sea fishing fit for the east coast of Scotland where Jamie was
then working, and a play on the cliché 'for pity's sake'.

In recent years Jamie has published more prose than poetry. Eight years separate *The Overhaul* from her previous collection, the prize-winning *The Tree House*. So she may not have had much influence on women poets who have emerged since the millennium, and who use forms of play and surreal imagery in their work. This new cohort ranges from Helen Ivory and Suzanne Batty, both in their forties, to Heather Phillipson and Annie Katchinska, graduates of the Faber pamphlet scheme, and Liz Berry and Emily Berry, relatively recent creative writing MA graduates. All are producing work that is somewhat whimsical; a kind of surrealism lite. They are not shoring fragments up against their ruin, or radically questioning orthodox coherence, so much as simply playing. Often charming and successful, the work employs an aesthetic, rather than a methodology. It's ditzy and frequently endearing: the verbal equivalent of boho chic. In Liz Berry's 'The Patron Saint of School Girls':

> My miracles were revelations.
> I saved seventeen girls from a fire that rose
> like a serpent behind the bike sheds,
> cured the scoliosis of a teacher
> who hadn't lifted her head to sing a hymn
> in years. I fed the dinner hall
> on one small cake and a carton of milk.
>
> A cult developed. The Head Girl
> kissed my cheek in the dark-room,
> first years wrote my name
> on the flyleaf of their hymn books,
> letters appeared in my school bag,
> a bracelet woven from a blonde plait.

This very feminized imagery – those school crushes, that 'one small cake and a carton of milk' – resembles less the furious psychodramas of Frida Kahlo than Leonora Carrington's delicate, whimsical, hybrids. Despite her own brushes with serious mental illness and war, Carrington, the English surrealist writer and painter, who lived from 1917 to 2011, reclaimed and juxtaposed images in often amusing ways, not least in fiction including *The Hearing Trumpet* (finally published in English in 1976).

Like a cabinet of curiosities, this technique invites images to cohabit. But what makes them match and belong is their very idiosyncrasy. The potential for mismatch is always already incorporated by this style. Disparity is play: not dissonant but a sign of liveliness. This is a feminine, conservative strategy, which joins up the 'more' of variety and makes it safely 'less'. It's a different game from that being played by Kathleen Jamie, Pascale Petit, Selima Hill or Medbh McGuckian. But it's not necessarily an unrelated one. We are still in a postmodern, as well as a post-feminist, moment. What was earlier deeply interrogated and hard-won is now available to browse and sample. Perhaps, after all, the middle generation are material enablers for the new decorative poetics.

Deep play is a strategy that has been adopted largely by women poets born since the Second World War. The division along gender lines is unusual. Only among the Oxford elegists and the modernists do strong female role models seem to be missing; and even here it could be argued that the modernist tradition in British verse has not only included, in the recent past, Rosemary Tonks (*b.* 1932) and Veronica Forrest-Thomson (1947–75), but has influenced contemporary poets as various as the early Gwyneth Lewis or Jo Shapcott. Whether consciously or not, surrealism and deep play echo the playful subversion embraced by feminist writers who came to prominence in the Eighties; not only the Parisian intellectuals who would explicitly influence radical women poets of the Eighties and Nineties, and their American peers, but British novelists like Angela Carter, Michèle Roberts and Jeanette Winterson. Apart from Selima Hill, who does belong to that artistic generation, British women poets largely took up this sense of the capacity of play a decade later. The transmission may have been a creative coincidence rather than a philosophical move, but it is easy to see how playfulness is most attractive for speakers, such as women, who have less – dignity, status – to lose.

The conspicuous exception to this pattern is the Pulitzer prize-winner, Princeton Chair and former Oxford Professor of Poetry, Paul Muldoon. It is impossible to ignore the influence of this tremendous game-player, on not only fellow Northern Irish poet Medbh McGuckian, or even simply the poets of this chapter, but nearly every poet writing in Britain today. Particularly since *Moy Sand and Gravel* (2002), Muldoon (*b.* 1951) has transformed himself into a trickster-poet, consistently pulling the riddling rug from under the reader's feet in collections which include *Horse Latitudes* (2006) and *Maggot* (2010), and in his lectures as Oxford Professor of Poetry, collected as *The End of the Poem* (2006). Exhilarating, dazzling: Muldoon's writing changes what literary language does as cannily as Samuel Beckett did and in analogous ways. It denies the usual affective grammar that allows statements to convey emotional and relational intelligence. World-class though he may be however, he has lived and worked in America for so long that we simply cannot call him a British poet.

It is to three poets who remain here, working on various margins of the contested parallelogram called Britain, that we turn instead. Ciaran Carson, native of Belfast, the Iranian-born Mimi Khalvati in London, and Dundonian Don Paterson have each been hammering out new approaches to strict form that seem to offer a curious counterpart or even counter-argument to post-surreal play. Perhaps it's no coincidence that poets in such edgy positions should work hard to develop a territory of certainty within and of their verse itself.

11

THE NEW FORMALISTS

Poets turn out to have several reasons for writing in the ways that they do. These include both a zeitgeist – whether that be the Festival of Britain or post-feminism – and the influence of writing from other eras. Sometimes, experience seems to trump all existing poetics, breaking them open and renewing them. That was the case with the Romanian Jew Paul Celan's fractured German verse in the years between the Second World War and his suicide; one thinks also of W.H. Auden's famous verdict on W.B. Yeats: 'mad Ireland hurt you into poetry'.

In contrast, because they argue that form is the very nature of poetry, the new formalists' writing springs directly from the way they view verse itself. Consciously taking responsibility for an active renewal within contemporary poetics, their writing and thinking is almost the complete opposite of today's widely published poetry of inertia. Often perfectly acceptable, if perhaps a little comfortable in tone, inert verse has something in common with the contents of a notebook. The writing, unformed although it probably includes pleasant enough lines, is produced by individuals who don't accept that making a poem involves transformational effort. If poetry is one kind of writing that somehow differentiates itself from others – surely a minimal definition – this could almost be seen as a disavowal of poetry itself. So it's hard to avoid the suspicion that sometimes verse remains inert simply because neither its own intentions, nor its author's, have become conscious. But an actual resistance to transformation may accompany a belief that what's important in a poem is its sensibility; and that such a sensibility needs to be somehow authentic to the author.

One result of such an almost childish 'accept me as I am' approach is of featurelessness. Like the woman who forgot her make up, this kind of poem does not *make itself visible*. It stays within the comfort zones. The verse is unformed, and the phrase-making and sentiments are off-the-peg. They appear as cliché within literary writing because they are, quite simply, cosy: middle-brow, anti-experimental, anti-intellectual and anti-formal. (The exhausted workshop forms of pantoum, villanelle and the palindrome verse, heavily reliant on repetition, add no formal 'charge', but simply prolong the text.) It is, alas, sometimes women who fall into the temptation of producing writing that remains diaphanous, under-resolved and, in the Mary Archer sense, 'fragrant'. Indeed, proponents of this kind of writing have been known to 'police' those who work a little harder, accusing them of 'writing like men'. This is a particularly unfortunate piece of false consciousness since, historically, the trail-blazing great women poets – from Elizabeth Barrett Browning and Emily Dickinson through Elizabeth Bishop and Sylvia Plath – have had to be consummate technicians and formal innovators in order to be heard.

Today, exploring and reviving strict form, Ciaran Carson, Mimi Khalvati and Don Paterson are leading the new formalism. While Carson experiments with a range of self-devised structures, Khalvati practises traditional discipline, using the sonnet and ghazal with fidelity to an immaculate ear. Yet it is Don Paterson (*b.* 1963), who has written specifically and polemically about the uses of strict form, who has become its leading contemporary practitioner-advocate. In 'The Lyric Principle' he says that:

> The most powerful mnemonic devices are brief speech, patterned speech and original speech. Brevity of speech is the poem's most basic formal strategy; originality of speech, its most basic literary

virtue; patterned speech, its most basic identifying feature. The mere act of making brief speech often produces both original and patterned speech, the former by expedient necessity, the latter by physical law. All three arise naturally from the compositional process, but we can also employ them as deliberate strategies . . . Language behaves in a curiously material-like way and, placed under the dual pressures of emotional urgency and temporal limit, will reveal its crystalline structure and intimate grain.

(Poetry Review 97:2)

Paterson's own formalism can be seen most clearly in his work since the millennium, where it emerges from the more generalized economy and focus of his first collections, *Nil Nil* (1993) and *God's Gift to Women* (1997).

A good place to observe this development at work is in *Orpheus* (2006), a version of Rainer Maria Rilke's *Die Sonette an Orpheus* (1922). All translation operates a system of concealed levers by which a translator pits his weight against the original; and when a poet as influential as Paterson squares up to one of the greats, something like a trial of contemporary poetics ensues. The fifty-five *Sonette*, written at speed while he was completing the *Duino Elegies*, concentrate Rilke's extraordinary, expansive metaphysical imagination, and his ability to render the material world hyperreal, within a more traditional form. They allow us to see Rilke (who would be dead within four years of their composition) as a post-Romantic; a post-Christian chromaticist who occupies a pivotal position at the entrance to modernity, rather as Gustav Mahler does in music.

Rilke – and by extension Paterson, himself a musician – seems to have little difficulty identifying with Orpheus. Though the poems of Part One are largely addressed *to* that 'lost god, you eternal trace' ('The Trace'), those of the second half come close to inhabiting the Orphic role. Such stakes are exceptional in contemporary British verse:

> Breath, you invisible poem –
> pure exchange, sister to silence,
> being and its counterbalance,
> rhythm wherein I become,
>
> ocean I accumulate
> by stealth . . .
>
> ('Breath')

This shift or enlargement is characteristic of Rilke's symbol-building. Characteristic too is a doubling, or doubling-back, of metaphor. By the end of the poem this list of the poetic qualities of breath itself includes what it has *been* all along, 'the leaf and rind / of my every word'. Translating such doublings requires real precision, yet at the same time a lack of laboriousness. His 'Afterword' tells us Paterson was aiming for 'just a little of the self-sufficiency of the German – meaning [a version] I could memorize, and carry round in my head.'

When a sonnet works, the whole sounds to one note. Paterson's versions vary in metre, rhyme scheme, tone and diction, though not in stanzaic arrangement. But virtually every one of these versions occupies its own tone and thought so thoroughly as to ring true to itself. To combine this with fidelity to the complex thought-progressions of the original is extraordinary. In some places, a patter of half-rhyme is almost subliminal: 'Mirrors: no one's had the skill / to speak about your secret lives. / Doors cut into time, you're filled / with nothing but the holes of sieves –' ('Mirror'). Elsewhere, as in 'Flight', the writing handles pun as if it were metaphor: while air's 'gracile and pliant' qualities unfold from 'wind's lass', the aspirant who must 'outstrip the weather / to be his flight's end' brings us both conclusion and purpose on this last word. Paterson's verse displays its usual hammered line of argumentation to 'praise all things wrested from doubt' ('The Sarcophagi in Rome'). But it also enlarges itself towards territories new to the poet – the rhythm of speech, the *purely* concrete apprehension:

I remember one Spring, in Russia . . .
It was evening, and at the first star

a white horse
crossed the village square, one fetlock hobbled
for a night alone in the field . . .

('Horse')

Perhaps it's not surprising that *Orpheus* seems to have led Paterson into a prolonged fascination with the sonnet form (he had already edited *101 Sonnets* in 1999). His *Shakespeare's Sonnets* (2010) is a geeky, idiosyncratic, *poet's* reading of that canon. It may have shocked some scholars – this intrusion of a real working apprehension of poem-building into the library must have seemed a threat to some of the archivists working there – but the book bravely attempts to build bridges between poems written 'then' and 'now'. Paterson's next move has been to embark on an extended sonnet sequence.

Orpheus left behind Paterson's earlier forays into translation whether true or imagined: from a 'Poem (after Ladislav Skala)' in his debut *Nil Nil* to *The Eyes*, his 1999 version of and homage to Antonio Machado. In these books, Paterson seems to be tracing a way to clarity and economy through pure fidelity to the sequence of images. It seems as though he is shaking off the hum of expression, the busy need to say things for and of oneself – which includes expressions of cleverness:

Traveller, your footprints are
the only path, the only track:
wayfarer, there is no way,
there is no map or Northern star,
just a blank page and a starless dark

('Road')

Distillation produces a poem that feels not cosy but inevitable: as if it had already been written. That in turn can seem close to a conservative sensibility – with which Paterson is increasingly charged. In fact, something more knowing and radical is going on. While the third line wakes up the 'way' in 'wayfarer', that word would be arguably too risky to use in a poem he signed as his own – as *contemporary*. Writing by way of Machado, though, gives the poet an alibi for big-breath words and the ideas this kind of note exacts from language. The poem's last line is riskier still: 'wayfarer, sea-walker, Christ'.

Here too, Paterson clarifies both his project and his view of poetry in an 'Afterword':

> This interdependence of form and content means that a poem can no more be translated than a piece of music . . . A poem derives much of its depth and complexity by developing the relationships between the vast entourage of semantic, acoustic and etymological friends, ghosts and ancestors that one word introduces to another.

We can see this idea pass over to Paterson's own poems. The dandified brilliance of his first two collections allowed casual readers to mistake him for a wizard of poetry lite. Very few of the pieces in *Nil Nil* go over the page: this crude thumb-measure instantly reveals a steely, wired-tight sensibility. Paterson's debut matters because it refuses to go with the grain of a then-usual rhythmic music, and because of a shameless brilliance to his phrasemaking. These often coincide. In 'Graffito', 'each dumb caress seared through him like sciatica' is a great description of the sexual jolt. So much the better that it produces the answering rhyme of 'her arse's silk-smooth hieratica', and though the rhyme *sciatica/hieratica* may be rhythmically untidy, that untidiness acts like an upward, opening inflection at the line's end. In the well-known 'Seed', about bachelor terror of Cyril Connolly's 'the pram in the hall', lines rhyme in pairs but the number of stresses in those lines remains uneven: 'it is I who just escape with my life. / My child is hunting me down like a thief.' Few young poets are prepared to be as confidently cavalier with slant-rhyme and metre, and the effect is expansive.

By *God's Gift to Women* (1997) this vigour has begun to infuse increasingly regular metre and a proverbial note. 'Buggery', in strict ballad-form, arrives on what is clearly meant as a poetic definition of the act – 'hold me when I hold you down / and plough the lonely furrow' – but also suggests a more general grief for loneliness unassuaged by love. Sui generis the book may be, but it is also host to a variety of tropes that run from volume to Patersonian volume. Orpheus makes his appearance ('The Undead'), as does the Alexandrian Library; Ladislav Skala makes another bow, in a self-referential piece which is indeed a 'Private Bottling'; while 'To Cut it Short' is an end-of-the-affair *'companion piece'* in both senses, as its epigraph states, to the first book's 'The Trans-Siberian Express':

> We may infer, from its caterwauling,
> its sugared windows and scorched livery,
> the grievous excess of its final night.

This is metaphor as code: the train engine and the sound of its brakes a stand-in for the soundtrack of break-up rows. The Paterson of this early-middle period is delighted by such codification, which also produces such textual jokes as the blank page of 'On Going to Meet a Zen Master in the Kyushu Mountains and Not Finding Him' or the mad place names of '14.50: Rosekinghall'.

Landing Light (2003) marks a transition, bringing that virtuosity to bear on increasingly complex material, including parenthood and fidelity. A more generous book in several ways – it is longer, and its emotions seem steadied by the often-extended pieces which make up those extra pages – it is also still the work of a youngish man in love with being on the road ('The Last Waltz', 'The Black Box'), with the idea of the guitar hero as Orpheus ('The Landing', 'The Box'), with sex ('My Love', 'The Wreck', 'Letter to the Twins') and – not least in another instalment of 'The Alexandrian Library' – with the glamour of writing itself. Iambic pentameter makes a more sustained appearance, inhabited with ease not only in the terza rima of 'The Last

Waltz', but in the six-page 'A Talking Book', which convincingly 'thinks aloud'. This is also the volume that cracks the carapace of poetic cool by including love poems to Paterson's twin sons.

Far from any Shakespearean emissary of gentleness, Paterson's *Rain* (2009) is grainy as a black-and-white movie: 'I love all films that start with rain'. Though the book extends and deepens *Landing Light*'s project, it is also a lament for Paterson's comrade-in-arms, the poet Michael Donaghy, who died in 2004. In the title poem, water cleanses a human state of something like Original Grief: '*all was washed clean with the flood / we rose up from the falling waters / the fallen rain's own sons and daughters.*' But the book's centre of gravity is the seven-part 'Phantom'. In a chiaroscuro meditation on presence and absence, 'The night's surveillance' denotes the way we're haunted by grief, fear and regret. Death undoes not only the self but the meaning that self brought to things: 'it reached into the room / switched off the mirrors in their frames / and undeveloped your photographs'. 'Michael Donaghy the poet' speaks to – and through – the grieving narrator. Like Dante's Virgil, he has become an expert guide to the nature of death, which is to say of life.

This is symbol-formation indeed. And, in a remarkably Hughesian foundation myth, '[Matter] *made a self to look at death, / but then within the self it saw its death; / and so it made a soul to look at self, / but then within the soul it saw its death; / and so it made a god to look at soul.*' What stops that *sounding* like Ted Hughes is Paterson's characteristic iambic metre, which evokes the authority, and the formalizing, distancing qualities, of tradition. But this is not traditional elegy, with its comforting closure. Paterson shines the 'black sun' of 'the void' on the living too: 'We come from nothing and return to it. / It lends us out to time . . .' Demanding not intellectually but emotionally, this troubled, troubling sequence is a contemporary, secular equivalent of Gerard Manley Hopkins's 'Terrible Sonnets'.

For all his light touch with precursors, though, Paterson is doing something all his own. *Rain* includes a cluster of poems 'after' (with Paterson, one can never be quite sure the original exists) Desnos, Cavafy, Li Po, Vallejo, Quasimodo and Robert Garioch. These versions reveal a poetry exploring and extending its capacities in the face of what a more glib writer might have called 'the inexpressible'. As in his versions of Rilke, the metaphysical tradition haunts the diction of poems such as 'The Error': which other contemporary would risk borrowing Eliot's 'eye-beam'? Here paradox, a form most associated with the Metaphysical poets, is transformed by a highly contemporary sensibility into images of opposition and reflection. For Paterson doesn't look for the nostalgic trope, but modernizes the past. That contemporaneity is showcased by the Forward Prize-winning 'Song for Natalie "Tusja" Beridze', a joyous master-class in rhyme and electro-geekery. Joyous too is 'The Handspring', with its 'world swung up on your fingertips'; as deft as the cartwheel it captures in four lines. In two other poems, 'The shudder in my son's left hand / he cures with one touch from his right' represents not only 'all / (thank god) his body can recall' of a momentary oxygen-starvation at birth, but a glancing tribute to friendship, 'the one hand's kindness to the other'. It's hard to imagine a more tender leave-taking than 'The Swing', a *man's* poem about a termination. These are lyrics, poems which perform the trick of simultaneous narrative that song lyrics so often stage-manage. A story is told as a situation that, replacing the straggle of 'and then . . . and then', encapsulates the narrative that has led to this point. It's the technique many a country-and-western songwriter adopts – think of songs like 'Jolene', or 'Angel of Morning' – not surprising, perhaps, given that Don Paterson has been an accomplished and successful composer and song-writer.

Mimi Khalvati's lyrics are also poised in a single temporal moment, but they work the opposite way, escaping story for the pleasures of pattern. There are artists in every genre whose work is neither argumentation nor narrative, but instead operates a series of tableaux. In operas including *Punch and Judy* and *The Minotaur* Harrison Birtwistle is fascinated by irreconcilable difference itself, rather than by character-led progression. Countless Romanesque and Gothic Madonna-and-Childs contain, rather than resolve, their moment of sacred-secular paradox. Arabic calligraphy, working in ways analogous to traditional textiles, allows the piece to be experienced *as a whole* as well as line by line. The register, range and indeed the beauty of what we might call

simultaneous art is various and complex. It is, though, less common
in the Western Enlightenment tradition, which tends to portray the
world as a linear series of problems and solutions. When it escapes
such concerns with progression, art presents us with the *given*-ness of
the world, and all that this may imply for fatalism, a tragic imagination
or even ego-lessness. The simultaneous is, therefore, the opposite of
trivial. But it is also rare in British poetry and, in a narrowed poetic
economy where a few models do wide service, Mimi Khalvati's whole
project, with its minutely attentive gaze, elegant diction and above all
rigour, has often been missed.

The title sequence of *The Meanest Flower* (2007) is a set of twelve
sonnets about childhood. Apparently autobiographical, they are also
an *ars poetica*, expressed in resolutely metaphorical, non-technical terms:

> For this,
> you are thankful: earth's horizontal shelves
> standing, like a glass museum case, open.

and:

> The garden is timeless.
> Time is in the refuse, recent, delinquent.

and:

> Cup your face as the sepals cup the flower.
> . . . This is a gesture of safety,
> of happiness.

'Frowning and impenetrable', childhood is invoked as the model of
how to let 'the earth's dimensions, / of which you know so little, rise
to greet you'. Each sonnet ends on the word 'open'. The 'Tintinnabuli'
of the Estonian Arvo Pärt are another model, revealing that 'the biggest
mystery in music / is something about . . . how to enter / a single

sound'. In this palimpsest poem, which uses multiple speakers, the composer:

> . . . has to love
> each sound, each sound – so that
> every blade of grass would be,
>
> Pärt adds, as important as the flower . . .

Perhaps it's not surprising that a poet who writes of echoes that she wants to 'reel them in / like a curing-song in the creel of my ear' – orchestrating a lovely curve of alliteration and rhyme – should recruit music to her cause. Painters, too, see as Khalvati would have us do – with 'the love you will lose'. 'How do you see this tree? Is it really green? / Use green, then, the most beautiful green on your palette' are the 'Lines from Paul Gauguin' on which she builds a pantoum bursting with colour.

The form with which Khalvati (born in Tehran in 1944) is most associated, though, is the ghazal. Chiming and melodic, hers differ more in diction than in sensibility from the poems that surround them. Something loose-limbed and playful seems to enter the line even of 'To Hold Me', whose sadness – 'I want to be held' – is subverted by exaggeration. In 'I want all that has been denied me. And more,' that last irrepressibility still makes us smile. But there's deprecation in these strategies, too; a refusal to *confess*. Sadness is cumulative in *The Meanest Flower*; coalescing in its third section around complex poems of motherhood. The illness which overtakes the poet's son has the savagery of a Massacre of the Innocents. Elsewhere, children are killed 'on old battlegrounds' or stare out of Sebastiao Salgado's Oxfam photos from the camps they live in. In a book remarkable for its sequences, the twelve-part 'The Mediterranean of the Mind' is a farewell to, and in memoriam for, the poet Michael Donaghy. Tenderness and deft evocation combine: 'Michael and Ruari / going down to the almond grove, // their voices drifting up from below.' As the beautiful mid-life poem 'Come Close' asks, 'What went wrong?':

> Some lives fall, some flower. And some are granted
> birthrights – a verandah, a sunken quadrant
> of old rose trees, a fountain dry as ground
> but still a fountain, in sense if not in sound.

This delicate image alludes to both the Eliot of *Burnt Norton* and, reclaiming her poetic starting point, to Khalvati's own childhood. Such in-every-sense reflective writing develops further in the largely sequential new poems which appear in *Child: New and Selected Poems 1991–2011*. Moving between North America, Crete, France and Spain, the extended perspectives of these reflections have been laid out by the slow processes of bereavement, loss and the passing of time. The long view they reveal is static, and shadowed like evening light: 'Come and sit here with me on the old stone wall, / half wall, half rubble' ('The Poet's House').

Earlier books contain the seeds of this approach. The first collection of Khalvati's mature middle period, *The Chine*, has a crown of lively, talkative sonnets, 'Love in an English August', which evoke the doubled stasis of late summer, and of an ending relationship. Encompassing 'Hatred, revulsion, rage', their two hundred and ten lines are sandwiched between iterations of 'Twice I've gone as far as the High Street phone' (this is, we suddenly realize, a volume published in 2002; a time, however, when even poets mostly had phones). The hermetic density of writing itself is evoked in 'Writing Letters':

> After chapel on Sundays we wrote letters,
> . . .
>
> Those who remembered their first alphabet
> Covered the page in reams of squiggly letters
> . . .
>
>   caught between
> two alphabets, the back and front of letters.

Appropriately, this poem is a sestina: that densely self-referential, inward-looking form. *The Chine* is full of such clues about the way a culture is reified by distance.

Whatever stops taking a live part in subjective experience does become an *object* of that experience. Even language gets denaturalized, ceasing to be representational and becoming ornamental. Which is not to say that it is trivial, but that it becomes a thing whose beauty is an end in itself. Sometimes, Khalvati wreaks this transformation on a single term – 'Darling' or 'Tenderness' or *'si morgh'* – and sometimes a whole meditation riffs like a *Samā* on an idea: about elephants or a daughter's pregnancy. The telling sixteen-line 'Lyric' is, not least by virtue of its title, a beautifully infolded *ars poetica*. While Don Paterson (embroidering William Carlos Williams) has called a poem 'a small machine for remembering itself', Mimi Khalvati here describes it as 'a small three-dimensional plane' with its own 'memory'. For her, 'the lyric is designed to be seen / against self', and is a vehicle for integration: since whatever can't be integrated 'flies out of frame'. In Khalvati's poetics, movement and mismatch break up a poem and its complex system of interdependencies. Therein lies the risk to this work, which could – were she to take her eye off the poetic life of the line – be tempted into self-restraint and false limitation. Instead, a subtle judgement keeps her verse taut and alive.

Ciaran Carson's debut, *The New Estate* (1976), appeared fifteen years before Khalvati's; but it was with his second and third collections, *The Irish for No* (1987) and *Belfast Confetti* (1989), that he shot to prominence as a poet who can make elastic connections between stories, scenarios, ideas and images. *Belfast Confetti* uses Whitmanesque long lines to shepherd literate, clever allusions and gritty reality. Sometimes these elements turn to each other and make a snug fit, as in 'Queen's Gambit', a poem about the game police, soldiers and terrorists play with each other, whose title invokes the British crown as much as a chess move:

. . . As someone spills a cup of tea on a discarded *Irish News*

A minor item bleeds through from another page, blurring the
 main story.
It's difficult to pick up without the whole thing coming apart in
 your hands.

But at other times the mix is less predictable. The poems are arranged
in sections which counterbalance their explicit Belfast settings with
Japanese verse epigraphs. 'Ambition' is a poem about the author's
father; it is also about the family's place in a divided society and –
circling deeper through the perhaps purgatorial circumstance of the
Troubles – mortality. At its conclusion, the poet's father isn't exemplar,
but guide:

I found him yesterday a hundred yards ahead of me,
 struggling, as the blazing
Summer hauled him one step at a time into a freezing
 furnace. And with each step
He aged. As I closed in on him, he coughed. I coughed.
 He stopped and turned,
Made two steps back towards me, and I took one
 step forward.

Fifteen years later, in *Breaking News* (2003), Carson (*b*. 1948) riffs on
the way that the streets near Queen's University Belfast (which the Seamus
Heaney Centre for Contemporary Poetry has formalized as a powerhouse
for contemporary Northern Irish verse) are named for towns in the
Crimea. In a riskily exoticizing strategy, he lets an account of that brutal
nineteenth-century campaign stand for the Irish conflict. This is not a
locked-tight metaphorical association – plainly the two conflicts had very
different forms and causes – but it is a loose association of clustered
resonances.

The 'otherness' of the Crimea – fruit rotting on hot quaysides, an unfamiliar language – is brought vividly to life; yet that life has something of the heightened colour of a film set or a nineteenth-century painting of some half-imagined landscape by Caspar David Friedrich. This East-West image transfer can make the post-colonial reader a little queasy. War is, like the past, a foreign country; but isn't it perhaps *more* foreign than a society that just happens to be bordered by the Black, instead of the Irish, Sea? When his verse-mystery *For All We Know* (2008) uses wartime France in a similar way, this feeling of unease subsides. It seems that Carson is, after all, simply using 'elsewhere' as a symbolic space – a place both for the imagination and for the concentrating power of symbol – rather than reducing particular examples of that space to exotica. The clear lines of well-known conflicts, whether the Crimean War or the Second World War, are there to help his audience 'read' what he wants to say about the Troubles. These symbolic equivalents aren't chosen at random: the Belfast street names show how Britain implicated that city in its imperial project. This kind of thematic interweaving, never explicated but tracing a pattern, has something in common with Khalvati's vision of the lyric as a self-referential unity. Like Khalvati's, Carson's books hold themselves in tension. But for both poets, themes – whether of individual or communitarian identity – are, though compelling, not the furthest extent of pattern forming. Pattern is revelation, after all: it is the *Aha!* of a completed, not a partial, vision. A sonnet becomes a sonnet when it clicks shut its final rhyme.

Formalism resists the timeline of conventional storytelling. Underlying all strict form is a poetics of simultaneity. The formal poem – even the whole sequence or book – has to exist entire in the mind's eye for the complete form to be experienced. This is a radically additional take on the old axiom that a poem should 'show not tell'. It means that, in formal verse, ideas *can* be directly expressed. Questions and statements don't disrupt the way the poem's material shows itself – and shows itself off.

Carson's *For All We Know* (2008) contains love poetry as elegant and mysterious as his heroine, Francophone Nina, whose perfume 'opens with luminous bergamot /and rosewood, developing a bouquet of gardenia, // violet, jasmine and ylang ylang'. But this verse novel is also an intricately worked psychological and political thriller, in which bombs in the streets of Seventies Belfast echo the firebombing of Dresden. An exquisitely layered narrative sequence is composed, in the tradition of Renaissance verse, around a series of formal conceits. Some of these are numerological. The book's seventy poems are a series of sonnets, double-sonnets and once even a triple, written in paired seven-stress lines and split halfway through the book into a second part whose titles repeat those in the first. This multiplication of governing sevens makes the sonnet form, with its traditions of courtship and love, the book's harmonic ground. It is joined and deepened by pairs: couplets, the book's paired sections and of course the two protagonists. Couplets often struggle, like couples, to come together. They also represent the Janus-faced coin of truth. And this is a marvellously shifty book, in which every narrative may be a lie – 'But was I really from Ireland? That was hard to believe, / my French was so good. Your French is very good too, you said, // I'd never have guessed you were from where you said you were from' – and even a love affair is composed moment by moment, like an alibi: 'this story we've been over so many times, inventing // that which we might have been . . .'

These formal games are the opposite of arid. As in a madrigal or parterre, intricacy heightens and illuminates the poems' flair and fetch. Another set of conceits are the book's recurring symbols: a watch, perfume, a patchwork quilt, a Mont Blanc pen, Bach's fugues, the French folk song which is one of the book's epigraphs. Repeated alone, each of these would be resonant; together they create a strategy that doesn't illustrate this shadowy story but deepens and complicates it. In a classic fugal displacement they serve both to evoke continental glamour and as palimpsest of a wartime past: in which that quilt was sewn by the heroine's widowed aunts; one aunt, 'who had died for the Résistance', also wore both the aptly named *L'Air du Temps* and the watch: 'Omega. White gold bezel / With black guilloche enamel inlay. Porcelain dial. // Arabic numerals, alpha hands. Seventeen jewel / movement.'

For All We Know is rich with mystery, wise to the shadows events and possibilities cast on each other; its writing coloured by a religious 'Lenten violet' and the 'Blue' which 'stands for eternity, its gaze plumbs infinity. // To penetrate the blue is to go through the looking glass'. But the book's resolution is satisfying and necessary even as it throws the reader back on herself and on big human questions about time, identity and the 'Forest of Language'. It's the uniqueness of its form, though, that is the key signature of Carson's work. He adopts a new pattern in every volume, and his relationship with formalism is a playful flirtation with many tropes and styles.

Perhaps this formal ease comes from Carson's other life as a performer of folk music; that Don Paterson has had a significant career as a jazz-folk musician lends substance to this theory. Mimi Khalvati, too, was first an actor and director, and it's hard to avoid the conclusion that she acquired an equivalent performer's sense of form through this work. Certainly, while the new formalists don't surrender to the kind of swoon, rap or riff so often associated with musicality in verse, theirs is arguably the most profoundly *musical* of today's British poetries – because it is structured by abstract form. Music is, after all, rarely representational. What it represents is *itself*. Understood as a term for abstract form, 'musicality' pushes its way into poetics somewhere between aesthetics and the legacies of particular poetry movements.

This thought is a useful introduction to the next chapter, which looks at the expanded lyric and its relationship to breath – and hence melody – and to the notion of improvisatory composition 'on the lips'. The new formalism and the expanded lyric, both deeply sensual poetics, face each other across a divide of balanced virtues. A lift-off of aural pleasure that is more than the sum of its parts, and the discipline of a poem's foundation in its own prior, abstract logic, are contesting yet profoundly important elements in the very best writing. One important question for today's poetics might be how to combine them in a genuinely contemporary way. Poets who have tried to do so in the past are as varied as Edward Thomas, with his 'sound of sense' and the Romantic poets, who tried to combine 'rapture' with blank verse and other strict forms – leading, at worst, to excessive length; a self-generating overspill entailing more – and more – lines.

Before moving on, though, we must briefly salute the impeccable verse of Wendy Cope (*b.* 1945), who attempts no such excess. Cope's readership, numerous and adoring, is the envy of most poets. It's easy to assume we know why this is. After all, the poems are often very funny and deliver their emotional intelligence as memorable bursts of pleasure. *Making Cocoa for Kingsley Amis* (1986) was a triumph of a debut, whose literary pastiches remain as finely judged and funny today as they were then:

> If men deride and sneer, I shall defy them
> And soar above Tulse Hill on poet's wings –
> A brother to the thrush in Brockwell Park,
> Whose song, though sometimes drowned by rock guitars,
> Outlives their din. One day I'll make my mark,
> Although I'm not from Ulster or from Mars
>
>   ('Strugnell's Sonnets' VI)

Yet Cope's real strength lies not in charm or insight but in the pitch-perfect exactitude of her writing. It's not only the formal technique that is immaculate; although she's glad to point it out, as in the wry model 'Villanelle for Hugo Williams': 'These lines, if not polite, / Will be of use, I hope. The rhyme-scheme's right.' There's more to Cope than the wit for which she's famous. She has also written confessional love lyrics, in *Serious Concerns* (1992). Her more recent and telling territory is a precisely captured autobiography. In 'Boarders', from 2011's *Family Values*, 'Copper' avoids the bullies who 'decided / That I used too many long words'. She is avoiding them still: 'I soon learned not to. / Look at how I write.' It's as important not to be confessional as it is not to stand out: 'Tears disarrange / my manners.'

Cope is an acute, if not an innovatory, formalist, but it's not just good behaviour that makes her a significant presence in British poetry. An author whose pillow talk includes discussions of rhythmic variation truly understands that the poem is in the art. 'At the Poetry Conference' is a long-distance love poem – 'I need to write a poem but I've written it / Already: 1989, LA' – which consoles itself:

> . . . You see I'm alternating
> Two kinds of rhyme, the way you recommend.
> I trust you'll give these lines a Grade A rating
> And that of course, will cheer me up no end.

Like all formalists, Cope reminds us that poetry brings form to chaos: 'I'm living with Uncertainty and Fear. / I need to say their names and make them rhyme.'

12A

THE EXPANDED LYRIC

An unintended consequence of the recent interest in formalism – and perhaps, too, of the patronage system that can arise all too easily in a writing workshop culture – is the caution audible in some contemporary verse. No doubt the forgotten majority of poets in any era are poetically well-behaved. But there are striking echoes, in some of today's writing, of the Georgian moment in early twentieth-century verse. Then, one response of British poetry to the hurly-burly of a new internationalism – not least the shock of the First World War – was a careful, conservative turn towards nuanced perspective, and traditional form used without bombast. That turn would generate both the lyric lucidity of Edward Thomas and, in a slightly different key, Ivor Gurney; and the more limited, even inhibited, verse of Lascelles Abercrombie. A century later, recalibration in the similarly overwhelming era of globalization has given us Don Paterson, and those of his peers who favour thrilling clarity over a loose and rather risky grandiosity. But it also seems to have left us with the oxymoronic concept of a cool poetry, limited in affect and range. This makes a poetics which has the kind of capacious generosity that Les Murray calls 'sprawl', or Edmond Rostand's Cyrano de Bergerac 'panache', particularly significant.

Bold, and even radical, lyric expansion has become a flamboyant presence in the centre ground of British poetry. Recognizable by its unusually rangy scale and wide, synthesizing intelligence, the expanded lyric often enters contemporary verse speaking with an Australian accent; although I suspect that British practitioners, certainly of the established middle generation, may see themselves as more influenced by a varied North American pantheon that includes Robert Hass, Anne Carson, Kay Ryan and Jorie Graham. Both inter-continental traditions belong beyond the remit of this book, but it's important to note the particular context created by the exuberant eco-riffs of the hugely productive Australian John Kinsella. He combines profound intelligence, political conscience and a sort of Shelleyan rapture in a fast-moving hyper-lyric which prickles with detail and idea. Even the lyrics of recent collections like *Shades of the Sublime and Beautiful* and *Armour* display a speedy brilliance that sometimes seems as though it 'doesn't touch the sides' of their lyric music. More level in tone, but thoughtful and capacious, are Kinsella's compatriots Martin Harrison and Chris Wallace-Crabbe. Perhaps the best-known of this quartet, Les Murray, has not only produced *Fredy Neptune* (1998), a great war novel in verse, but expanded poetic convention to include his own signature view of the world; one that is animist-autist and strangely literal.

Also beyond the geographical scope of this book, Paul Celan's European heirs, descending by way of Ingeborg Bachmann, are highly significant but, being largely female, are often overlooked as an international school. Nevertheless, they include the Slovak Mila Haugová, a major figure in Central Europe, and her literary heir the Slovak-Slovene Stanislava Chrobáková Repar and, in France, Claire Malroux and – largely writing prose – Hélène Cixous with her 'strategy of celerity'; not to mention a wider international tradition that takes in poets like Gloria Gervitz in Mexico. Perhaps it's no coincidence that the two British poets most identified with this kind of writing, Lavinia Greenlaw (*b.* 1962) and John Burnside (*b.* 1955), both have unusually strong European links: Greenlaw has lived in Europe, Burnside is a linguist by training, and both have won major European prizes for their work.

How easy is it to import literary influence? In the five collections published during the first decade of this century – the prize-winning *The Asylum Dance* (2000), *The Light Trap* (2002), *The Good Neighbour* (2005),

Gift Songs (2007) and *The Hunt in the Forest* (2009) – John Burnside's
expanded poetics are immediately visible. Long, often stepped lines, in
poems that frequently work as sequenced lyric interludes, take up
spacious room on the page. There's a lot of white paper: it suggests
air, space or a resonating chamber. This space between and around
the lines means that, even at a distance, these 'early-middle' poems
appear under-determined. On the other hand, they guide the eye, and
in that sense 'conduct' the reader. The stepped lines, in particular,
resemble arrows:

> He has come to a halt in the woods:
> snow on the path
> 				and everything gone to ground
> in its silken lair;
>
> gone to ground
> 			or folded in a death
> so quiet, he can almost taste the fade
> of hair and vein
>
> 						('Saint Hubert and the Deer',
> 							*from The Hunt in the Forest*)

The effect of following these directions for reading is so clearly musical
that we should better call them scoring.

   To obey their musical logic, though, is to listen-in on an accelerated,
slippery tunefulness. This poetry's central gesture is a kind of topple,
something utterly removed from the steady gait and equalizing tensions
of pentameter. John Burnside is a poet of surrender. Far from producing
certainty, his writing is continually in flight from it, as if from a false
consciousness. Each image is a temporary habitation, if not for meaning,
then for reflective awareness:

> Something that runs to copper
> or cornflower blue,

> a live creature bounding away
> from the glare of my headlamps
>
> and, when the engine stops, a sudden
> quiet that waits to be filled
>
> by owls, or cicadas;
> . . .

This passage from 'Dirt Road', the third part of 'By Pittenweem' from *Gift Songs* (2007), is about both one single instant of glimpsing, and a whole series of experiences: one colour, then another, 'a live creature bounding away', headlamps, sudden quiet, owls, cicadas. These can't be integrated into a single picture but instead track the consciousness that bounds from one thing to another: the true 'live creature' of the poem.

That kind of bounding trajectory might appear to refuse the poem's basic task of unity, and it can certainly seem as if a Burnside poem also escapes from *itself*; a sensation underscored by virtuoso use of extended, sometimes poem-long, sentences. ('Dirt Road' is one such. The 'By Pittenweem' sequence contains several sentences of more than a page in length.) But unity isn't stasis, and these concertinaing techniques heighten what we could call longitudinal unity. One part of the poem is explicitly joined to the next – couplet, stanza, phrase – by *aural* logic.

In part this is achieved by the rhythmic balance Burnside's phrases strike. In the opening couplets of 'Stalkers', from *The Hunt in the Forest*, the balanced alternation of two-stress, three-stress lines is further inflected by nursery anapests:

> Tell me again
> the stories you tell a child
>
> when the season begins
> and the hunters are out on the moor

Often, though, that balance is less regular:

> . . . That *self* is metaphor
>
> and what he mistakes for himself
> > and the presence he loves
> are different
>
> > as emptiness and form
> give rise to one another ceaselessly
>
> the shaper shaped
> > the lines
> identical.

('The Myth of Narcissus', II, from *The Good Neighbour*)

Here the to-and-fro of phrases – with lines stepped even across the stanza break – satisfies because the sense it makes is ear-led. Though not grammatically independent, each phrasal line represents a 'step' of understanding. In fact, the absence of an active verb in the two final phrases has a unifying effect, making them seem 'brushed in the same direction'. The sense of movement is reinforced by the oscillation when first *sh/a* and then *i/l* sounds and signs are repeated. That repetition also means each phrase must slow to mid-line pause between *shaper* and *shaped*, and *lines* and *identical,* creating a sense of something that is as much separate as joined.

This is no accident: the half-line is the secret generator of much British poetry. Its twin roots can be found in the assonantal forms of Anglo-Saxon and mediaeval Welsh verse, and in the parallelism of psalmody, widely adopted in Christian liturgy. In assonantal forms the second half-line repeats the sound, in parallelism the sense, of what has just been said. Burnside's decompressed lyric frees itself from the obligation to keep looking backwards through repetition, but it retains the cumulative impetus that comes from a shared 'direction of travel'. This doubling impetus, that second bounce at the line's caesura, also characterizes the work of poets as various as David Harsent and Geoffrey

Hill. It is in Burnside's work, though, that its role as accelerator emerges most distinctively. In large part this is because his poetry strips out many of those grammatical and semantic structures, such as qualifying clauses, that might set up cross-rhythms to the line's trajectory.

This constant longitudinal shifting is reflected in the poet's characteristic chain-link imagery, which sets up a continual transfer of imagistic, and often metaphorical, currency. Conventionally, poets enter a metaphor and then leave it after a short or extended passage, closing it behind themselves as if this were a particular kind of parenthesis that had opened up within the poem. Rather than generating a narrative or ideational movement, in other words, the metaphor traditionally drops anchor at one expository spot. Contrast this with the movement of sequential metaphor that the Russian Acmeist Osip Mandelstam discusses in his 'Conversation about Dante':

> Imagine to yourself an aeroplane . . . which in full flight constructs and launches another machine. In exactly the same way, this second flying machine, though completely absorbed in its own flight, manages to assemble and launch a third. [This] assembly and launch . . . forms an absolutely essential attribute and part of the flight itself . . .

In a sequence which works just this way, Burnside's 'Ars Moriendi . . .' – in 'An Essay Concerning Time' from *The Hunt in the Forest* – the art of dying is 'Like going to meet a friend / . . . though no one is there, at last, in the quiet room / that so much resembles / the room you have just abandoned'. Or else death, or the room, is like the 'space long-abandoned' of a 'hut at the end of the track / that runs through the woods' where among souvenirs 'a music that nobody hears' comes in through the open door. Each of these images – the feeling of anticipation, the empty and the familiar rooms, the hut at the end of the track, the unheard, mysterious music – both links back to the start of this thought sequence as a direct metaphor for death, and is a simile for its own immediate precursor.

The insights that result are evanescent and also evasive, a recurring
fantasy of escape through dissolution: 'the shift / from here to there,
from near to almost gone' ('Kronos'). They portray a world of flux and
dream, whose sources may be as various as drug culture (as the poet's
second volume of memoir, *Waking up in Toytown* (2010), suggests) or
scientific ideas of flux and contingency. But Burnside is also establishing
a position in relation to meaning-making. Like much secular spirituality,
his ecological, almost pantheistic beliefs are undoctrinal, even anti-doctri-
naire. His poems rarely state beliefs or arrive at conclusions, either
narrative or intellectual. The 'Essays' in *The Hunt in the Forest* and the
major, multipartite 'Responses' and 'Four Quartets' of *Gift Songs* – his
most explicitly theological and philosophical book to date – are expansive explorations rather than narrowing to examination and solution. In
this he is part of a wider tradition. In late-modern European philosophy
both Friedrich Nietzsche and Martin Heidegger struggle against a
prevailing belief in the truth of labels: what their inheritor Jacques
Derrida would call a 'metaphysics of presence'. Their prose tied itself
in knots as it tried to avoid treating language as 'true'. Burnside's poetry
is unknotted and jargon-free, yet it allows us to glimpse how words might
be contingent, fleeting devices for dealing with the world. Composing
'on the ear', he is a Shelleyan whose strategic evocations of speed bring
together the flux and contingency of the world and of experience. That
poetry must be in and of its world, and that the world it responds to is
unstable, is a modernist insight. But if Percy Bysshe Shelley was in some
ways neo-modernist, John Burnside is a late Romantic, who looks to his
own responses to replace both an absent God and the realist contract.

The much-awarded *Black Cat Bone* (2011) suggests a return to more
apparently conventional verse forms. There are fewer stepped lines in
this collection, and some poems – 'The Listener' and the stanzaic
'Pieter Brueghel: Winter Landscape with Skaters and Bird Trap, 1565'
– are baldly columnar in a way that almost seems like an exasperated
challenge to conservative readers, as if the subtle delineation of half-
line breaks had been brusquely redrawn by yoking everything back to
the left-hand margin:

. . . something like the absence of ourselves
from our lives,
some other luck
that would not lead
to now.

and:

the long-dead blanking the roads
and everything
disloyal to the earth
it came from . . .

('The Listener')

The book's two most significant poems, though, are both written in tercets. Of these, the introductory five-part 'The Fair Chase' is a cross between ballad and folk tale in which the protagonist, a sort of holy fool – 'flycatcher, dreamer, dolt, / companion to no one, / alone in a havoc of signs' – observes the hunting traditions of family and community, and 'becomes / the thing he kills'. This kind of transubstantiation isn't new in Burnside's work, but its explicitly *narrative* working-out – owing as much to Ovid as to the Hungarian Ferenc Juhász and the Brothers Grimm as to his own distinguished parallel career as a novelist – is a seam he's left largely untouched in verse since the title poem of *The Asylum Dance*. That much-shorter piece, written a decade earlier and in loosely blank verse, shares the narrative structure of 'The Fair Chase': in each, the critical encounter is succeeded by an extended, dream-like longing for reprise. Burnside's 'pearl-effect' sensibility is well-adapted to this patterning of regret.

Yet *Black Cat Bone*'s most important departure is the poem in which the eponymous Bone makes its appearance: the thirteen-line 'Hurts Me Too'. If this love poem is a sonnet – its opening declaration *I love my love with an X* repeated at the traditional point of the sonnet turn – it is one that has been exploded. Its dispersed sense, in the second stanza for example –

> Rain on the yards; a cuckoo in the meadows;
> I look in my bed tonight
> > and find
> my brothers and sisters gone

– is retroactively gathered to the explosive point of the last line:

> she thinks [my mouth] is safe
> > until I drink her in.

Something has broken through both form and register, and the stippled grace of much of Burnside's earlier verse falls away at its blunt touch.

Perhaps, it has taken so long for a group of poets directly influenced by Burnside's work to appear because the project of joining multiple impulses to each other, rather than focusing on a single principle as lyric has largely done, is profoundly thorough-going. We can glimpse its radicalism through Anthony Caro's analogous role in shaping British twentieth-century sculpture. As a lay audience, we automatically think of sculpture as a single, unitary density; Caro transformed all this in the Sixties, when he started making sculptures, such as the famous straggling red forms of 'Early One Morning' (1962), that display a *series* of impulses. Whatever the reason, it is very new poets like Maitreyabandhu and Kim Moore, poets of light touch like Janet Sutherland, and the secular visionaries A.A. Marcoff, Alan Stubbs and David Briggs, whose work most distinctively exhibits the kind of scope – in theme, flexibility of image and movement of thought – Burnside permits. Although it is too early to know whether, and how, their work will develop, these writers are recognizably Burnsidian in their use of the suspended grammatical phrase and 'floating' imagery to evoke the underdetermined nature of experience or, in the case of Maitreyabandhu, an ordained monk who runs the London Buddhist Centre, of spiritual enquiry. Maitreyabandhu has also learnt from Burnside's use of colour and his unexpected, almost category-busting, similes for mood or feeling:

just *there*

like the shadow of a church

or a quiet brother.
And how I saw you, in the mess of things,
was as a slant of grey,
the perfect grey of house dust,
an absolute neutral, with no weaving,
no shimmer of cobalt
and light years away from Byzantium.

('Visitation')

Lavinia Greenlaw does not belong among Burnside's disciples. On
the contrary, her influences come more directly from European intellectual and musical culture. Especially since her third collection, *Minsk*
(2003), she has experimented with liminal themes and a suggestive
stepping back from regular metre. Though she doesn't replace conventional forms with conspicuous formal gestures of her own, as Burnside
does, this quiet clearing away of the particular music and associated
expectation of much formal convention has made space for a subtle,
exploratory poetry to emerge.

Greenlaw's subject is often the underdetermined element within an
experience. In *The Casual Perfect* (2011) the sequence 'Winter Finding'
reveals a 'watercolour' landscape of estuaries and shores: 'Maeshowe',
'Fal Estuary', Blakeney Point' and 'Severn'. 'Blakeney Point' opens,
'Such constancy is no celebration.' The 'constancy' in question is,
presumably, that this point of land continues to go out to meet the
sea, since the poem continues, 'Under this careful light / it is only
earth we walk on.' This delicacy is always at risk of inundation. In the
next poem, 'Severn':

Each time the tide overtakes itself
what's worked loose is moved inland
on river over-running river

This is a fine description of the mysterious, almost paradoxical, sight of the Severn Bore overtaking itself as it races upriver. But the meanings of these poems aren't always so straightforward. Back at 'Blakeney', in the poem's resolve,

> A cure for the visible.
> Fern seed gathered in this midsummer midnight
> would render us as clear.

Fern seed, in superstition, conveys invisibility, not visibility; so this 'clear' means a clearing of everything away, not the kind of 'getting things clear' that we associate with puzzles and questions, such as the one that directly precedes this stanza: 'Is this love?'

If not quite concerned with actual self-extinction, these middle-period poems do feel attenuated to a point of extreme fragility. Why is this? In the magazine *Mslexia*, Greenlaw has talked about writing *The Casual Perfect* out of the resonant fuzziness of language, rather than from its simple denotative capacities: 'My sense of it was of words that are deep in the shadows of themselves and so carry a feeling of still emerging "out of the impenetrable wood".' The collection also evokes other marginal landscapes – a Siberian spring in 'Otolith', the distinctive smell of air 'On the Mountain' – and several poems are set at night or dusk. What all these settings have in common is that they are, bluntly, hard to see.

A poet's themes don't necessarily form part of a poetics, but here the preponderance of ideas about ungraspability, mutability and absence does amount to a project. Greenlaw's poetic concerns in this collection are with colour and mood, and with the mystery or the incomprehensibility of much experience – which renders it inarticulable. It matters that words are 'deep in the shadows of themselves' because this reveals something about the world. Perhaps it also suggests something about the nature of poetry. Maybe, like John Keats, Lavinia Greenlaw is using 'doubts and uncertainties' to create poetic breathing room. Or could it be that this is a complex poetry of disavowal, which is trying not to say what it has to say: replacing 'This *is* love' with 'Is this love?' for example? 'A Circle Round Our House', at the collection's conclusion, describes how:

> Because we do not live together, we describe a circle
> round our house. Like the unpaid milkman
> we hurry past . . .

Sometimes, these poems seem to 'hurry past' bald truth or confession, to the welcoming shelter of aphorism or beautiful phrase-making: 'How long the sky retains its brightness / when sky is so much of it'; 'the hidden continuous'; 'I take a drink to fix myself inside / what's left of night'. They have moved a long way from Greenlaw's 1993 debut *Night Photograph*, whose fine, quiet yet compacted diction tells history stories ('The Patagonian Nightingale'); borrows fabular forms from both the European Aesopian tradition and the more playful, and local, poetry of her then-editor Christopher Reid ('The Astronomer's Watch', 'Night Parrot', 'Moby Dick Suite'); and includes travel poems like 'Anchorage' and 'Linear, Parallel, Constant'.

It's an irreproachable and then-fashionable mix; but interesting poets are always more than simply irreproachable, and Greenlaw was here already rehearsing the privacy, mystery and a kind of looping metaphor that have come to mark her work. In 'Galileo's Wife', for example, simple costume drama is transformed:

> He can bring down stars.
> They are paper in my hands
> and the night is dark.

This opening tercet, with its innocent-seeming, almost monosyllabic diction, takes three giant steps. In the first line Galileo's star-mapping is metaphorically transformed; then that metaphor is either enlarged – as 'paper' star charts – or overstepped, as the image is turned inside out, so that a man's gifts (achievements) are measured only by whether they are gifts (presents) for his wife. The third line takes another step: back to stargazing and at the same time – 'the night is dark' – into a sexy suggestiveness. Yet all of this is a prelude to a feminist fable in which Galileo's discoveries are in fact his wife's. Still, the telling is unschematic; and this doubling, as much as the frank mystery of her recent poems, has Lavinia Greenlaw pushing sideways at the lyric line. Through radical under-determination of both form and content, she allows the lyric to expand into a suggestion of enormous capacity. And this, of course, is what the expanded lyric is *for*.

12B

THE EXPLODED LYRIC

Because the lyric tradition conflates poetry's music and its sense, an expanded poetic line is all too easily heard as something that destabilizes conventional meaning. John Burnside's and Lavinia Greenlaw's verse may be rich with *particular* themes and resonances, but it doesn't have a complicated *relationship* to those meanings, which it denotes and evokes in the conventional way. Yet any deviation from straightforward realism seems to arouse anger or even fear in poetry commentators. It's as if such alternatives as dream, thought-experiment or abstraction are too complex even to contemplate. Yet – forms as various and familiar as instrumental music, the dramatic monologue and confessional verse have long shown – there's a great deal more to artistic convention, across all genres, than simple reportage. Experiment is often dismissed as 'postmodern', but a conscious postmodernity already exists within contemporary British poetry.

The tradition of the exploded lyric demonstrates how arbitrary the relationship between words and the world they're supposed to describe can be. Putting sense in question like this entails an implicit, and sometimes an explicit, critique of most mainstream poetics. The techniques this tradition adopts are not new, but they are radical in the narrower sense of forming part of a continually reactive practice. The exploded lyricists see themselves as engaged in critique, in a way that no other contemporary school does. They mark out an alternative poetic lineage, identifying themselves as the heirs of a discrete set of radical traditions.

Although British radical poetics of recent decades have largely been concerned with the impossibility of communicating and denoting, radicals who emerged in the Sixties, like Harry Fainlight (1935–82) and Barry MacSweeney (1948–2000), by contrast practised a kind of hyperbolic 'over-saying'. That plenitude – of words and possible meanings – has been succeeded by what can seem like dearth. In a second moment, in the Eighties and Nineties, it is a poem's silences that make space for multiple meanings, as in 'The Separable Soul' by Elisabeth Bletsoe (b.1960):

> seepage

> like the memory of water
> an interstitial filtrate between stones, within speech

> the weight of absence,
> of meaning implicit in

> these empty spaces

In this century a third moment in post-war radical poetics has arrived, and is characterized by a kind of 'automatic writing' that seems to mimic the generative capacity and quasi-autonomy of the digital realm. Poets, some of whom founded Reality Street and Equipage, and others who are associated with another independent press, Shearsman, are interested in 'gesture', 'trace' or 'text': in what we might call the *outside* of the poem, as it runs through a series of grammatical tasks or takes up space on the page, rather than in the possibility that it might in itself create readerly experience, evoke insight, give pleasure or even argue a case.

Unifying these radical generations there is also J.H. Prynne: long seen as the central figure in radical British poetics, not least because of his widely documented generosity as a teacher at Cambridge, where he is a Fellow of Gonville and Caius College. Like John Fuller in Oxford, Prynne has gained disciples among his students. He has also developed wider regional loyalties; befriending Barry MacSweeney, for example, when the latter was training as a journalist at Harlow Technical College. But Prynne's poetry itself displays a mandarin, leaderly quality. His diction is formal, richly furnished and not at times tremendously removed from that of Geoffrey Hill. He has also achieved real literary longevity: his first collections, *Kitchen Songs* and *Day Light Songs*, appeared in 1968, and he is still publishing at the height of his powers today.

Prynne's contemporaries in the radical Sixties were rather more creatures of their own era. Barry MacSweeney's 1997 *The Book of Demons*, which appeared towards the end of his abbreviated life, was named for his battle with alcohol; a struggle as public as Harry Fainlight's had been with drugs and bipolar illness. Despite their differing backgrounds – the Anglo-American Fainlight was a brilliant Cambridge undergraduate, while MacSweeney grew up in a working-class district of Newcastle and left school at sixteen – both poets emerged from the new egalitarianism of the Sixties. For, as society grew more flexible, figures like R.D. Laing encouraged its mainstream to believe that psychological 'demons' could be part not of pathology but of personality: *The Divided Self* was published in 1960, and Laing co-founded the experimental community Kingsley Hall in 1965. Recreational drug use became increasingly public. Instead of being marginalized, troubled individuals could be admired. These attitudes gave permission for a certain amount of acting-out by artists and entertainers. They also encouraged an interest in Outsider Art, especially work by people with mental health problems: paintings and drawings had been archived by asylums since the nineteenth century and Roger Cardinal's 1972 book *Outsider Art* brought Jean Dubuffet's theories of *art brut* to an English-speaking public; by 1981 Victor Musgrave had founded the Outsider Archive.

A frequent symptom of bipolar disorder is an inability to distinguish between internal and external stimuli: the cliché of 'hearing voices'. During my years spent working in this field I found that

writing by people who are in the acute phases of illness often takes
the form of stream-of-consciousness fantasy; it resembles those
'internal out-loud' monologues which are a symptom of the condition. The note of such writing may be highly focused, for example
by repetition and heightened register, but its relationship to things
external or prior to it, such as accurate observation or logic, is
profoundly unstable. Just like visual *art brut*, it occupies the very
threshold between conventional denotation – a shared language game
in which the group understands what the individual is saying – and
the private dream-life of symbol or symptom. This makes it extraordinarily seductive for poets.

In one of MacSweeney's versions of Apollinaire, posthumously
published in *Horses in Boiling Blood* (2003):

> We want new sounds not neat Faber and Faber
> We want new sounds no Simon Armitage
> with hands in the pockets of his suit in Paris
> half a pound of badly fried chips on each shoulder
>
> I say: Fight the language which is nailed and then driven down!
> ('Victory Over Darkness & The Sunne')

Echoing *art brut*'s pre-war discovery by modernist artists like Pablo
Picasso and Joan Miró, but working in tandem with popular music of
the Sixties and Seventies, MacSweeney's poetry borrowed tropes of
delusion and hallucination to 'fight the language which is nailed and
then driven down'. This could lead to a wild lyricism:

> Hammers and pinions, sockets, fatal faces
> and broken bones. That was after Pearl.
> All mornings the sapphire sky, judge wig clouds, here
> to Dunbar, made especially gentle because
> turned left towards Ireland and soft rain, air delicious
> with scent of borage and thyme, dreaming, dreaming,

dreaming and dreaming of Pearl. She gripped her Co-op coat
and she gripped me, bonds not lost in azure eternity.

('Pearl And Barry Pick Rosehips For The Good
Of The Country')

Part of the wildness of this writing is to be found in the sheer range
of its images. The diction – nothing more complicated than commas
separates the elements of what is, in fact, a list – suggests an artless
tumbling together of figures and sensations that have 'raced by like a
Hexham builder's van / late for lunch'. But, in fact, the juxtapositions,
like that of the blue 'Co-op coat' and 'azure eternity' are absolutely
artful.

Here and elsewhere, MacSweeney repeatedly yokes 'the emotions
of literate people' to 'my often gobsmacked face'. The gesture is partly
aesthetic, partly political. He was, with Tony Harrison and Ian Duhig,
the major poet writing directly about class in post-war Britain, but he
also sets up a non-stop oscillation – between the 'poetic' dream and a
sometimes brutal quotidian – that allows the writing to keep revisiting
archaism, and indeed beauty:

O just to vex me inside the bottle the wind stayed still,
and left correct my cheap Woolworth accoutrements.

('Up A Height And Raining')

Uncompromising juxtaposition and lengthy, often over-comprehensive,
sentences are nothing new in twentieth-century verse. They're central
to the rhetoric of the Beat poets, whose appearances in Donald Allen's
1960 *The New American Poetry 1945– 60,* and at 1963's takeover of the
Albert Hall for the International Poetry Incarnation, seem to have
opened the door to the publication of more radical forms in the UK.
MacSweeney's own first book, *The Boy from the Green Cabaret Tells of
His Mother,* appeared from a trade publisher, Hutchinson, in 1968,
and in the US in 1969, and was accompanied by the kind of

reputation-manufacturing publicity (an appearance in *Vogue*, candidature for the Oxford Professorship of Poetry) we tend nowadays to associate with a post-Nineties loss of literary innocence.

Though it adopts a flexible inner/outer boundary, Beat poetry resolves this flexibility *within* a relatively straightforward relationship to language by owning its confessional element. The narrator of a poem like *Howl* is an 'I', substantially characterized by the text. MacSweeney, too, writes almost exclusively in the first person, but in his poems subjective apprehension leaks into omniscient narrative. There isn't always a character located within the text who is 'having' these sometimes idiosyncratic insights. In 'Demons In My Pocket',

> The emerging lance-heads of the chives are so
> beautiful tonight . . .

works straightforwardly enough, because that 'tonight' locates the speaker within the frame of the poem. But something else is happening in 'Sweet Jesus: Pearl's Prayer' also from *The Book of Demons*, with its strange paranoia:

> When the borage flowers closed at night
> she moved against me, rain lashed facing
> west to the law, whispering: There is so much
> wickedness.

For a more dangerous legacy of the Beats than hyperbole was their fetishization of personal dysfunction. Harry Fainlight, who spent three years in New York from 1962, recorded this fascination in poems like 'Mescalin Notes' and 'The Spider', which describes an acid trip:

> So is my spiderhood a whole new mythology – a cavern full of
> wicked sisters, a whole new breed of them mutated by this new
> hallucinogenic vitamin which I hereby christen SPIRITLECT

Fainlight also participated in the zeitgeist in happier ways. In New York he had contributed to *Fuck You* magazine and become friendly with Allen Ginsberg, who called him 'the most gifted English poet of his generation'; in London he co-founded *International Times* and took part, though not comfortably, in the Albert Hall Incarnation. His Cambridge friend Ted Hughes even asked Faber to publish him, but the young *poète maudit* repudiated the gesture.

This was an overwhelmingly masculine scene; though MacSweeney had the good taste to marry not one but two fellow poets, Elaine Randell and Jackie Litherland. By contrast, many of the most interesting figures to have emerged during radicalism's second moment in the Eighties and Nineties are women; among them Wendy Mulford (*b.* 1941), who had already published three volumes in the Seventies, Denise Riley (*b.* 1948), Frances Presley (*b.* 1952) and Elisabeth Bletsoe (*b.* 1960). Riley's other life as a theoretician casts some light on this apparent coincidence. One enduring legacy of *les événements* of 1968 was the rise of a generation of women philosophers and psychoanalytic theorists working in France during the Seventies. By the Eighties, Julia Kristeva, Hélène Cixous and Luce Irigaray had all appeared in English-language editions by pioneer advocates like Toril Moi, Mary Eagleton and Gillian C. Gill, and were influencing feminist scholars – and so, university students – and writers in the anglophone West with their critique of the realist contract. Importantly for poetry, their work combined to suggest that using language as if it can map reality is just one practice, rooted in a particular belief system. The increased attention to the music, resonance and sheer pleasurability of language that they offered in place of these beliefs was clearly encouraging for serious, bookish young women interested in verse. However, some of this thinking went one step further. The essentialist idea of 'writing the body' suggested that women could and should use language in ways reflecting their experiences of embodiment. A resulting interest in transgression, playfulness and the impossibility of trusting language formed the background to the work of European women poets born in the Forties and Fifties, like Antonella Anedda and Mila Haugová, who play with symbol and disrupt the lyric line: using for example stepped lines, spaces and inverted brackets. A parallel movement in North America, whose most consistent expositor is perhaps Jorie Graham, has been similarly informed but looks back further, to the famous gasping fractures of Emily Dickinson's verse. Showing the reader that some things (horrifying inhumanity, or the nature of God) really are inexpressible, this approach takes the evocation of mental processes as the basis of its poetics.

The British mainstream has not yet admitted women with similar ideas. The bully boys of the blogosphere, who call this kind of writing 'Burnside lite', simply assume a male poet is being imitated. But as Denise Riley asks in 'Oleanna', 'suppose you stopped describing / something, would stopping free you from it, almost as if it hadn't happened?' In Eighties and Nineties Britain such work got written anyway, but it was kept in the radical margins.

In her theoretical prose studies *War in the Nursery* (1983) and *Am I That Name?* (1988) Riley expanded her critique of the assumption that things have stable identities which can be fixed by a name. She pointed out that this would have to include the 'identities' of selves, too: I know to whom the name 'Fiona Sampson' refers, but I certainly don't feel identical with the person I was ten years ago or in my teens or childhood. Similar concerns are worked through in Riley's verse. 'Dark Looks' opens:

> Who anyone is or I am is nothing to the work. The writer
> properly should be the last person that the reader or the
> > listener need think about
> yet the poet with her signature stands up trembling, grateful,
> > mortally embarrassed
> and especially embarrassing to herself, patting her hair
> > and twittering If, if only
> I need not have a physical appearance! To be sheer air,
> > and mousseline!
> And as she frets the minute wars scorch on through the
> > paranoias of the unreviewed
> herded against a cold that drives us in together . . .

This is a funny as well as apt description of the public world of poetry. The poem's long sentences and lines – especially their loose-limbed enjambments, that imply something is being tossed over the line's shoulder like a throwaway remark – suggest languid, dry observation. But, of course, 'the poet with her signature' comes straight from the author's theoretical concerns (*Am I That Name?* indeed), as does her character's ambivalence about embodiment: 'patting her hair', yet wishing, 'if only / I need not have a physical appearance!'

Much of Riley's writing concerns the impossibility of human contact or communication. In 'Oleanna', a poem about looking, naming and communicating, spectacles are a symbol of this impossibility: 'Steel-rimmed the hole at the centre / through which all hopes of contact plummet down in flames.' In 'Knowing in the Real World':

> I'm not outside anything: I'm not inside it either.
> There's no democracy in beauty, I'm following
>
> human looks, though people spin away, don't
> be thrown by their puzzling lives, later the lives
>
> secrete their meaning. *The red sun's on the rain.*
> Where do I put myself, if public life's destroyed.

For all their poetic caution, these are big-picture, universalizing claims.

At first glance, then, Frances Presley seems a more conservative poet. But her anti-photographic approach to landscape evokes both a consciousness that has become disunited and the contingency of such external stimuli, however beautiful:

> *Here ti (l) la*
> my deepest breath
> startling deer

> stertling roil
> on the ridge
>
> she's here at last
> the 'veiled lady'
>
> shepherde of the stream
> no strange or rambling . . .

('West Anstey Longstone', from Lines of Sight, 2009)

Perhaps not coincidentally, this is close to the reflexive, ruminative work of post-war French poets like Yves Bonnefoy, who had been the subject of Presley's MPhil thesis. Its understatement and apparently fragile, fragmentary lines conjure what is inconstant, rather than what is certain, in experience. Such writing is antithetical to the Romantic tradition, which though it too explores the effects of a place on an observer, rather than the place itself, assumes those effects to be a continuing given – to be 'true'. In Percy Bysshe Shelley's 'Mont Blanc', William Wordsworth's *The Prelude* or even in Samuel Taylor Coleridge's 'Kubla Khan', landscape is an external, character-forming principle.

Presley's mildly spoken uncertainty has more in common with the work of her peers like Wendy Mulford whose 'Goblin Combe', written in the Seventies, was published in *and suddenly, supposing: Selected Poems* (2002):

> in the steep always damp of the gorge-cleft
> the violet-bunch clinging at the rockface wild
> garlic & uprooted hellebore –
> such richness is & light why do our days stony?

These destabilizing line breaks ('at the rockface wild / garlic') and grammatical compressions ('why do our days stony?') suggest the slipperiness of experience. They also evoke in turn the work of Gillian Allnutt, fine poet of the numinous:

delphinium

the heart, fleet, in its large domain

a *grand meaulnes*

summer, recalled, a light blue lent sea

of dust and shadow, now, the house

of doubtfulness

                                                        ('in her kitchen')

Yet Allnutt (*b.* 1949) belongs in the lyric mainstream, alongside other masters of the carefully poised, expanded lyric. Though her work proceeds by evocation rather than logical argument, it evokes images from the concrete world. Moreover, these images have a transparent emotional logic; which is not to say that they are unsubtle or clichéd, but that her line breaks (and increasing use of double-spacing to underline those breaks) serve as a rhythmic guide to their unfolding connections. Rather than mystifying or disrupting itself, her verse encourages us to follow the imagery's rhythmic logic.

Allnutt's proximity to this second wave of radical poets indicates just how much their work shares with the conventional lyric. Specifically, there is a care for tone and a delicacy in the selection of both image and vocabulary. This careful interplay of poetic elements has been overthrown by the new, reactive poetry. Angry not-so-young men – like Keston Sutherland (*b.* 1976), a senior academic whose career was launched with a doctoral thesis on *J.H.*

Prynne and Philology, Chris McCabe (*b.* 1977), who occupies a senior position as Joint Librarian at the UK's national Poetry Library, and Matthew Welton (*b.* 1969) – whose second collection, titled *We needed coffee but we'd got ourselves convinced that the later we left it the better it would taste, and, as the country grew flatter and the roads became quiet and dusk began to colour the sky, you could guess from the way we retuned the radio and unfolded the map or commented on the view that the tang of determination had overtaken our thoughts, and when, fidgety and untalkative but almost home, we drew up outside the all-night restaurant, it felt like we might just stay in the car, listening to the engine and the gentle sound of the wind* appeared in 2009 – are unafraid of resistance. In fact, they are particularly interested in writing that resists what they see as the mistaken beliefs of other linguistic and poetic ways of working. Patterned sound, and sense sustained for more than one phrase at a time, are often put to one side in the cause of non-collusion in such beliefs. To the usual problematic attempts to define what makes a poem, this group seems to add a definition of their own: a poem is a text which renounces any other discursive purpose.

A long untitled poem by Keston Sutherland, published in 1998 in the Australian magazine *Jacket*, starts:

> To evade cinereous ice which cut
>   back repro were they set
> up for retraversing as
>   if incomparably or mute her
> skips a beat, recall it were the attached
>   remit-plaudition to faded
> trust to appear refreshed, her for
>   skips back put allayed in
> stantial, should there ever be
>   come back as a choice, now I adore
> her will not be remote fast to
>   hide which cut
> remark . . .

Serious thinking underpins what is a postmodern project of continuous play. This writing continually eschews anything beyond the surface of language: such as the possibility that the meaning each phrase brings with it willy-nilly, by virtue of language's denotative history, might become a starting point for the next. But after all, play *within* language is *not* limitless: it has to retain certain configurations of grammar and vocabulary in order to *be* language rather than the oral nonsense linguists call lallation. Perhaps it is more useful to think of this kind of poetry as a *practice*, one whose poetics may exist more in the process than the product. It bears comparison with the process paintings of an artist like Jackson Pollock. An image such as the famous *Blue Poles* (1952) may be the traces of a process, but the process is one that has knowingly introduced a pleasurable coherence of rhythm, texture, form and colour. The newest radical poets on the other hand resist pleasure, in either sound or content, seeing it as one of language's old tricks. The result is a text that can only 'play' – and therefore only 'happen' as postmodern poetry – for the poet himself, as it is being written. .

It is a relief, therefore, to turn to J.H. Prynne, whose work from more than four decades exhibits the kind of characteristic, unifying tone we call 'voice'. J.H. Prynne's is alert, intelligent and *sensible* in the original sense. In the young poet, its busy, renovatory quality is equally evident through the questioning 'thinking aloud' of *Kitchen Poems* (1968):

> As you drag your feet or simply being
> tired, the ground is suddenly interesting;
> not as metaphysic but the grave maybe,
> that area which claims its place like
> a shoe . . .

> ('A Gold Ring Called Reluctance')

and the thin-skinned poise of *Day Light Songs*, published in the same year:

> The leaves make drops, drop
> > down the great
> tent of falling, the
> > twigs are inside
> > us, we the
> branches beyond which
> > > by which through which
> > ever the
> > > > entire brightness ex
> > tends

In this untitled 'song' Prynne makes explicit how radical poetry takes notice of the way image and symbol form part of, rather than existing independently from, the observer's mind: 'we the / branches . . . through which / [the] brightness ex / tends'. Such attentiveness is a far cry from the colourful pathology that marked the work of Barry MacSweeney or Harry Fainlight. Here, consciousness is presented as both responsive (well-attuned and undistorted) and responsible, able to take on existential meaning-making rather than abjuring responsibility for even conventional comprehensibility.

A 'song' is also – and the context makes this non-trivial – a poem that has been composed with intention and formal care. Those leaves, twigs and then branches make a sequence that has image logic (it's the order in which they're arranged on the tree, after all), but also beautifully, and filmically, extends to show how an apprehension works – at the same time as *providing* just such a mental experience. These details are not an extended metaphor, but a trope that trembles on the boundary between representations of two different things – the way we see and the way we are – in a duo-metaphor. As his appearance among the mythopoets revealed, the Swedish Nobel Laureate Tomas Tranströmer does just the same. In his poem 'Romanesque Arches', an arcade is both the artefact a group of tourists apprehends, and the structuring character *of* those apprehending minds. To use an image in this way is to symbol-form in the round, since the resonance of symbol comes both from the metaphorical or encapsulating work it does, and from its already being so used.

Prynne's line break at 'ex / tends' restores the original, bipartite sense of that word to give us the sense of a 'brightness' that both shines out ('ex') and moves ('tends') in a particular direction. It's a tending, shepherding principle that is often present in his verse. Throughout the Seventies this principle coalesces, if not in narrative then through the *situated* character of the verse; as a series of openings from 1974's *Wound Response* reveal: 'Through the window the sky clears', 'So the tenant comes back under his arch / of blood, affirming its pulse', 'Shouts rise again from the water / surface and flecks of cloud skim over / to storm-light'. It would be easy, and glib, to think of these poems as a set of thought-experiments carried out on the reader: what can I make him or her go along with? More useful is to conceive of Prynne's poems, and their by-and-large increasing semantic complexity, as entering consistently deeper into privacy. The intelligence is conscientious and speedy – 'Nerve / and verve broke for lunch & were gone' is the terrific, and indeed verve-filled, ending to his long poem on 'tribe' and kinship, *News of Warring Clans* (1977) – and it does not gloss over the necessary origin of a poem's ideas, images and symbols in the author's own psyche.

Increasingly, we find the poet exploring this personal, contingent origin to the poem, rather than attempting to change readers' minds. What produces semantic complexity in middle-period Prynne is simply the apparent lack of connection between parts of a poem: all our psyches, after all, are both incoherent and cluttered with *stuff that only I know*. Unlike Selima Hill and Medbh McGuckian, J.H. Prynne is not, in effect, an abstract expressionist. We cannot rely on an emotional logic to decode his argumentation – not least because it *is* argumentation, not confession. Instead, once again, the shepherding principle – and beyond it that characteristic 'voice' – are what we have to rely on to see us through:

> The scores read like this: word ranking
>   under the Sentences Act gives a choice

of tempers, arbiter's freedom to set out
where the deepest shadows shall fall.

(untitled, from *Triodes, Book III*, 2000)

This could simply be a poem about the coercive power of language, but it develops that theme along the lines of Dylan Thomas's 'The Hand That Signed the Paper': 'in order/ to renounce the use of arms / it is necessary to have weapons to hand / and in hand, preferably / bloodied beyond a doubt' is made analogous with 'the crime of the rational script'.

Not all Prynne's later poems are so single-minded. In an untitled poem from 2004's *Blue Slides at Rest*, 'Each one tissue-wrapped phoneme sedative to give out / for slip finish her nest, henny-penny unfolds a share / on a tribune team. Anyway burnt to ashes slant paper / whether not free of risk. Well not stapled . . .' This seems to suggest a quite other thought about the ways in which language fails to act in the world. It implies that its sound ('phoneme sedative') is a kind of drug, which – by way of the pun on 'slip', which is both slippage and the clay 'mortar' to 'finish [a] nest' – becomes commodity. She who 'feathers her nest' looks after her own material advantage, as do those who buy shares. Linguistic pleasure – so, that's *poetry* – is complicit in the commodification of the world, just as language's legislative power makes it complicit in worldly violence and power. But the poem that articulates this idea has all the condensation (and, later, expansion through examples) of self-thought. It is not expository. Discreet as a college servant, it neither confesses nor seeks to persuade. Prynne's verse seems to say that we must each be allowed our own worlds.

Yet sometimes even Prynne can't resist the 'tissue-wrapped phoneme'. Characteristic brevity means that most of his pamphlet collections are through-composed – more sequences than collections – and strongly unitary in character. Some – particularly those like *A Night Square* (1971), *Down where changed* (1979) or, to a lesser extent, *The Oval Window* (1983), which are characterized by short untitled poems – take a stride into what clearly knows itself to be beauty. In a love lyric from *A Night Square* the hallucinatory quality of cycling is evoked, and quickly put to symbolic use:

> . . . the
>> path still as
>>> still rising over the
>>> wheel so were it
>>>> almost
>> a part of what you say
>>>> you tell me
>>> every third day

In *Down where changed*, a hospital visit piles up images:

> By the pure fluke
> of the introit now
> into the NHS cathedral
>
> the bundle of new
> roses in their Trauersaft
> hits peak fluid
>
> and shatters softly
> like a blue vase

Passing from hand to cultural hand, an accelerated metaphorical currency unifies this thought. 'Introit', an opening processional music, announces the 'cathedral' of the next line; *Trauersaft* (grief-juice) suggests not only tears but the elegiac form of *Trauermusik*, composed by both Wolfgang Amadeus Mozart and Paul Hindemith. Their solemn musics also seem to be evoked by the processional gait of this short-lined poem, in which the roses' sudden 'going over' into a fall of petals is evoked by the surprising comparison with a vase: that would 'shatter' in a completely different way from the flowers, but is linked to them by its use for them, and their *Trauersaft*.

Through-patterned with mutually resonating images, this is writing as capacious, and dense with purposive pleasure, as any great European poetry, and it's here, rather than through the diminishing returns of some of Prynne's imitators, that the exploded lyric contributes much to what we might hope for the future of British poetry.

AFTERWORD: ELECTIVE AFFINITIES

Poetry is no more composed independently of context than are volumes of philosophy, or recipes. That undramatic observation underlies this book, in which I've tried to outline the networks of alliance and influence, both on and off the page, that produce the poetry we enjoy in Britain today.

Perhaps all avid readers are interpreters, eager to make the best of many different kinds of writing. Some of those who read and review poetry, however, seem less than sure-footed: stuck, like character actors, within the comfort zone of a familiar style. When I started writing *Beyond the Lyric* I was certainly avid, and did think of myself as an interpreter. I was tired, though, of the way in which even brilliant poets, critics and editors would sometimes conflate and confuse questions of taste and merit. The map of British poetry reminded me of nothing so much as Italy in the Quattrocento. Terrific art was going on inside – indeed, in celebration of – a series of city states, each with its own leader. These charismatic (male) figures seemed to have arisen in a number of ways: through creative revolution (Michael Donaghy, Don Paterson) or diplomatic campaign (Robin Robertson), with post-Marxist historical inevitability (Sean O'Brien), by secession (J.H. Prynne) or succession (Ian Hamilton, Blake Morrison, Alan Jenkins, Andrew Motion). Each practised a generous integrity within their own poetic community, but some of their followers at least seemed less aware of – or equipped to deal with – what lay beyond the city walls.

Editing a magazine which was supposed to have no house loyalty should have allowed me to move freely in and out of these fortifications. It took a while, however, for my pass to be accepted at all gates. It wasn't simply being a woman editor that elicited the assumption that I must be 'so-and-so's creature'. Even the notion of a critical lingua franca seemed, at times, unimaginable. My own writing was scrutinized for signs of poetic loyalties. And of course, like all poets, I am what I read. But poets who emerge without early mentorship – many of us do, incomprehensible as this may seem to those for whom that privilege was formative – have a relationship to influence that is more enthusiastic than blindly obedient. Our enthusiasms are mobile, transferable – and conditional. They encourage scrutiny of the admired object. In fact, they are *founded* in such scrutiny.

It's certainly true that the experience of editing is one of close reading. Sometimes that feels like parsing, at others like divination. A poet like J.H. Prynne or Geoffrey Hill can require us to throw our intuitions and observations ahead of ourselves, across the gap left by conventional denotation or shared cultural referent. A different problem is posed by a John Stammers or a Mark Ford. Their work isn't grammatically or denotatively obscure, but its tendency to cite stories or themes from contemporary culture in a non-reflexive manner gives those references (here a movie name-checked, there an anecdote retold) the feel of found objects or texts, leading to the question, 'What for?' We are a long way after Marcel Duchamp's ready-mades and it feels necessary to ask why such material is framed as poetry. Sometimes, again, it is simply a problem of sensibility. How can I *feel* the hare in a poem by Pauline Stainer, and the very different, equally tremulous one in a poem by David Harsent, in ways which I can put together: can I respond authentically to both? Is it possible to fit both these responses into a unified experience of poetry, or am I somehow betraying my reading of the one when I read the other with equal pleasure?

The longer I've worked on this book, the more I've realized that the best way to make sense of what an individual poem is doing is to read it for degrees not of separation, but of connection. Theory has taught students not to assume intention; not to think, in other words, that the authorial purposes which precede a poem form part of that poem. But poems *themselves* declare their intentions: though some do so more successfully than others. For example, a fourteen-line rhyming love poem in iambic pentameter is declaring its intention to be a sonnet. A fourteen-line unrhymed poem which is not in pentameter, and which appears to be about hate, may also see itself in these terms. But what if it is unmetrical – yet still has a *volta*? . . . Sometimes, the clues to poetic intent are straightforwardly comparative: we find the source of this poem's identity in (other) sonnets. Sometimes they're more contextual: it's only by knowing about her work on Marina Tsvetaeva that we understand how Elaine Feinstein's work suddenly swerved away from modernism to explore personal material.

Just as the composition of Elizabethan actors' companies affected Shakespeare's plots – all those boy-women – so the books they read, and the company they keep, affect what today's writers ask their poems to do. As I've worked on, I've also become aware of the importance of poetry kinship: within city states maybe, but also in other, looser alliances; affiliations that move back through recent literary history, as well as on to embrace new, emerging talents. These literary friendships aren't purely practical. Each represents not simply hours on the phone or in the pub, gossiping and putting the literary world to rights, but a web of shared ideas about what makes a poem; ideas hammered out through examples and reactions, the checks and balances that another mind exerts on individual instincts. In the early twentieth century there was a fashion for artistic manifestos, put together by groups of bright young things eager to change the literary world: F.T. Marinetti's 1909 Futurist Manifesto, the Blast Manifesto of 1914. This kind of transformation is exciting and energizing and it captures journalists' attention, but it's not the only way that schools of poets and of poetics emerge. Most develop more organically. For example, the Oxford elegists were brought together by a cultural like-mindedness which enabled their exchange of ideas and influences. But behind John Fuller stands the figure of his father, Roy, who moderated the influence of the Movement with his own brand of intellectual lyricism. The elegists shared – and learnt from – his resistance to the Movement's economizing principles. Peter Porter occupies an arguably even more influential position behind several of the surviving modernists and iambic legislators, sometimes as mentor and sometimes as example. Ian Duhig, Sean O'Brien and Gwyneth Lewis each see him as their own.

Like family histories, such 'vertical' influences generally branch between several different heirs. Duhig and Lewis are as dissimilar from each other as from O'Brien, who himself emerged as the most passionately engaged of the Hull Poets of the Eighties. This group included Peter Didsbury, Douglas Houston and John Osbourne: intelligent, angry-ish young men a decade and more junior to Douglas Dunn, who both studied and worked at the university, and from different stock than Andrew Motion, who taught there from 1976 to 1980. O'Brien's *primus inter pares* model of poetic leadership is similar to that developed by Michael Donaghy, an American whose arrival in 1985 reconstellated British verse. Donaghy was not simply a very fine poet, conspicuously within the British tradition of the narrative, rather than abstract, lyric, but he had also been the editor of the *Chicago Review*. He knew how to read poetry discerningly, and also, perhaps more importantly, how to build a poetry community. His immense gifts of personality meant that, until his premature death in 2004, his sometimes appeared to be the only community within British poetry.

These kinds of influence and affiliation are unmysterious and, ultimately, transparent. Theory may have taught us not to confuse the text with its author, but it has also shown how texts are decoded by their contexts. Poems are written in codes that continue beyond the margins of the page – into social mores and shared cultural knowledge, for example. Literary biography itself is nothing more or less than the story of how these influences move on and off the page.

Despite such precedents, thinking about poetry as this book does means making a conceptual shift, into understanding it as a shared culture. That's the opposite of how it is often imagined, and means tearing ourselves away from the idea of poetry as a form of exceptionalism. A poem does not record the unmediated descent of a muse. Every writer has moments of grace, but poem-making largely involves the craft with which this book is concerned. True, talent is one kind of ultimate limit. No amount of wilful imitation can conjure what's not there to *be* conjured. The poet-editor Ian Hamilton's own writing has survived his death, but that of some of his imitators at the *Review* and *New Review* has lasted less well. Still, the idea of a poetry culture – and the notion that contributing to this might be worthwhile *in itself*, regardless of the wing-beats of literary reputation – seems to be oddly foreign not only to onlookers, but to many protagonists of British verse.

Young poets, in particular, often fuss over the distinction between their 'own work', and other parts of a well-rounded poetic practice, such as reviewing, essay-writing and translating – as if these were non-authorial, neither 'theirs' nor 'work'. Attitudes elsewhere are somewhat other. The European notion of the writer-and-intellectual may be biased towards the cerebral, and fail to recognize other aspects of a poetic role, such as that of the 'troubadour' performer travelling from gig to gig. But it is at its most helpful as an idea about a thickened-up poetic practice, a professional collegiality in which reviewing, for example, is a serious act of critical engagement rather than a simple barter-system, and where poets both young and established display a genuine and continuing curiosity about our limitless genre and the world beyond it. Connective, discursive, public and *written*, such a poetry culture isn't founded solely on gossip and personality. It affords space for young talent to articulate sophisticated, energetic challenges to existing poetic establishments, instead of leaving them with an incoherent sense of being baulked, and it encourages establishment figures to stay on their toes, rather than stick with a trademark trick.

Such poetic practice, enriched by care for poetry itself – beyond and as well as simple ambition for one's own poems – doesn't of course prevent fierce professional rivalries. But perhaps more radical still is the idea that poetry is *essentially* collaborative. In this way of thinking, writing a poem is not an act committed *against* other, rival poets – as it can be in the expedient, power-driven British scene – but an act *towards* them. An astonishing new development by one does all of us good; we need only remember what a poem like Sylvia Plath's 'Daddy' or T.S. Eliot's *The Waste Land* has released in countless other writers. The effect, and indeed one point, of the exception is to 'purify the dialect of the tribe', as Eliot himself said, in *Little Gidding*.

In his famous essay 'Tradition and the Individual Talent', Eliot acknowledges the way that a young poet falls in love with – identifies with – a poet already in the canon; and how talent can be shaped by that relationship. But as he points out, this kind of monogamy must also be outgrown. As Percy Bysshe Shelley observes in 'Epipsychidion', his shameless polemic for free love:

> True Love in this differs from gold and clay,
> That to divide is not to take away.
> Love is like understanding, that grows bright,
> Gazing on many truths . . .

It might be more useful to think of each poet as engaged in a whole web of dialogue with poets both canonical and living. In Eliot's words:

> the historical sense, which we may call nearly indispensible to anyone who would continue to be a poet past his twenty-fifth year . . . involves a perception, not only of the pastness of the past, but of its presence; the historical sense compels a man to write not merely with his own generation in his bones, but with a feeling that the whole of literature . . . has a simultaneous existence and composes a simultaneous order.

For some poets in some places, this web of responses and reading is so dense that it seems to make a continuous fabric: as in the marital and creative partnership of Penny Shuttle and Peter Redgrove, or close literary friendships like that between Michael Donaghy and Don Paterson. Poet-editors like Paterson, or Robin Robertson, may not prescribe their personal practice as a model in the way that Ian Hamilton did, but young poets entering their lists must make an individual *poetic* relationship with their editor if their work is to thrive.

But even beyond such 'super'-connections, all poets write in relation to each other. Understood this way, a multiplicity of influences is a sign of poetic strength; and so is a poetry culture dense with cross-reference and multiple allegiances. Contemporary British poetry should take pride in both the variety and the consistency of its strengths. Today's British society is complex, various and interdependent. It is also, arguably, a fraction less hierarchical than in past centuries. Culturally porous, it absorbs both the dominant world culture of the US, through the usual media of film, music and TV, and the many cultures of citizens with hybrid backgrounds. Fairly obviously, such a society can no longer be univocal: if indeed it ever truly was. There is no longer only one shared cultural transition underway at any one time. The twentieth century's world wars and the societal shifts they triggered were a kind of 'trump' that affected all writers and artists; but today's cultural and social influences are a great deal more piecemeal, and produce a palette of variation rather than absolute differences.

Ultimately, then, this is a book about the great web of tradition. Within that web the poems themselves create a series of dialectics. When I read a poem by Colette Bryce it reminds me equally of Jo Shapcott and of Fleur Adock – though for different reasons – and thus, in reading Bryce, I reawaken both older poets. All three are held together in my reading experience. This kind of overlapped differentiation, a sort of half-step change of gears, isn't a sign of the exhaustion of invention but, on the contrary, of how unexhausted the resources within contemporary poetry are. At its most radical, it is a kind of co-creation.

Perhaps all this sounds wilfully optimistic. Of course, it is a model; a perspective. It's a way of interpreting what goes on. Such willed choices are, though, how we make things happen. They are, in a small but exact way, political. And this book, because it's written by someone who has always worked in roles that assumed there was such a thing as collective poetic responsibility – community artist, editor – is in some similarly small-scale way political, too. The case *Beyond the Lyric* makes is for poetry as a fundamentally communitarian, connected and responsive form. Rather than a blank page on which the drama of individual egos can be played out, poetry is, I would suggest, a collective practice, which is always already going on.

Poetry is written on the tilt, biased towards the other who listens to it and to whom it listens. I suspect this used to be easier than it is today. Poets could routinely rely on the consolations of religion (as some still can): for John Donne, or John Milton, the listening other was God. Emily Dickinson and Gerard Manley Hopkins could write in apparent isolation because their Ideal Reader was already to hand. Not only did He have a perfect ear, but omniscience meant that He would always understand what a poem was doing, however revolutionary its technique. Nowadays it is mostly our peers to whom we must entrust this role of Ideal Reader. Our poems still tilt towards the readers, and this purposive predisposition is intimate, inclusive – and a sign of respect. Poets and their readers form – at least according to the genre itself, if not always by custom and habit – a mutually respectful community. Providing that respect *is* mutual, this does not lead to conservatism and 'dumbing down', but the kind of shared trust that allows for real artistic adventure and experiment.

The work of a poem *is* to face towards a reader, whether real or Ideal. Its task is to create a small synaptic jump of recognition and co-thought between writer and reader. Poetry is not the inconsolable wail of the only child. It can be the hum of neighbourly voices in a meeting-hall. To be welcomed in, all you need do is open the door.

ACKNOWLEDGEMENTS

I am grateful to the Institute of English Studies in the School for Advanced Study at the University of London for a Visiting Fellowship, which enabled work on this book. Earlier versions of some of the material in this book were published in *The Sunday Times*, *Times Literary Supplement*, *Guardian*, *Independent*, the *Irish Times* and *Agenda*.

For permission to reprint copyright material the publishers fully acknowledge the following:

Dannie Abse: lines from 'Song for Dov Shamir', 'Leaving Cardiff', 'Remembering Miguel Henandez' and 'Portrait of the artist as a middle-aged man' taken from *Collected Poems 1948-1976* (Hutchinson, 1977); lines from 'Lachrymae' and 'Letters' taken from *Two for Joy* (Hutchinson, 2010). Reprinted by permission of The Random House Group Limited. **Fleur Adcock:** lines from 'Against Coupling', 'For a Five-Year-Old' and 'The Video' from *Poems 1960-2000* (Bloodaxe, 2000); lines from 'Dragon Talk' taken from *Dragon Talk* (Bloodaxe, 2010). Reprinted by permission of the publisher. **Gillian Allnutt:** lines from 'in her kitchen' reprinted by kind permission of the author. **Moniza Alvi:** lines from 'Fighter Planes', 'Rolling', 'You are Turning me into a Novel', 'All Fours', 'Substance' and 'Storyteller' taken from *Carrying My Wife* (Bloodaxe, 2000). Reprinted by permission of the publisher. **Simon Armitage:** lines from 'You're Beautiful', 'The Patent', 'Pheasants, iii: Brace' taken from *Tyrannosaurus Rex versus the Corduroy Kid* (Faber, 2006);

lines from *Gawain* (Faber, 2007) reprinted by permission of the publisher. Lines from *The Twilight Readings* published by Yorkshire Sculpture Park, 2008. **W.H. Auden:** lines from 'In Praise of Limestone' taken from *Collected Poems* copyright © The Estate of W.H. Auden 1976, 1991. All rights reserved. **Liz Berry:** lines from 'The Patron Saint of School Girls' reprinted by kind permission of the author. **John Betjeman:** lines from 'Business Girls' taken from *Collected Poems* (John Murray, 2006). Reprinted by permission of John Murray and The Betjeman Estate. **Sujata Bhatt:** lines from 'A Poem Consisting Entirely of Introductions' taken from *Augatora* (Carcanet, 2000). Reprinted by permission of the publisher. **Ruth Bidgood:** lines from 'Burial Path' taken from *Selected Poems* (Seren, 1995). Reprinted by permission of the publisher. **Elisabeth Bletsoe:** lines from 'The Separable Soul' taken from *Landscape from a Dream* (Shearsman, 2008). Reprinted by permission of the publisher. **Alan Brownjohn:** lines from 'His Compliment' and 'December 31st 2009' taken from *Ludbrooke and Others* (Enitharmon, 2010); lines from 'On Dancing' and 'Somehow' taken from *The Saner Places* (Enitharmon, 2011). Reprinted by permission of the publisher. **Basil Bunting:** lines from 'Briggflatts' from *Complete Poems* (Bloodaxe, 2001). Reprinted by permission of the publisher. **John Burnside:** lines from 'The Myth of Narcissus' taken from *The Good Neighbour* (Jonathan Cape, 2005); lines from 'Pittenweem' taken from *Gift Songs* (Jonathan Cape, 2007); lines from 'Saint Hubert and the Deer', 'Stalkers' and 'Ars Moriendi...' taken from *The Hunt in the Forest* (Jonathan Cape, 2009); lines from 'The Listener', 'The Fair Chase' and 'Hurts Me Too' taken from *Black Cat Bone* (Jonathan Cape, 2011). Reprinted by permission of The Random House Group Limited. **Ciaran Carson:** lines from 'Queen's Gambit' and 'Ambition' taken from *Belfast Confetti* (Bloodaxe, 1990); lines from 'L'air du temps', 'Redoubt', 'Treaty', 'Second Hand', 'Peace', 'The Present', 'Never Never' and 'The Assignation' taken from *For All We Know* (Gallery Press, 2008). Reprinted by permission of the publisher. **Gillian Clarke:** lines from 'Dream', 'In January' and 'Blaen Cwrt' taken from *Collected Poems* (Carcanet, 1997). Reprinted by permission of the publisher.

Wendy Cope: lines from 'Strugnell's Sonnets' taken from *Making Cocoa for Kingsley Amis* (Faber, 1986); lines from 'Villanelle for Hugo Williams', 'Boarders', 'At the Poetry Conference', 'The Health Scare' taken from *Family Values* (Faber, 2011). Reprinted by permission of the publisher. **Fred D'Aguiar:** lines from 'Airy Hall's Dynasty' taken from *Airy Hall* (Chatto & Windus, 1989). Reprinted by permission of The Random House Group Limited. **Ian Duhig:** lines from 'Róisín Bán' and 'Jericho Shandy' from *Pandorama* (Picador, 2010). Reprinted by permission of the publisher. **Douglas Dunn:** lines from 'Re-reading Katherine Mansfield's *Bliss and Other Stories*' taken from *Elegies* (Faber, 1985); lines from 'Dante's Drum-kit', 'Audenesques for 1960' and 'Kabla Khun' taken from *Dante's Drum-kit* (Faber, 1993). By permission of the publisher. **Carol Ann Duffy:** lines from 'The Captain of the 1964 *Top of the Form* Team', 'Room', 'Prayer', 'Disgrace' and 'Mean Time' taken from *Mean Time* (Anvil, 1993); lines from 'Text' and 'The Love Poem' taken from *Rapture* (Picador, 2005). Reprinted by permission of the publisher. **T.S. Eliot:** lines from 'Tradition and the Individual Talent' taken from *The Sacred Wood* (Faber, 1997); lines from 'Burnt Norton' taken from *Four Quartets* © The Estate of T.S. Eliot and reproduced by permission of the publisher. **Harry Fainlight**: lines from 'The Spider' published in *Fuck You*, A Magazine of the Arts, no. 5, vol. 7 (Sept. 1964). Reprinted by kind permission of Ruth Fainlight. **Ruth Fainlight**: lines from 'My Position in the History of the Twentieth Century', 'Or Her Soft Breast', 'Brush and Comb' and 'The Rings' taken from *Collected Poems* (Bloodaxe, 2010). Reprinted by permission of the publisher. **Paul Farley:** lines from 'Eaux D'Artifice' and 'A Minute's Silence' from *The Boy from the Chemist is Here to See You* (Picador, 1998); 'The Sea in the Seventeenth Century' from *The Ice Age* (Picador, 2002). 'Tramp in Flames' and 'Civic' from *Tramp in Flames* (Picador, 2006). Reprinted by permission of the publisher. **Elaine Feinstein:** lines from 'The Visit' from *Talking to the Dead* (Carcanet, 2007); lines from 'Heaven' from *The Russian Jerusalem* (Carcanet, 2008); lines from 'An Attempt at Jealousy' taken from *Bride of Ice* (Carcanet, 2009); lines from 'Lublin, 1973' from *Cities* (Carcanet, 2010). Reprinted by permission of the publisher. Interview with Elaine Feinstein, published in 'Close to the Bone', in *Poetry Review* *96:2*. **John Fuller:** lines from 'Excitement' and 'Ghosts' taken from *Ghosts* (Chatto & Windus, 2004); lines from 'The Solitary Life', 'Arnold in Thun', 'Coleridge in Stowey' and 'Thun 1947' taken from *The Space of Joy* (Chatto & Windus, 2006); lines from 'Piano Masterclass' taken from *Pebble and I* (Chatto & Windus, 2010). Reprinted by permission of The Random House Group Limited. **W.S. Graham:** lines from 'Malcolm Mooney's Land' taken from *New Collected Poems* (Faber, 2005). Reprinted by permission of the publisher. **Lavinia Greenlaw:** lines from 'Blakeney Point', 'Severn', 'A Circle Round Our House', 'A Dutch Landscape for Isla McGuire', 'Superlocution' and 'English Lullaby' taken from *The Casual Perfect* (Faber, 2011); lines from 'Galileo's Wife' taken from *Night Photograph* (Faber, 1993). By permission of the publisher. Quote from interview taken from *Mslexia*, issue 52. **Tony Harrison:** lines from 'The Railway Heroides', 'The Blasphemer's Banquet', 'Loving Memory', 'Bye-Byes' and 'Confessional Poetry' taken from *Selected Poems* (Penguin, 2006). Reprinted by permission of the publisher. **David Harsent:** lines from 'Punch in the Ancient World: Patmos', 'Punch's Nightmares 6', 'Bonnard: Breakfast', taken from *Mr Punch* (Oxford University Press, 1984); lines from 'Dawn Walk' taken from *Selected Poems 1969-2005* (Faber, 2007); lines from *Marriage* (Faber, 2002); lines from 'The Hut in Question', 'The Garden Goddess', 'Night', 'Elsewhere', 'Abstracts: Red', taken from *Night* (2011). By permission of the publisher. **W.N. Herbert:** lines from 'A Breakfast Wreath', 'Cromag' and 'In Memoriam Bill Burroughs' from *The Laurelude* (Bloodaxe, 1998). Reprinted by permission of the publisher. **Geoffrey Hill:** lines from 'Mercian Hymns', 'Two Formal Elegies: For the Jews in Europe' and 'XXXVI' from *Orchards of Syon* in *Selected Poems* (Penguin, 2006); lines from 'Lachrimae: 2 The Masque of Blackness' and 'Florentines' taken from *Tenebrae* (1978) and lines from *Speech! Speech!* (2000) taken from *Collected Poems* (Penguin, 1985). Reprinted by permission of the publisher. **Selima Hill:** lines from 'The Holy Brains of Snails', 'Aeroplanes', 'Violence', 'Penetrative Sex and Housewifery' and 'Turpentine', taken from *The Hat* (Bloodaxe, 2010); lines from 'My

Sister Calls me Darling', 'Red Cows' and 'Portrait of my Lover as Hildegard of Bingen' taken from *Gloria* (2010). Reprinted by permission of the publisher. **Miroslav Holub:** lines from 'Brief reflection on cracks' taken from *Poems Before and After* (Bloodaxe, 2nd edn. 2006). Reprinted by permission of the publisher. **Frances Horovitz:** lines from 'Vindolanda – January' and 'Orkney' from *Collected Poems*, ed. Roger Garfitt (Bloodaxe, 2011). Reprinted by permission of the publisher. **Ted Hughes:** lines from 'Widdop', taken from *Collected Poems* (ed. Paul Keegan, Faber, 2003) © The Estate of Ted Hughes and reproduced by permission of the publisher. **Kathleen Jamie:** lines from 'The Way We Live' taken from *The Way We Live* (Bloodaxe, 1984); lines from 'The Queen of Sheba' taken from *The Queen of Sheba* (Bloodaxe, 1994); lines from 'Ultrasound' taken from *Jizzen* (Picador, 1999); lines from 'The Galilean Moons', 'Materials', 'Swifts' and 'Halfling' taken from *The Overhaul* (Picador, 2012). Reprinted by permission of the publisher. **Alan Jenkins:** lines from 'Climber' reprinted by kind permission of the author; lines from 'Poetry' taken from *The Drift* (Chatto & Windus, 2000); lines from 'Orpheus', taken from *A Shorter Life* (Chatto & Windus, 2005). Reprinted by permission of The Random House Group Limited; lines from 'A Canterbury Tale', 'The Lost World', and 'Little Men' taken from *The Lost World* (Clutag Press, 2010), reprinted by permission of the publisher. **John Idris Jones:** lines from 'To Ioan Madog, Poet, Ancestor' taken from *Accord* (Cinnamon Press, 2011). Reprinted by permission of the publisher. **Jackie Kay:** lines from 'My Face is a Map', 'Stars, Sea', 'First Light', 'George Square', 'Condemned Property', 'Maw Broon Visits a Therapist', 'Twelve Bar Bessie Blues' and 'Spoons' taken from *Darling* (Bloodaxe, 2007). Reprinted by permission of the publisher. **Mimi Khalvati:** lines from 'The Meanest Flower', 'On Lines from Paul Gauguin', 'Ghazal: To Hold Me', 'The Mediterranean of the Mind', 'Come Close', 'The Poet's House', 'Love in an English August', and 'Writing Letters' taken from *Child* (Carcanet, 2012); lines from 'Lyric' taken from *The Chine* (Carcanet, 2002). Reprinted by permission of the publisher. **Linton Kwesi Johnson:** lines from 'Interv Mervyn Morris',

'Five Nights of Bleeding' and 'Bass Culture' taken from *Hinterland* (ed. E.A. Markham, Bloodaxe, 1989). Reprinted by permission of the publisher. **Philip Larkin:** lines from 'An Arundel Tomb' and 'Aubade' taken from *Complete Poems* © The Estate of Philip Larkin and reproduced by permission of the publisher. **Gwyneth Lewis:** lines from 'Welsh Espionage', 'A Golf-Course Resurrection', 'Illinois Idylls' and 'The Soul Mine', from *Parables and Faxes* (Bloodaxe, 1995); lines from *A Hospital Odyssey* (Bloodaxe, 2010); lines from 'Remission Sevillanas' taken from *Sparrow Tree* (Bloodaxe, 2011). Reprinted by permission of the publisher. **Tim Liardet:** lines from 'A Futurist Looks at a Dog' and 'Lumm's Tower' taken from *To the God of Rain* (Seren, 2003); lines from 'Mirror Angled at Sky' taken from *Competing with the Piano Tuner* (Seren, 1998); lines from 'Wormwood' taken from *Fellini Beach* (Seren, 1994); lines from *Priests Skear* (Shoestring Press 2010), reprinted by permission of the publisher. **Herbert Lomas**: lines from 'Greenwich Park', 'Something, Nothing and Everything', 'Three Prayers for Children', 'All that's Transitory is only a Trope' and 'The Month of Holy Souls' taken from *A Casual Knack of Living* (Arc Publications, 2009). Reprinted by permission of the publisher. **Michael Longley:** lines from 'Phoenix', 'Mole', 'The Exhibit', 'Harmonica', 'Heron', 'The Wren' and 'The Leveret' taken from *Collected Poems* (Jonathan Cape, 2006). Reprinted by permission of The Random House Group Limited. **Sarah Maguire**: lines from 'Mist Bench' taken from *The Invisible Mender* (Jonanthan Cape, 1997); lines from 'From Dublin to Ramallah', 'Landscape, with Dead Sea', 'Petersburg' and 'Europe' taken from *The Pomegranates of Kandahar* (Chatto & Windus, 2007). Reprinted by permission of The Random House Group Limited. **Maitreyabandhu:** lines from 'Visitation' reprinted by kind permission of the author. **Toby Martinez de las Rivas:** lines from 'Penitential Psalm' reprinted by kind permission of the author. **Barry MacSweeney:** lines from 'Pearl And Barry Pick Rosehips For The Good Of The Country', 'Up A Height And Raining', 'Demons in my Pocket' and 'Sweet Jesus: Pearl's Prayer' taken from *The Book of Demons* (Bloodaxe, 1997); 'Victory Over Darkness & The Sunne' from *Horses in Boiling Blood* (Equipage, 2004).

Reprinted by permission of the publisher. **Glyn Maxwell:** lines from 'Raul fixing a Cosmopolitan' and 'Granny May at the Scene' from *The Sugar Mile* (Picador, 2005); lines from 'Tale of the Mayor's Son' from *Tale of the Mayor's Son* (Bloodaxe, 1990); lines from 'A Play of the Word', 'Flags and Candles' from *Hide Now* (Picador, 2008); lines from 'Come to Where I'm From' © Glyn Maxwell. Reprinted by permission of the publisher. **Medbh McGuckian:** lines from 'Sagrario', 'Studies for a Running Angel: 2 A Chrisom Child', 'Closed Bells', 'In the Ploughzone', 'The Parents of Dreams', 'The Saints of April', 'St Faith' and 'Turning the Moon into a Verb' taken from *The Book of the Angel* (Gallery Press, 2004). Reprinted by permission of the publisher. **Andrew Motion:** lines from 'This is your subject speaking' taken from *Natural Causes* (Chatto & Windus, 1987), reprinted by permission of The Random House Group Limited; lines from 'Fresh Water' taken from *Selected Poems 1976-1997* (Faber, 2002). **David Morley:** lines from 'November the Fourteenth, Nineteen Forty-one' taken from *The Invisible Kings* (Carcanet, 2007). Reprinted by permission of the publisher. **Wendy Mulford:** lines from 'Goblin Combe' from *and suddenly, supposing: Selected Poems* (Etruscan Books, 2001). By permission of the publisher. **Grace Nichols:** lines from 'Because She Has Come', Without Song' and 'Tropical Death' from *I Have Crossed an Ocean: Selected Poems* (Bloodaxe, 2010). Reprinted by permission of the publisher. **Sean O'Brien:** lines from 'The Railway Sleeper', 'The Underwater Songbook' and 'Lines on Mr Porter's Birthday' from *Downriver* (Picador, 2001); lines from 'Ryan's Farewell' and 'A Rarity' from *Cousin Coat* (Picador, 2002); lines from 'The Them', 'Blue Night' and 'Blizzard' from *The Drowned Book* (Picador, 2007); lines from 'The Citizens', 'On the Toon', 'Europeans', 'Leave-taking', 'Elegy', 'Matinee' and 'Sunday in a Station of the Metro' from *November* (Picador, 2011). Reprinted by permission of the publisher. **Bernard O'Donoghue:** lines from 'Kilmacow' from *Here nor There* (Chatto & Windus, 1999). Reprinted by permission of The Random House Group Limited. **Alice Oswald:** lines from 'When a Stone was Wrecking His Country', 'Sea Sonnet', 'The Glass House' taken from *The Thing in the Gap-stone Stile* (Faber, 2007); lines from *Dart*

(Faber, 2002), lines from 'For Many Hours there's been an Old Couple Standing at that Window', 'Field', 'Three Portraits of Radio Audience', 'Ideogram for Green', 'Poem for Carrying a Baby out of Hospital', 'Solomon Grundy' taken from *Woods, etc* (Faber, 2005); lines from *A Sleepwalk on the Severn* (Faber, 2009) reprinted by permission of the publisher. **Ruth Padel:** lines from 'Heatwave' and 'The Eyes' taken from *Rembrandt Would Have Loved You* (Chatto & Windus, 1998); lines from 'On Not Thinking about Variation in Tortoiseshell', 'A Desperate Way to Avoid Paying your Tailor', The Devil's Chaplain' taken from *Darwin* (Chatto & Windus, 2010); lines from 'Breaking the Bond' taken from *The Mara Crossing* (Chatto & Windus, 2012). Reprinted by permission of The Random House Group Limited. **Don Paterson:** lines from 'An Elliptical Stylus', 'Graffito', 'Seed' taken from *Nil Nil* (Faber, 1993); lines from 'Buggery', 'To Cut it Short' taken from God's *Gift to Women* (Faber, 1997); lines from 'Road' and 'Afterword' taken from *The Eyes* (Faber, 1999); lines from 'Breath', 'Afterword', 'Mirror', 'Flight', 'The Sarcophagi in Rome', 'Horse' taken from *Orpheus* (2006); lines from 'Rain', 'Phantom i', 'Phantom vi', 'Phantom v', 'Correctives' and 'The Circle', taken from *Rain* (Faber, 2009). By permission of the publisher. Quote from 'The Lyric Principle' in *Poetry Review,* Autumn 2007. **Pascale Petit:** lines from 'House of Darkness', 'The Love Embrace of the Universe, the Earth (Mexico), Diego, Myself and Senor Xólotl', 'My Mother's Perfume' and 'The Mirror Orchid', taken from *The Huntress* (Carcanet, 2005); lines from 'Self-Portrait with Monkey' and 'What the Water Gave Me IV' taken from *What the Water Gave Me* (Carcanet, 2010). By permission of the publisher. Lines from 'The Second Husband' by kind permission of the poet. **Jacob Polley:** lines from 'Economics' taken from *The Brink* (Picador, 2003). Reprinted by permission of the publisher. **Peter Porter:** lines from 'Throw the Book at Them', 'Ranunculus Which My Father Called a Poppy', 'The Sanitised Sonnets 4', 'Cat's Fugue', 'Death in the Pergola Tea-Rooms', 'After Schiller', 'An Angel in Blythburgh Church' and 'Streetside Poppies' from *The Rest on the Flight: Selected Poems* (Picador, 2010). Reprinted by permission of the publisher. **Frances Presley:** lines from 'West Anstey Longstone' taken from *Line's of Sight* (Shearsman, 2009). Reprinted by permission of the publisher. **J.H. Prynne:** lines from *Kitchen Poems* (1968), *Day Light Songs* (1968), *Night Square* (1971), *Wound Response* (1974), *News of Warring Clans* (1977), *Down Where Changed* (1979), *Triodes* (2000), *Blue Slides at Rest* (2004), taken from *Poems* (Bloodaxe, 2005) © by J.H. Prynne. Reprinted by permission of the publisher and the author. **Craig Raine:** lines from 'A Silver Plate', 'Arsehole' 'The Grey Boy', 'Rich' taken from *Rich* (Faber, 1984); lines from *A la Recherche du temps perdu* (Picador, 1999); lines from *History: The Home Movie* (Penguin, 1994); lines from 'Redmond's Hare' taken from *Clay, Wherabouts Unknown* (Penguin, 1996). Reprinted by permission of the publisher. **Tom Raworth:** lines from 'Logbook' taken from *Collected Poems* (Carcanet, 2003). Reprinted by permission of the publisher. **Christopher Reid:** lines from 'Strange Vibes', 'The Old Soap Opera', 'Ransom and Rescue' taken from *Arcadia* (Faber, 1979); lines from 'The Liarbird' taken from *Alphabicycle Order* (with Sara Fanelli; Ondt and Gracehoper, 2001). By permission of the publisher. **Maurice Riordan:** lines from 'Idyll 6' taken from *The Holy Land* (Faber, 2007). By permission of the publisher. **Denise Riley:** lines from 'Dark Looks', 'Oleanna' and 'Knowing in the Real world', reprinted by kind permission of the author. **Carol Rumens:** lines from 'De Chirico's Threads', 'East Ending', 'The Concentration-Camp Poplars Remember their First Gardeners' and 'Dipthongs' taken from *De Chirico's Threads* (Bloodaxe, 2010). Reprinted by permission of the publisher. **Robin Robertson:** lines from 'At Dusk' and 'Flaying of Marsyas' from *A Painted Field* (Picador, 1997); lines from 'Sea-Fret' and 'Actaeon: The Early Years' from *Swithering* (Picador, 2006); lines from 'Kalighat', 'About Time' and 'Alice' from *The Wrecking Light* (Picador, 2010). Reprinted by permission of the publisher. **Neil Rollinson:** lines from 'Hubris', 'Away with the Mixer', 'Chaos Theory at the 4.20 Handicap Chase at Haydock Park', 'Onions', 'Demolition' and 'Waiting for the Man' taken from *Demolition* (Jonathan Cape, 2007). 'In Bed', 'The Good Old Days', 'The Wall' taken from the poet's own pamphlet *Talking Dead*. Reprinted by permission of The Random House Group Limited and the author. **Jo**

Shapcott: lines from 'Deft', 'Of Mutability', 'Viral Landscape', 'Procedure', 'The Bet', 'All Flesh Is', 'Piss Flower', 'The Death of Iris', 'St Bride's' taken from *Of Mutability* (Faber, 2011); lines from 'I'm Contemplated by a Portrait of a Divine', 'Brando on Commuting', 'The Mad Cow Tries to Write a Good Poem', and 'The Mad Cow Believes She is the Spirit of the Weather' taken from *Her Book: Poems 1988—1998* (Faber, 2006). By permission of the publisher. **Pauline Stainer:** lines from 'Keats on Iona', 'Herman Melville jumps ship', 'Song without voices', 'Sourin', 'The Borrowdyke' and 'Voltage' taken from *The Lady & the Hare: New & Selected Poems* (Bloodaxe Books, 2003); lines from 'Dowland at Elsinore' taken from *Crossing the Snowline* (Bloodaxe, 2008). Reprinted by permission of the publisher. **John Stammers:** lines from 'Mother's Day' taken from *Stolen Love Behaviour* (Picador, 2005). Reprinted by permission of the publisher. **Chloe Stopa-Hunt:** lines from 'The Illustrated Compendium of Russian Fairy Tales' reprinted by kind permission of the author. **Anne Stevenson:** lines from 'Utah' and 'By the Boat House, Oxford' taken from *The Collected Poems 1955-1995* (Bloodaxe, 2000); lines from 'Before Eden' and 'The Enigma' taken from *Stone Milk* (Bloodaxe, 2007). Reprinted by permission of the publisher. **Keston Sutherland:** lines from untitled, published in *Jacket* 1998, reprinted by kind permission of the author. **Michael Symmons Roberts**: lines from 'Carnivorous – iv', 'Ascension Day' taken from *Corpus* (Jonathan Cape, 2004). Reprinted by permission of The Random House Group Limited. **George Szirtes:** lines from 'Canzone: Architecture', 'The Burning of the Books: Consuming Passion', 'Sudek: Tree', 'Kértesz: Latrine' taken from *The Burning of the Books and other poems* (Bloodaxe, 2009). Reprinted by permission of the publisher. **Wisława Szymborska:** lines from 'Hatred' from *Poems New and Collected* (Faber, 1999). Reprinted by permission of the publisher. **Anthony Thwaite:** lines from 'Mr Cooper', 'The Art of Poetry', 'Leavings', 'Spring', 'Accumulations', 'House for Sale', '1936' and 'Reformation' taken from *Collected Poems* (Enitharmon, 2007). Reprinted by permission of the publisher. **Tomas Tranströmer:** lines from 'Winter's Code' taken from *The Deleted World*, trans. Robin Robertson (Enitharmon, 2006). Reprinted by permission of the publisher. **Harri Webb**: lines from 'Synopsis of the Great Welsh Novel' and 'Thanks in Winter' taken from *Collected Poems* (compiled and edited by Meic Stephens, Gomer, 1995). Reprinted with kind permission of Meic Stephens. **Ahren Warner:** lines from 'Between' reprinted by kind permission of the author. **Hugo Williams:** lines from 'Interval', 'Rhetorical Questions' and 'Congratulations' taken from *Billy's Rain* (Faber, 1999); lines from 'Wow and Flutter', 'Toilet' and 'In the Seventies' taken from *Self-Portrait with a Slide* (OUP, 1990); lines from 'A Conjuring Trick' taken from *West End Final* (Faber, 2009). By kind permission of the publisher. **Raymond Williams:** lines from *The Country and the City* (Hogarth Press, 1973), reprinted by permission of The Random House Group Limited.

Every effort has been made to trace and contact all the copyright holders prior to publication. If there are any inadvertent omissions or errors, the publishers will be pleased to correct these at the earliest opportunity.

INDEX